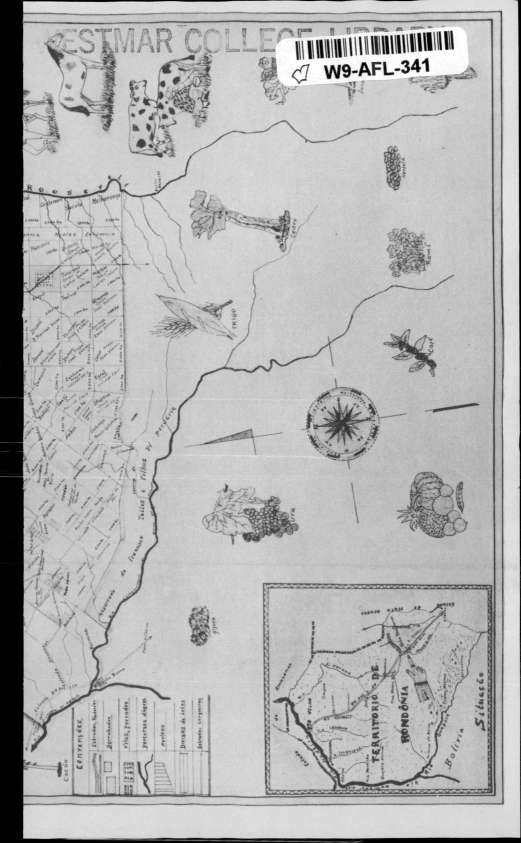

Unless something is done soon, the remaining tribal Indians of Brazil will die out.

This book describes the author's visit to Brazil to check whether the recommendations by the International Red Cross for the improvement of the Amazonian Indians' lot had been implemented by the Brazilian Government. To his consternation he discovered that not only had the recommendations been largely ignored but that the whole future of these tribal peoples was being jeopardized for the sake of progress. Roads are being driven through their territories, land belonging to them has been divided into plots and sold to developers and speculators, and the roots of their culture are being torn up and destroyed before they have had time to assimilate and adjust to the new way of life which is being imposed upon them.

If a global economic balance sheet were to be drawn up, it would show the world – as the ethnobotanist Conrad Gorinsky has pointed out – much indebted to the South American Indian. Cocoa and peanuts, tomatoes, cashews and avocados, are all of Amerindian origin; cocaine derivatives are used as local anaesthetics in dentistry; curare helped give surgery its present standing; the common insecticide Derris is derived from plants used by the Indian to stun fish; modern chemotherapy owes much to quinine; what little we know about the biochemistry of mental disease has been developed from the use of compounds of plant origin, such as mescalin and bufotenine. Yet in return the Indian has received only disease, expropriation and death. He has no natural immunity to many of the diseases carried by the white man. Settlers shoot him and then express surprise that the Indians are counted as human beings at all. Often, the so-called pacified tribes are reduced to beggary and prostitution. Little wonder that the few remaining uncontacted tribes avoid approaching civilization.

A QUESTION OF SURVIVAL

Civilization, however, is fast approaching them, and *A Question of Survival* poses the dilemma which faces Western civilization and all who adhere to its philosophies: that in the name of progress and technological advance we are destroying all cultures in any way different from our own, even though they constitute the roots from which we have sprung and without which our own stability and sense of continuity are threatened. It is, therefore, not just a question of survival for the South American Indian that the author is raising but, by implication, the survival of mankind as a species.

Robin Hanbury-Tenison was born in 1936, grew up in Ireland, and was educated in England. He has traveled widely and adventurously throughout the world and has taken part in, or led, over a dozen expeditions.

The Chairman of Survival International and a member of the Council of the Royal Geographical Society, Robin Hanbury-Tenison is married to writer Marika Hanbury Tenison. They have two children and live on a farm on the edge of Bodmin Moor, in Cornwall, England.

By the same author

THE ROUGH AND THE SMOOTH

ROBIN HANBURY-TENISON

A Question of Survival

FOR THE INDIANS OF BRAZIL

❧

*Foreword by H.R.H. The Duke
of Edinburgh*

CHARLES SCRIBNER'S SONS
NEW YORK

For Marika

NOTE

There are about one hundred and fifty different tribes of Indians in Brazil. They vary racially, linguistically and culturally as much as any people on earth and the conditions under which they find themselves living today vary as much. It is therefore dangerous and misleading to generalize about them but, since they are, in Brazil, an easily identifiable section of the community, it is almost impossible not to do so. During the journey which this book is about, we travelled over a large part of Brazil, a country bigger than the USA (discounting Alaska) and the text follows the geographical order in which we visited tribes. No attempt has been made to classify the thirty-three tribes we saw as regards their origins. To have done so would have only made it more confusing.

Anyone interested in studying the anthropological and historical aspects of the subject further should refer to the following: *The Situation of the Indian in South America*, Department of Ethnology, University of Bern on behalf of the World Council of Churches, Geneva: 1972, (The full text of the Declaration of Barbados); Farb, Peter, *Man's Rise to Civilization*, Secker and Warburg: 1969; Furneaux, Robin, *The Amazon*, Hamish Hamilton: 1969; Hemming, John, *The Conquest of the Incas*, Macmillan: 1970; Hopper, Janice, ed. & trans., *Indians of Brazil in the Twentieth Century*, Institute for Cross-Cultural Research, Washington: 1967; Maybury Lewis, David, *The Savage and the Innocent*, Evans Bros: 1965; Meggers, Betty and Evans, Clifford, *Aboriginal Cultural Development in Latin America*, David and Charles: 1969; Melatti, J. C., *Indios do Brasil, Brasilia*: 1970; Ribeiro, Darcy, *Os Indios e a Civilização*, Ed. Civilização Brasileiro, Rio de Janeiro: 1970; Steward, Julian H. and Faron, L. C., *Native Peoples of South America*, McGraw: 1959.

Contents

❧

Illustrations

❧

The colour illustrations are between pages 88 and 89 and pages 168 and 169 and are by Robin or Marika Hanbury-Tenison except where stated. *end papers*: A map produced by a local property development company in Rondônia marking out the plots of virgin jungle sold to settlers and which is occupied by the only recently contacted and hostile Cinta Larga Indians (see page 164)

Maps

Foreword
by H.R.H. The Duke
of Edinburgh

❦

Many people are concerned with the survival of wildlife, even more people are worried about the environment, but there is one desperately difficult problem of survival which gets very little attention at all. The survival of primitive people in the face of the overwhelming onslaught of a relentlessly advancing technological civilisation.

This problem has existed for hundreds of years as Europeans have explored, traded and settled in every accessible and interesting part of the world. North American Indians, Polynesians, Australian Aboriginals, Africans and many others have all had their cultures and ways of life changed or seriously influenced by European infiltration. In the early days, European certainty of superiority masked what is now recognised to be a mixed blessing at best and total disaster for the primitive people at worst.

Latin America, since the arrival of the Spaniards and Portuguese, has witnessed the most violent clashes between cultures and a complete transformation in its racial pattern. The Brazilian Indians are the last tribes of primitive people to come in contact with a rapidly developing and pioneering nation. The outcome, even if the clash is made gently and gradually, is a foregone conclusion; the tribes will disappear, their cultures will vanish, save for a few artifacts in museums, and their races will be absorbed into the 'melting pot'. The question is whether it is right that this should happen, and if it is not, then what alternatives should be considered. If modern medicine, technology and integration spell ruin, is it morally and ethically, and in-

9

deed practically, possible to keep these people isolated from the rest of the world?

These and many other ideas will be stirred up in the minds of the readers of this fascinating book.

October, 1972

Preface

❦

THE survival in question in this book is not that of the whole world, but of the remaining pre-Columbian peoples of Brazil. Their physical survival depends to a large extent on whether their culture is preserved for long enough for them to be able to face our overwhelming technology and withstand the shock. Conversely, most of their varied and often highly developed cultures will vanish with them when they die. No detailed anthropological study of a tribe, for all its interest and value as a record, can ever equal the living example of a people who are the heirs to a thousand generations of evolution.

If we, who call ourselves civilized, deserve the name at all, then we should no longer seek to destroy all the products of other cultures in the blind search for material prosperity. Doing so will only hasten our own destruction. The remaining tribal peoples of the world present no threat to us. On the contrary, there is much they can teach us. The world no longer consists of isolated pockets of enlightenment surrounded by barbarian hordes who will overrun us if we do not use all our wits to subdue them first. Instead, from Peking to Paris, from Copenhagen to Cape Town and from Alaska to Tierra del Fuego, materialism (whether dialectical or otherwise) reigns supreme, and it is the few surviving examples of alternative cultures and philosophies which face their final extinction.

I do not set out to prove that they are better or worse than we are. I do not believe that at birth they are any different. What I do believe is that imposing alien standards upon whole peoples too fast, and with little or no understanding or respect for who and what they are, will destroy them and all their evolution will have been in vain.

Throughout history, millions have died as a result of this process just as millions of species have become extinct since life first appeared on earth. Perhaps it is inevitable that modern civilized man will destroy all opposition in the human, animal and plant world until he stands alone. I hope not.

Robin Hanbury-Tenison 1972

PART ONE

Beginnings

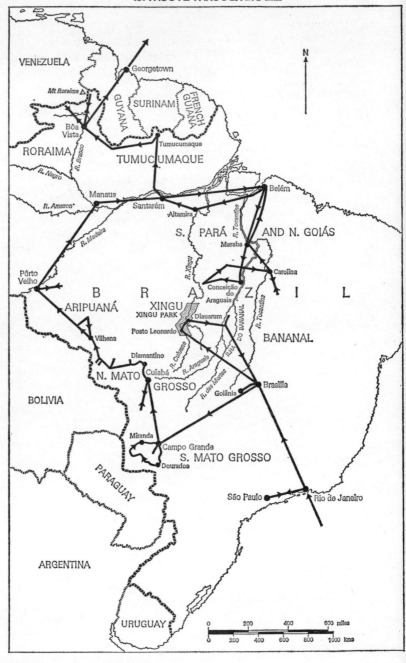

Beginnings

❧

AT the age of six I made my first voyage of discovery. In the middle of the lake below the house stood a small, wooded island. Generations had picnicked on its rocky shore on hot summer days, surrounded by the still dark water in which the tall beeches and fringe of alders at the lake's edge were reflected. My braver elder brothers and sisters caught freshwater crayfish under the stones, cast for fat, bony perch and trolled for giant pike from the boat. They built bonfires in which to roast potatoes and came and went from school and later from the war.

As far as I knew, no one ever went to the middle of the island. One day I crawled under the thick, high barrier of brambles, pushed my way through bulrushes, nettles, honeysuckle and wild rose, and reached a small clearing. Out of it grew an immense beech tree, below which the earth was bare and fringed with short grass. I liked the place and when it was time to go home for tea, begged to be allowed to stay. Bad parent that she was, my mother agreed and returned later in the boat with tent, dachshund and muffins. It became my own private world and when, later, a visiting 'Tarzan manqué' built for me a solid, dry house thirty feet up in the giant tree, my kingdom was complete.

Waking up alone on an island as the morning mist lifts off the water and otters make vees on the surface is an addictive experience. I believe that the pure joy of those first frightening mornings is what has made me want to travel since and visit wild and lonely places. I learnt as a child that occasional solitude makes the human race seem more attractive and I was lucky in having a mother who not only understood this feeling but actively encouraged it. On leaving school and university I travelled round the world, first driving a leisurely and ancient jeep to Ceylon, detouring to cross the central desert of Persia, explore the highlands of Afghanistan and climb a little in the Himalayas. Then I wandered through Indo-China and the Far East by country bus and bicycle, by river-boat on the Irrawaddy and in Borneo, and hitch-hiking, to the amazement of the still-occupied Japanese, through Japan. I worked my passage 'before the mast' on a most modern and comfortable Norwegian cargo-boat across the Pacific and then crossed the United States to Mexico.

Much to everyone's surprise I came home after a year in order to ask Marika to marry me. She accepted, but was not over-pleased when I confessed that I was just off to Brazil with Richard Mason – a friend from Oxford days – on an expedition that would take six months. This journey, by jeep, was to be the first land crossing of the South American continent at its widest point. Of the 6,000 miles we travelled, nearly half was through country where our jeep was the first vehicle ever to have penetrated and as a result we were out of touch for most of the time. (The full story of this and a subsequent 6,000-mile river journey from the Orinoco to the Plate is told in my book, *The Rough and the Smooth*, published in 1969 by Robert Hale.) I arrived home just in time for the wedding and Marika dutifully married me. After a short spell at agricultural college, we began to farm at 800 feet on Bodmin Moor in Cornwall and I thought that my exploring days were over.

Richard Mason, with whom I had jointly received one of the Royal Geographical Society's annual awards, returned to Brazil with John Hemming (another close friend – the three of us had shared digs at Oxford) on a major expedition to the River Iriri and was tragically ambushed and killed by a hunting party of Kreen Akrore Indians. These Indians have still never been contacted, in spite of many years of effort by the Villas Boas brothers. It is ironic, but entirely fitting, that a large part of the energy which I am now (1972) expending on trying to help primitive tribes, is being devoted to raising the necessary funds to give the brothers another chance to reach the Kreen Akrore before they are massacred or otherwise destroyed by settlers.

Marika, who had spent much of her childhood in Devon but the larger part in London, took to Cornish life with even more enthusiasm than I did. She loves Maidenwell, the house and farm, fiercely and passionately and has made her own highly successful career as a writer. It had never occurred to me that she might also have a desire to travel and explore and I don't think that to begin with she did. Later, when I took part in several other expeditions, I saw the corrosive effect which shared isolation and discomfort can have on relationships and felt it might not be a good idea for us to try it. It was only in 1971, when the three-month journey to Brazil, which is the subject of this book, came about that she finally came with me. The fact that we both enjoyed it so much, and that this was largely due to our being together, only goes to show how wrong I was; or perhaps it would be truer to say that a couple who have shared twelve years of marriage can survive anything.

During those twelve years I began, inevitably, to travel again. A desire to see and film the innumerable and beautiful prehistoric paintings and drawings of the Sahara took me on three expeditions across and through the vast empty wastes of the greatest desert in the world. Once I crossed the Libyan desert with John Hemming, riding for seven days on the top of an Arab truck, jostling for space with thirty Tibbu tribesmen, before climbing up into the Tibesti mountains in Chad. Twice I went alone, travelling for several weeks by camel in the company of a Tuareg warrior, first in the Tassili N'Ajjer in Southern Algeria and then in the Aïr Mountains of Niger. These journeys not only taught me to understand the attraction and the magic of life in the desert but also to respect and admire the people who live in one of the most inhospitable regions of the world and do so with elegance and grace.

My long river journey through South America followed. At first I was with Sebastian Snow, who had organized the expedition, but when he fell ill and had to return home I was alone, often seeing no other human being for many days at a time. Later came the two hovercraft expeditions when, by contrast, I had to learn to cope with the pressures and problems of travelling in a large group of people with dissimilar characters and objectives.

All this was very exciting and gave me plenty of experience, but something was lacking. My part in every journey so far had been pure exploration; a search for adventure, a desire to tread where no foot had trod before, see things few had seen, do things no one else had done and meet people who had a fresh and uncynical view of life. Sheer physical exploits, the search for adventure and danger began to seem pointless, selfish and unsatisfying. Others – geologists, botanists, surveyors – endured as much, and more, in the legitimate course of their scientific work, and what they did had a purpose and a usefulness. Neither mountaineering nor lone ocean voyages have ever held much appeal for me, but these are the only two fields in which the simple pitting of oneself against the elements is generally recognized as an end justifiable in itself.

With the remote and isolated peoples living in inaccessible deserts and jungles I had felt at home; the Tuareg in the Sahara, the hill tribes of Afghanistan and Kashmir, the Dyaks in Borneo and the Indians of South America. It was during the first hovercraft expedition, as a result of some side trips by canoe up tributaries of the Orinoco that my interest in these Indians suddenly developed.

Conrad Gorinsky, an ethnobotanist studying Indian plant medicines, and I had left the main party for a few days and visited some very primitive Waika Indians and later two Piaroa villages on a tributary of the Ventuari. Conrad, himself of part-Indian descent, talked and I listened – a state of affairs, as I have since learnt, not unusual where Conrad is concerned. I had met Indians before, from the tough naked Xavantes of the Mato Grosso to the sturdy Andean Indian peasants, and they had interested and excited me with their strange beauty and aloofness, their sense of colour and their skills. I had known, too, that many of them had been exploited and enslaved and I had seen the despair and squalor of a group of 'settled' Xerente. But I had never felt that any of this was my concern or indeed that anything could be done about it.

Conrad's enthusiasm was infectious. The scope of the problem was far greater than I had imagined and the situation far graver. With the sudden rapid increase of activity in South America directed towards development and exploitation of the remaining virgin lands and the enormously improved technological means available, the Indians stood little chance of having any land left before long. Without land on which to hunt and fish, the remaining forest Indians would soon die because it takes time to change a whole culture and way of life. When all the motive for continuing to live has been removed and nothing put in its place, the Indian is susceptible to exploitation and oppression. His lack of natural immunity to Western diseases lays his people open to decimating epidemics and he finds himself unable to compete effectively in a world he no longer understands. This was sad, I felt, but surely inevitable in a world where superior civilizations have always destroyed inferior ones, and where the exploding population of the world needs every acre of land to feed itself. How can one argue that a few Indians are more important than the starving masses of the coastal strip and of the shanty towns? Conrad did so, and convinced me.

The Indian, he claimed, might well hold the key to our own eventual survival on the planet. Every time a tribe dies out a whole vast unwritten library of knowledge, skill and experience dies with it. The Indian, although not living in the paradise conveyed by the concept of the 'Noble Savage', does live in a balanced relationship with his own environment. We do not. We have a great deal to learn from him, both in practical terms and about life itself.

It was on the practical matters that Conrad impressed me most. During the days we spent together in our canoe he produced a staggering list of examples of ways in which primitive societies have contributed to modern life. Practically all our major food plants and many of our medicines were discovered by primitive man and have only been improved by us. Some foods, like maize, are unknown in the wild state, having been developed from foundation stock which has now vanished. Aspirin only exists because a certain Dr Bayer was interested in folk remedies and studied the properties of willow bark, prescribed in the middle ages to be chewed in case of headaches.

The tribes we were travelling among on the Upper Orinoco and its tributaries have long known how to make curare and they still use several different forms with which they treat their arrows so as to paralyse game. From samples of the finished products – always the outcome of elaborate processes of preparation – scientists have recently isolated quite a few chemicals now used clinically in Western medicine. The most important of these so far is d-tubocurarine, which has played a vital part in heart transplant operations. Without the clues given by curare this drug would not exist today.

The Indians' knowledge of the manufacture and use of hallucinogenic drugs is unequalled in the world – something which it is vital for a society only now discovering them, and grossly misusing them, to study. When Conrad and I were on the Ocamo River, we witnessed the use of a complex hallucinogen commonly known as Yopo. One of the potent ingredients used to prepare the Yopo is a resin obtained from the inner bark of a tree known as Ebene (Virola sp.) which they also use as a curare to tip the points of their arrows. However, when demand is great for its use in ceremony, such as during their endo-cannabalistic festivals, the Waika warriors scrape the resin directly off the tips of the arrows as a fine powder for use as a hallucinogenic snuff. This demonstrates a supreme confidence in the knowledge and use of these materials of which we are still basically ignorant.

Because of these talks I began to believe that it might be possible to persuade governments that eliminating their indigenous populations, whether deliberately or accidentally, might not be in their best interests. After all, if the intention is to extract the maximum from the remaining jungles and deserts of the world, who best to turn to for advice and information than the people who live there and know the value of every animal and plant? Destroy them and nothing but a limited resource is left. Encourage and protect their knowledge and way of life and a bottomless fund of wisdom can be tapped producing unlimited potential benefit.

We agreed that something must be done.

At about this time, news was coming out of Brazil of the disbandment of the Indian Protection Service due to the fact that it had been found to be riddled with corruption. One hundred and thirty-four of its functionaries were being prosecuted for crimes ranging from murder to theft. Several European newspapers carried stories of atrocities committed against the Indians and began to speak of genocide. In February 1969, an article by Norman Lewis was published in *The Sunday Times Magazine* about the situation of the Indians in Brazil, and the following week a letter appeared in the same paper signed by Nicholas Guppy and Francis Huxley saying that an international organization for the protection of primitive peoples should be formed. Both had written very good books on Amer-indian tribes (*Wai Wai* by Nicholas Guppy, published in 1958 by John Murray; *Affable Savages* by Francis Huxley, published in 1963 by Rupert Hart-Davis) and I already knew Nicholas, through having asked his advice before one of my expeditions. We made contact and, during the summer, a series of meetings took place in my London flat to which many of those interested in the subject came and a great many ideas were exchanged. Among these was my close friend and sometime travelling companion, John Hemming, who was just finishing his superb book *The Conquest of the Incas*, as well as anthropologists such as Audrey Butt Colson and James Woodburn; Teddy Goldsmith who was about to start the magazine *The Ecologist*; Adrian Cowell, recently returned from making his excellent award-winning film in the Xingu, *The Tribe that Hides from Man*, and, of course, Conrad. When over thirty people began to turn up and there was barely room to squeeze everyone in, it was decided to take premises and form a proper charity.

Largely thanks to Nicholas Guppy's efforts, sponsors of the highest distinction were persuaded to support us and from these, and our own ranks, trustees of 'The Primitive Peoples Fund' were appointed. Later, due to dissatisfaction, particularly in Africa and the USA, with the 'Primitive' part of our name, it was decided to change it to 'Survival International', but, as the charity had by then been registered and covenants received in the name of PPF, it was necessary for a time to use both names.

The object of the Fund was to raise money to help primitive peoples throughout the world; to arouse international public opinion about their plight and to promote projects and research into ways in which their lives and cultures could be saved.

A year passed, during which I went on another hovercraft expedition, this time through much of Central Africa including Lake Chad and the Congo. Wherever I went now I heard of cases where the Fund was needed and could, if it became rich and powerful enough, perform a useful service. The Pygmies were dying out in the dense jungles of the Congo and the Cameroons, and those in contact with civilization were being exploited and treated like animals. The remaining Bushmen of the Kalahari were disappearing and the survivors living as unproductive parasites in camps.

At home, however, it was proving, as is so often the case, much harder to raise money for human need than it would have been had our 'primitive' people in fact been animals. The World Wildlife Fund, whose president, Peter Scott, was one of our sponsors, had grown out of all recognition in the last few years and was doing an invaluable and admirable job, but we were dealing with an even more difficult and tricky subject than the preservation of species of fauna and results were much more difficult to achieve or even hope for. Although our first job was to work for the physical survival of the people we were concerned with, it was also necessary to look beyond that to the survival of their culture and pride, their skills and talents, so that they should not just enter our society at its lowest level, with no hope of rising any higher, but should at best be given the chance one day of joining us on equal terms, with a sense of identity with the past and a useful contribution to make to the future.

For me, Brazil was where it all began and so I was anxious to learn what was developing there. In the summer of 1970 a Medical Mission of the International Committee of the Red Cross undertook a 'survey of the conditions of existence and health of the indigenous populations in a number of different regions of Brazil'. They confined themselves largely to medical matters, but the news they brought back was disturbing. I was therefore delighted to be invited by the Brazilian Foreign Ministry to make a similar visit and write a report on the non-medical aspects of the situation and, in particular, the possibilities of co-ordinating international aid for the Indians of Brazil. Marika was also invited to come and write about the tour from a woman's point of view. I applied for a Winston Churchill Memorial Trust Fellowship towards the cost of the journey and they most generously gave me a substantial grant even though I had

to leave before the normal interviews took place. We left
England on the 5th January 1971.

The Brazilian government lodged us at the Hotel Nacional
in Brasilia, one of the best modern hotels in the world with
a large swimming-pool and every sort of comfort. I had
little time to enjoy all this, as every moment was occupied
in talks, discussions, plans and preparations.

We had spent a week in New York on the way which had
given me a chance to have some long and invaluable talks
with leading American anthropologists. I am not an anthropologist by training, and would have blamed no one for
resenting the fact that I was setting out to investigate a
situation concerning the remaining Indians of Brazil and
their future. Instead, I was given every possible help and
encouragement, and the fact that the Fund had come into
existence was welcomed. The American Anthropological
Association had already agreed to support Adrian Cowell's
and my effort in promoting a nomination for the Nobel
Peace prize for Orlando and Claudio Villas Boas, and I met
great enthusiasm for the development of a similar or related
body to the Primitive Peoples Fund in the USA. Only the
name was unacceptable and Survival International was
generally thought much better.

Besides meeting some of the world's leading authorities
on the Indians of the areas we were about to go to, we visited
the Museum of Ethnography in Philadelphia and the Pea-
body at Harvard, as well as the American Natural History
Museum in New York. The information, advice and contacts which resulted from these encounters made a tremendous difference to the whole subsequent journey, and I am
truly grateful to all those who helped me so generously.

I had previously corresponded with some of the people I
met, and to others I had letters of introduction. Dr Margaret
Mead, whom I finally tracked to earth in her extraordinary
gothic attic on the top of the American Museum of Natural
History, knew nothing about me, and could therefore not

be blamed for jumping to the conclusion that I was a crank 'do-gooder' representing a group of woolly-minded idealists who thought the Indians should be preserved because they are pretty. Trying to persuade her that this was not the case was a rather alarming experience.

After being put into the wrong lift and groping my way through an unlit and dusty library where I was in constant danger of tripping over and breaking one of the priceless artefacts littering the floor, I was shown into Dr Mead's office a few minutes late for my interview. I faced a small, beady-eyed dumpling of a lady who sailed into the attack as I came through the door, firing questions at me and then contradicting me and pulling me up on anything I said. No questioning of her criticisms was allowed and much was assumed without my saying it.

The main point that annoyed her was the concept, un-stated by me, that primitive peoples were any better off as they were. She said she was 'maddened by antibiotic-ridden idealists who wouldn't stand three weeks in the jungle', which was, I felt, a little unfair in my case. The whole 'Noble Savage' concept almost made her foam at the mouth. 'All primitive peoples,' she said, 'lead miserable, unhappy, cruel lives, most of which are spent trying to kill each other.' The reason they lived in the unpleasant places they did, like the middle of the Brazilian jungle, was that nobody else would. She said there were only two possible reasons for wishing to help them to survive. One was that their art, culture, dancing, music, etc. was pleasant and attractive and their grand-children might thank us for trying to preserve or at best record it now that we have the proper technical means of doing so. Secondly, there was the common cause of humanity. But she did not accept for one moment that they had any special reasons for being protected, as she denied any advantage of one race over another. She also claimed emphatically that they all wanted one thing only and that was to have as many material possessions and com-forts as possible. Those still running away in the jungle were the ones who had encountered the most unpleasant savagery from Europeans and even though they might be having no contact now, if they could possibly get hold of any aluminium pots or anything else they would use them. It was the memories of the horrors they had suffered which kept them from seeking contact.

She said that to protect them on the grounds that they could be useful to us or contribute anything was nonsense. 'No primitive person has *ever* contributed *anything,* or ever will,' she said. She had no time for suggestions of medical knowledge or the value of jungle lore. She was not impressed by curare and said that, 'Quinine was a positive disaster as it meant that Englishmen took their wives with them to foreign parts whereas previously they had interbred happily with the natives!'

During this onslaught it crossed my mind that I would love to get her together with Conrad Gorinsky as there seemed to be absolutely no point of contact, except that both felt so strongly about the subject. I suspected they might get on rather well. And, in fact, although time was very short as Dr Mead's secretary came in to tell her she should be leaving for lunch, we began to warm to each other. She said that if ever there had been a time when a movement such as ours stood a chance of being listened to it was now; that the climate was right now, as it had not been for thirty or forty years, for us to be reasonably effective. We agreed that the main justification for our existence was that it was bad for the world to let these people die and the effort to prevent their extermination was good for mankind even if it failed.

In the end I took her by taxi to her next appointment. I began to feel that she was not the dragon she had at first appeared to be, but brilliant and capable and, underneath her gruff manner, a highly likeable person. For her part, I hope she revised her first impression as to my crankiness and felt that I might be able to achieve something useful. We parted very amicably with her offering 'any help she could give', which, as she is the best-known anthropologist in

America, could be a very great deal.

In my conversations with other anthropologists in the United States much of the talk had centred on the question of national parks or reservations for the Indians. The suggestion that employing international aid to play a part in the demarcation and administration of such areas was made several times and there was general agreement that only through the enlightened provision and running of such areas would the remaining Indians stand any chance of survival.

When I arrived in Brazil and began to discuss the problem with experts in Rio de Janeiro and Brasilia, I again found this view emphatically supported. Although there was a wide level of disagreement on the ways and means which should be adopted to help the Indians, insulation from rapid change was a prime factor in all the expert opinion given me. Unfortunately, this view is apparently in direct conflict with the Brazilian national obsession with progress and development. I do not believe that this conflict need exist, nor that isolating and safeguarding the Indians' culture and way of life is detrimental to the country's welfare. Indeed, I passionately believe the opposite. But the fact that the vast majority of Brazilians are caught up in the nationalistic idealism of the country, and also know little or nothing about the Indian problem, or even that there is one, often makes discussion about the Indians very difficult.

There is considerable fear of Indians in Brazil. I was asked several times by people living in large cities whether I thought there was a chance of an Indian uprising. Considering the very small proportion of Indians in the population (less than 0·1 per cent), their very wide distribution over the large country, and the fact that they come from about one hundred and fifty different and usually inimical tribes, the idea is perfectly ludicrous.

In the interior the fear is slightly more rational as clashes have taken place, and still do, in which both *civilizados* and Indians are killed. But cases of Indian attacks on farms or villages are rare. More often, individuals or expeditions travelling into or through the territory of a particular tribe are massacred. It is unfortunate that the Brazilian population pioneering into these territories often consists of the least suitable representatives of Western culture to be making first contact with the Indians. The splendid lack of racial discrimination which is such a striking feature of Brazil, and which, even if not complete, puts most of the rest of the world to shame, sadly vanishes when it is a question of Indians. The desperately poor settlers on the fringe of civilization, whose standard of living, physique and culture is patently worse than that of the members of a thriving Indian community, *know* that those Indians are dangerous, unpredictable animals. And, whatever other possessions he may lack, the settler is sure to have a gun, which means that he is militarily superior at any meeting. In the long run he may be able to adapt sufficiently to his environment to extract a living from it. If this turns into a surplus it is most likely that he will use the profits from selling this surplus to hurry back to the cities of the coast.

The Indian, on the other hand, lacking resistance to the *civilizados'* diseases, needs civilization's medicines to cure or protect him against them. So either he runs further into the jungle, often taking the disease with him and spreading the epidemic to other groups, or he becomes dependent upon charity to be cured. If this is provided in an enlightened way it may be possible for him not to be destroyed in the process, but too often the overpowering demonstration of technological or moral superiority that goes with it destroys the Indian's self-confidence and he, too, grows to believe that there is something inferior and wrong with him. Once this happens there is little chance of his ever entering Brazilian society as an equal.

Those in the cities with an interest in exploiting the interior seldom see the Indian as anything but a menace.

His potential as a labourer is not great and anyway there is no shortage of manpower in the overcrowded coastal and north-eastern regions. This manpower is, however, reluctant to go where there may be danger from Indians. The Indian may have some value as a tool for extracting skins or nuts from the inhospitable jungle, but the profit motive is insufficiently present in his make-up to encourage him to produce a lot. Worst of all, he has an unforgivable tendency to live on, and lay claim to, land which others have 'legitimately' bought from a São Paulo property dealer, and to do so solely on the basis of two thousand years' occupancy and without a shed of documentary proof.

In Rio de Janeiro I met an American who, as part of a syndicate, was building up a chain of vast ranches in the Mato Grosso. He showed films of the beautiful country in which his herds of cattle roamed, but this was mostly taken from the air. He admitted that although he flew his aeroplane in regularly to inspect his properties, he seldom, if ever, spent a night there. Some Xavante Indians were, he said, 'allowed' to live on a corner of his land but he said they would have to go soon as he needed to clear the jungle there. He was proud of the way he had treated them, saying that every month or so he gave them a sack or two of rice and beans – and the current edition of *Playboy* magazine, which he showed pictures of them looking at, among hoots of laughter from the rest of the audience. He claimed to admire the Xavante, saying that they were very tough guys who were independent and had no wish to be assimilated, but he finally destroyed his credibility with his next remark.

'You can buy the land out there now for the same price as a couple of bottles of beer per acre. When you've got half a million acres and twenty thousand head of cattle, you can leave the lousy place and go and live in Paris, Hawaii, Switzerland or anywhere you choose.'

It seems a pity that the opening up of Brazil's interior should be in the hands of such men.

*   *   *

In Brasilia, most of my time was occupied in discussing and planning our itinerary and the arrangements for our visit to the interior. We were there at the invitation of Itamaraty, the Brazilian Foreign Office, and I spent many fascinating hours in talks with our host, Minister Alarico Silveira, an intelligent and most charming man. His complete grasp of the situation and of the international concern which lay behind my mission was very refreshing and through his patient and sensible arguments and explanations I learnt a lot about the most enlightened Brazilian attitudes towards the country's problems.

The detailed arrangements for our transportation were in the hands of the Fundação Nacional do Indio (FUNAI), in co-operation with the Brazilian Air Force (FAB), and here I was not so lucky. The recently appointed head of FUNAI, General Bandeira do Mello, made it quite clear that he did not approve of my mission or of me.

No sooner were we introduced than he reprimanded me severely for having gone to São Paulo for the day to visit Orlando Villas Boas and for having arrived in Brasilia a day early. He said that Orlando Villas Boas was just an ordinary FUNAI employee like any other and I should not have gone to see him. I pointed out that for nearly a year I had been working on the nomination for a Nobel Peace Prize for Orlando and his brother Claudio, and that it had been necessary to see him. I had also been commissioned by the Royal Geographical Society to deliver to Orlando his citation in connexion with that Society's Gold Medal.

The real storm broke when it came to discussing our itinerary. I had sent two proposed itineraries from England, one two months and one six weeks before our departure. During my visit to the USA, and as a result of further talks in Brazil, some very useful suggestions had been made as to ways in which our visit could be improved and the maximum number and variety of tribes seen. In particular, several anthropologists had urged that we visit some of the more acculturated Indians of the south, so as to be able to contrast their state with the more primitive tribes of the Amazon jungle. The General refused to consider the slightest variation from the original proposal, saying that the dates had been fixed and all the arrangements for our reception and accommodation along the route had been made and could not be changed. When I tried to explain how little difference the alterations would make and how little inconvenience it would cause, he became exceedingly angry and shouted that he would not allow us to go anywhere at all if we did not do exactly as he said. At this point, I was very near to replying that if he felt that way then perhaps I should return to England saying that it had proved impossible to prepare any report. Instead I managed to control myself and suggested that I go to another room to discuss the details with his staff.

This was agreed. Suddenly the atmosphere changed completely. Marika and I were formally welcomed to Brazil by the General and presented with black wooden Nambiquara wedding rings wrapped up in little boxes, tied with a ribbon and containing a prettily done message from the President of FUNAI.

In the other room I had a meeting at a round table, jokingly referred to as a 'Geneva Conference', with members of the General's staff. They could not have been more co-operative and we began to make excellent progress. I outlined my ideal plan and we worked out dates and distances on the map. The Air Force were consulted about planes and gradually a satisfactory compromise began to take shape.

At noon we had to break off as a formal luncheon was being given in our honour by Itamaraty. Among those present were the British Chargé d'Affaires in Brasilia and an Air Force general in full dress uniform. General Bandeira de Mello sat on my left and during the first course asked me politely about the background to my work. For a few moments he listened to my remarks about international concern over the problem of the Indians and the desire to co-operate and then, while I was in mid-sentence, abruptly turned his back on me, lit a cigarette and spent the rest of the meal talking to his other neighbour and chain-smoking.

When my talks with FUNAI resumed I was told that the General had vetoed a crucial part of the plan and so it was necessary to begin again. Eventually, after two days, we worked out a timetable which allowed visits to all the areas I wanted to see in the time available. It did not, however, allow any extra time at all and so we had to abandon our original idea of accepting an invitation to see the Carnival in Rio and link up there with John Hemming for the remainder of the journey. This was bad luck on Marika, who had been looking forward to the Carnival, but she claimed that she was really rather relieved as the Brazilian women were so elegant and beautiful that she was afraid to compete without spending a great deal more money than we had with us on clothes.

On the day after the luncheon I again had to leave the 'planning committee' for a meeting with the Minister of the Interior, Snr Costa Cavalcante. FUNAI is a department of the Ministry of the Interior and so the Minister holds overall responsibility for its actions. The General was there and, in fact, monopolized the conversation to a degree that I found surprising, considering the Minister was present. He is a very small and rather stout man with a loud voice and he became highly agitated when the question of the rate of integration came up. He seemed obsessed with the idea of speed and dismissed suggestions that there might be anything of value to preserve in the Indians' own culture.

In the past, in Brazil, first contact with Indian tribes has been brought about by a patient and long-drawn out process devised by Rondon, the great Brazilian explorer. Presents are left out and replaced when the Indians take them. Trust is gradually built up until the *sertanista* is invited to visit the Indians' village. Although the subsequent care of Indians thus pacified has often left a great deal to be desired, this method of contact is still today generally regarded as the best and the one most likely to give the Indians a chance of survival. It is the technique Meirelles, one of Brazil's leading Indian experts, has used successfully with several tribes in the past and is currently using with the Cinta Larga, a large, more recently-contacted group in the west. The Villas Boas brothers, too, have begun the process with the Kreen Akrore, based on their wide previous experience. Padre Calleri attempted a different system with the Atroari in 1968 and all but one of his party of twelve were slaughtered.

The General now shouted at me, 'It is no longer necessary to use the old slow process. Now we have new psychological methods for doing it in six months!'

I asked him what these were and he replied, 'We have applied psychology to the subject and we resettle them as quickly as possible in new villages and then remove the children and begin to educate them. We give them the benefits of our medicine and our education, and once they are completely acculturated we let them go out into the world as completely integrated citizens like you and me and the Minister here.'

I protested. Surely it was not quite as easy as that and would at least take longer than six months? But again he insisted, 'We can now bring totally isolated Indians into a state of full integration in a period of six months. We do not need the advice of European anthropologists and so-called experts.'

When pressed for examples, he said, 'We have been very successful with the Gaviões.'

He then began to attack me directly, saying that all I wanted to do was put the Indians in a zoo and treat them like animals.

The Minister then intervened, which was just as well as I was in danger of losing my temper, and said that surely in many cases the whole process would need to take as much as three generations. At this, the General interrupted and insisted, 'No! We can do it in six months,' and the Minister went on to say that of course it was necessary that the process should be as rapid as possible. He also said that it was an internal matter for Brazil to work out. To this I replied that, although the situations were totally different, the same could be said of South Africa, but that did not stop people in other countries being concerned.

'Although the United Nations is not yet very involved in the problems of primitive peoples,' I went on, 'a huge amount of concern and a deep desire to do something to help does exist in Europe, the United States and elsewhere. All I am trying to do is to see if this concern can be put to good use, rather than destructive criticism, and whether ways exist in which some of the large sums of money potentially available could be spent on behalf of the Indians of Brazil.'

The Minister replied that quite definitely the Brazilian government could not accept money but that medical aid and advice would be most valuable. 'We welcome advice of all sorts from lawyers, anthropologists, sociologists and anyone else, and we will consider this advice.'

I brought up the question of the new Indian statute which was in draft form before the Brazilian Congress and a copy of which I had just been given the previous day.

The Minister pointed out that under Article 198 of the Brazilian constitution the inalienable right of the Indians to the land they occupied was guaranteed. Fortunately I had my copy of the new statute with me and was able to point to Article 38 which stated that, 'An Indian, whether assimilated or not, who has built a house, even if in the manner used by his tribe, and has planted and cultivated land for five consecutive years, may own the property, up to a limit of five hectares.' This, I said, might be interpreted abroad and out of context as a case of racial discrimination in limiting the amount of land an Indian might hold where such a limit was not imposed on other Brazilians. After the vehement protestations of love and affection for the Indian which followed, and the affirmation that he had every opportunity to better himself and, indeed, more than the surrounding population, I was able to explain that this was not my accusation but simply how the law might be interpreted abroad in its present form.

The Minister said, 'It is a most excellent law and international advice from lawyers and experts all over the world has been taken in drafting it.'

I have not since then had any success in tracking down who these experts were and, in fact, it has become impossible to get hold of copies of the draft statute. The reply to my last application for a copy was, 'Since the statute has not yet become law and changes may yet be made in the final draft, copies are not available.'

More disturbing still, I did not find a single FUNAI employee, missionary, priest, doctor or anthropologist in all Brazil other than Brasilia who had seen a copy or knew what it contained. It seems to me that a document which sets out to 'regulate the rights and duties of Indians and indigenous peoples with respect to their integration in the national community' should have the widest possible airing among experts in the field before becoming law.

The Minister, who was most courteous and helpful throughout the meeting, offered us every facility during our visits, but made it quite clear that his concern was with the opening up of the interior of Brazil, the successful completion of road programmes and the resettlement of the dense coastal population. It is a mammoth task and one which Brazil, rightly or wrongly, is firmly committed to pursuing to the limit. Inevitably, this will mean disturbance of one sort or another to the Indians of the interior which would surely make it all the more vital that their interests are protected by an organ of the government whose sole preoccupation is their welfare, and which is not a part of the very movement which is bringing about the disturbance. At one time the old Indian Protection Service (SPI) was in this position and responsible only to the President direct. It abused that position in time but that is no reason for abandoning the principle.

Later, back in his office, General Bandeira de Mello and I examined the large wall-map on which some of the Indian tribes of Brazil had been marked with coloured pins. Several of these he pulled out and moved across the map explaining that this was how some of the tribes now in contact would be re-settled. On one occasion he explained that this involved taking interpreters from each tribe and bringing them together to see if they fought. If they did not, then it would be all right to re-settle both tribes in one new village outside the territory of either. I suggested that some tribes were nomadic and that it would take them time to adapt to the idea of being settled, to which he replied, 'They are perfectly free to wander off if they want to. We are not going to put a fence around them.'

On the question of reserving large areas as parks, both for flora and fauna as well as for the Indians already there, the General became very agitated and said, 'Do you mean to suggest that I should say to the President that he should not put a new road or a new development programme through this area just because I want to keep a few Indians and a few animals free from civilization?'

'Yes,' I replied.

The General made it quite clear to me that he did not have a high regard for the Villas Boas brothers. He repeated several times that they were just ordinary FUNAI workers like any others, and that their work in Xingu was much less effective than that being carried on elsewhere in Brazil. In particular he cited the island of Bananal as a model of what could and should be done and said that I would see for myself how much better the situation was there. He made great play of the assertion that the Indians, with all the benefits of Western medicine, live longer than those not yet contacted in the wild. I asked him whether any surveys had been made of the ages of groups of uncontacted Indians and he nodded dismissively saying, 'Oh yes, we know all about that.'

PART TWO

✦

Xingu–Posto Leonardo

Xingu–Diauarum

XINGU NATIONAL PARK

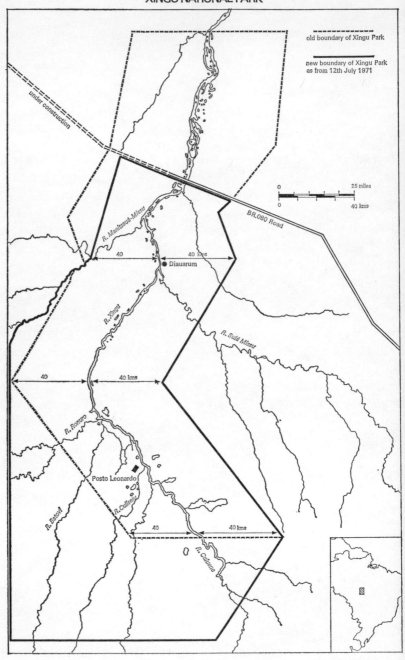

old boundary of Xingu Park

new boundary of Xingu Park
as from 12th July 1971

under construction

BR.080 Road

R. Manitsauá-Missú

Diauarum

R. Xingú

R. Suiá Missú

R. Ronuro

Posto Leonardo

R. Culiseu

R. Batoví

R. Culuene

0   25 miles

0   40 kms

40   40 kms

40   40 kms

40   40 kms

Xingu–Posto Leonardo

❧

THE Xingu National Park is unlike anywhere else in the world. The creation of Orlando and Claudio Villas Boas – and a third brother, Leonardo, who died of heart failure in 1962 – it is a legend and at the same time very much a reality. The brothers, members of an official expedition into the interior in 1945 which effectively began the process of opening up the whole area to development, were shocked by the effect their own well-intentioned contact had on the Indians they met on the way. They were even more appalled by the government's lack of interest in the people whose lives had been deeply affected by its expedition and its refusal to help those who were then dying of an epidemic brought in by its members. 'How can we send medicine for tribesmen when there is not enough for the slums of Rio?' was the reply to urgent requests for help. Many of the Indians died and the lives of the brothers were changed for good.

Since then, for twenty-six years, almost every waking hour has been devoted by the brothers to working and fighting on behalf of the Indians at tremendous cost to their health and often in considerable danger. The danger, often, has arisen less during their expeditions to hostile tribes than from the political and commercial interests waiting in the cities to knife them in the back. All the land in the park had been sold to property developers before these sales were invalidated by presidential decree when the park was created in 1961. People still hold these titles – and wait. Missionaries have never been allowed into the park and have at times formed a powerful lobby against it. And the brothers have never been afraid to condemn corruption in high places, the exploitation of the Indians, and mistaken policies. Not surprisingly, all this has earned them many enemies.

Their courage and dedication has been recognized, at times, as well. They were made members of the Honora e Merito of Brazil for work with the Indians in 1951 and chevaliers of the Order of Merit and Work in 1968.

The American Explorers Club made them honorary members and in 1967 the Royal Geographical Society gave them its highest award, the Founders' Gold Medal, 'in recognition of their distinguished contributions to exploration in the Xingu Region, Mato Grosso, Brazil, and of their devoted service to the welfare of the Indian tribes'.

Their work was already acknowledged by anthropologists all over the world as one of the most successful experiments in combating the destruction of a primitive people; and Adrian Cowell's superb film about them, *The Tribe That Hides From Man*, which was chosen as the best documentary of 1970, made them known to a wider audience. Their 1971 nomination for the Nobel Peace Prize had the backing of such distinguished, and different, authorities as Sir Julian Huxley, Professor Claude Lévi-Strauss, Dr Edmund Leach and Peter Scott, as well as the American Anthropological Association and the Societés d'Americanistes of France and Switzerland.

I had seen Adrian's film half-a-dozen times and felt I knew them already, but I had also heard some of the criticisms; the suggestions that they kept people out of Xingu for their own questionable reasons; that they had a secret gold mine there which had made them millionaires; that they were exploiting the Indians and deliberately holding back their development so as to get rich on the proceeds of photographs and articles about them. Finally, there had been the President of FUNAI's own damping comments.

My visit to Orlando had been brief. There had only been time to spend one day with him and he had looked ill and tired. His cataract had been troubling him and he was nearly blind. Almost the only time when I had seen signs of his famous exuberance and good humour had been when he drove me at speed through the terrifying traffic of São Paulo guided by a small Indian boy who sat next to him and told him whether the lights were red or green. Otherwise, he had been depressed and often silent. I had had much to tell him – messages and *abraços* to deliver from friends in Europe and the United States – and a thousand questions to ask. He had replied shortly, and had seldom elaborated on the subject. His mind had seemed preoccupied and weighed down with a great sadness. There was a bustle of activity in the small suburban house which was his office and doubled as a lodging for passing Indians. He cheered up a little back at his extremely simple and modest flat where I met his wife, Marina, and his two-month-old son, Orlando, of whom he was delightfully proud. But I felt that I had only seen a small corner of the picture. Orlando, ill and pensive in the bustling modern city of São Paulo, was not what the legend was all about. Now we were on our way to see the real thing. I hoped that I would not be disappointed, but was afraid that I would be. Few things can stand up to the sort of build-up which the Xingu had had for me since I had first heard of it when passing close by in 1958.

The aeroplane we had been given was a very comfortable twin-engined Beechcraft. It was piloted by two colonels of the Brazilian Air Force. With us was Edson Ramalho Junior, the FUNAI employee appointed to accompany us throughout our journey, and we were looked after during the flight by a young sergeant who, from time to time, poured us diminutive cups of excellent strong Brazilian coffee.

The flight to Xingu took nearly three hours and we flew first towards the island of Bananal. This is a huge island formed by the River Araguaia which divides, and then joins again some two hundred miles later. Richard Mason and I had reached the island in our jeep in 1958 – the first vehicle ever to do so – but it had broken in half there and I had had to ride for help while Richard had stayed alone until I returned in a second jeep fourteen days later. Flying back over the route I had ridden nearly thirteen years before was very exciting for me as, with the help of the pilots' maps, I was able to pick out points at which I had forded rivers on the horse I had borrowed from a settler at the southern end of the island; and then at last the very spot, or at least I was pretty sure it was the very spot, where the jeep had broken down. Near there was the beautiful little tributary in which we had swum and caught piranha.

We flew on down the Araguaia until the point at which the Rio das Mortes joins it. There we saw, below us, the new town of São Félix; and opposite, on the island, the Karaja village of Santa Isabel where I had filmed, in 1958, the witch doctors dancing. We were due to return in a couple of weeks to visit the Karaja, but now turned west and flew towards the Xingu. To begin with, much of the jungle had been cleared and we could see the rectangular shapes of new farms being carved out of the surrounding bush. Suddenly we came on the great scar of the Cuiabá-Belém road and in fact flew over it at the point where the spur road from Xavantina cuts across it to continue west into the Xingu Park. It was a rather terrifying sight from the air, a die-straight road of red earth two hundred yards wide slashing through the virgin jungle. I saw no more farms after this and, crossing the Suiá Missu River, we came eventually to the big lagoon which marks the edge of the Xingu River itself, at this point called the Culuene. We turned right, downstream, and soon had our first proper view of an Indian village from the air. The neat circle of huts holding back the surrounding jungle from the bare, beaten earth of the centre seemed right and natural in that environment.

Soon after, we saw a scatter of white buildings, some with corrugated iron roofs, perched on a bluff over a branch of the river. In spite of the romantic setting, they struck a jarring note. Here at last was Posto Leonardo. Circling to come in to land, we could see that there were Indian villages at varying distances from the post at three of the four points of the compass. Furthest away, down a long straight track, were the Kamayura on the edge of the large lagoon which plays such an important part in their lives. Much closer on either side of the post, opposite each other, were the small villages of the Txikao and the Yawalapiti.

We landed and I was able to pick out Claudio Villas Boas among the group of half a dozen or so Europeans and a rather larger number of Indians. He was less shy than I had expected and greeted us warmly. While our baggage was loaded on to the post's jeep, we all walked to the buildings which lay hardly two hundred yards from the runway. We passed three small aeroplanes sitting rather incongruously next to a thatched hut. Claudio said that two were out of order; only one was operating. The post itself formed a rough square with the main buildings overlooking a beautiful stretch of river with a sandy beach. We were shown to the simple guest hut which was comfortable and clean. Having unpacked the things we had brought for him, we went with Claudio to his office. There I presented him with the citation relating to the Gold Medal and a frame which I had had made for it in Brasilia; various letters and books which I had been asked to deliver by mutual friends; a bottle of twelve-year-old Scotch whisky; and the present which pleased him above all the others – the twenty-fifth anniversary issue of the American Gun Manual which I had bought in New York. We spent quite a long time looking at the pictures of guns in this. Claudio said, 'They are exquisite works of art and much too beautiful to be used for killing.'

He also made a very touching speech, saying how totally unworthy he was to have been given the Royal Geographical Society's award, and how deeply moved he was that I, and people like me, should be concerned with his, and the Indians', problems.

We arranged with the pilots to pick us up in a couple of weeks from Diauarum, and they took off again to fly back to Brasilia. Claudio and I went and sat in hammocks in the big open shed overlooking the river, and began to talk.

He was very angry and very desperate. He spoke of giving up and leaving the park. He was particularly bitter about the road which, in spite of all his and his brother's protestations, had now actually entered the park. When he had radioed Brasilia to say that this had happened, they had not even bothered to reply, let alone do anything to try and help. He said he realized that everybody in authority in Brasilia had turned against his policy, but he simply insisted that their ideas were wrong.

'It is stupid to try and integrate the Indian, for the Indian is better than we are, knows how to live better than we do, and has much more to teach us than we could ever teach him.

I am Brazilian and I love my country. I am not against progress, but my country's attitude is more under-developed than the country itself. The way it is going about exploiting its natural resources will inevitably drive the country towards Marxism, not just because it is being done in a capitalist way, but because the form of capitalism is so corrupt. It really is an extreme case of just a few people getting very, very rich on the pretence of helping other people to develop in the name of progress.

Who will benefit from the road? The Indians? Absolutely not! No. The land taken from the park will simply become three or four large *fazendas* and a few *Paulistas* will become rich.

The road cutting the park shows that there is no genuine desire to protect the Indian. If there *was* any concern for the Indian, and his way of life, and if this concern carried any weight at all in the face of the blind march of progress, then at least they would have hesitated on reaching the edge of the park and would have listened to the advice of the man who administers the park!'

But the authorities ignored his cable and the road came through. Claudio told me later that when he tried to sleep at night nowadays, he just lay awake seeing a great brown swathe two hundred metres wide cutting through the jungle

44

towards his Indians and destroying them wherever it came in contact with them.

'The time is coming, and very soon, when there will be no more Indians in Brazil,' he said. What he obviously found particularly frustrating and dreadful was that the solution to the problem was within our grasp. 'The Indians already have a perfectly-developed social system. They do not need change. Rather, it is we who need to change our attitudes towards them. The problem of primitive peoples in the world is a worldwide one and should not in any way relate to an individual government's own development programmes.'

It pleased and moved me very much to hear my own beliefs expressed so strongly by one who had lived with the problem for so long. Claudio did not entirely agree with the Marxist philosophy of Darcy Ribeiro, Brazil's leading anthropologist, that the Indian must die because he cannot withstand civilization. He said that this was a fatalistic approach and that if only the right policies were adopted all could be well and the Indian could grow and develop in the twentieth and on into the twenty-first century. This, he said, was fundamental to the issue and to the thinking behind the Xingu system.

'There really is no problem,' he said. 'It is only created by vast gestures towards progress, most of which will not do anybody any good, least of all the Indian.'

Only by changing attitudes towards the Indians could their extermination be avoided, he felt. Then it might be possible for Brazil to integrate the Indian properly. The frontiersmen and the people who are settling or being re-settled in the interior are often the worst products of our civilization so that at the moment the Indian is being integrated into a level of culture below his potential which will make him of less use to the nation. Even if the Indian is integrated effectively into these low strata of society, and does not die in the process, which is likely, he will certainly stand no chance of ever rising above this level. He is therefore doomed to remain below the lowest members of our society. This is the salvation we are offering him. This is the civilization, the opportunity, the education and the hope which we are giving to the Indian in the name of mankind and the name of progress.

I suggested that the painful and long, drawn-out process of integration might be avoided by taking the children away from the tribe and giving them the opportunity of education elsewhere. Claudio looked into my eyes for a long time without speaking. Even though I had been speaking as devil's advocate, I felt very ashamed when he said, 'Is that by any lights the way to improve a people's lot and to civilize them? To take away the children from a family? To remove children from the mother and father and to bring them up in an alien culture, so that their family, their tribe, their life, is lost completely?'

Indian culture has developed a system of myths, legends and cultural heroes, and everything they do is backed by this culture. Every action that the Indian takes in his normal life has a purpose and a meaning and is part of his system of life. Can the same be said any more of our lives? It is something that we have lost and should admire.

The settler population into which it is proposed to integrate the Indian has no knowledge, or respect, or the least understanding of what the Indian's culture and their way of life is all about. All it wants from them is the land they occupy, the women as prostitutes and the men as common labourers, and this is what it takes. The Indian is not regarded as a 'person' at all and therefore stands no chance of becoming one even according to the very modest criteria set by this population.

Claudio felt that if the Indian existed in Europe, or in England, where we have had our experience of destroying people and have perhaps learnt our lesson, where we have suffered through major wars, but, above all, where the standard of living and the attitudes that go with it are highly developed, then there would perhaps be a chance of integrating the Indian effectively into a society in which he could improve his situation. In the present Brazilian society he could only be destroyed. While expressing the deepest reservations about our own fitness to cope with the problem, and even more doubt about the ability of our so-called super-developed society to understand and assimilate the Indian successfully, I wholeheartedly agreed that only by giving ourselves time to study ways in which integration could come about, time during which attitudes could change, would the Indian and the other primitive people of the world stand any chance of effective survival. We agreed that the most vital priority was to protect the Indian's land rights, guaranteed in the constitution but so often abused.

As we talked, swinging in our hammocks above the river, people and animals came and went and the oppressive midday hum and heat of the jungle began to descend over the post. No one interrupted us for long, but minor administrative points were raised with Claudio, and from time to time naked Indians, who had walked from their often distant villages, arrived. After clasping Claudio's hand and exchanging a few words, they went and sat in a patch of shade and watched us.

Behind his small beard and dark glasses, Claudio was often silent for long periods of time, but never hesitated or seemed in doubt about what he wanted to say. I was deeply impressed by the sincerity with which he spoke.

The post's little troupe of comic parakeets kept up a constant chatter and activity in the background. Occasionally they climbed down my hammock rope in order to investigate me more closely and see whether I had any food in the hammock with me.

When we were called to lunch Claudio did not come but went off to his own quarters.

In the afternoon, when we were taking a short rest in our hammocks, Pionim, the head of the post – a Kayabi Indian – came and asked if we would like to go and visit the Yawalapiti village. We jumped into the jeep and drove perhaps a mile to the neat little circle of seven thatched huts, with one smaller hut in the middle. The whole area of the village and the beaten earth in the centre was spotlessly clean. Outside the central hut sat a row of twelve men with urucu, a red paint extracted from a fruit, on their bodies and feathers on their arms. They had bands of cloth tightly bound around their legs and wide, coloured bead-belts. Otherwise they were naked. They were muscular, healthy-looking and seemed big, although they were not tall. The chief, a young man of twenty-two, who came forward to greet us, was completely relaxed and at ease. He politely welcomed us to the village and took us round some of the huts to see their life. Everything was so right and perfect that it seemed almost like a stage set and I wondered if it had been laid on specially for our benefit. I learnt that it was in fact a special occasion and that a small feast was to be held that evening but that all this was in no way connected with our visit. I found on subsequent visits that the normal everyday scene was not so very different, except that most of the men would have been working or hunting away from the village, and their body decorations would not have been so fresh.

However, we were much too busy enjoying our first visit to a Xingu village to worry about this. There were virtually no indications of the twentieth century and no apparent need for them. The huts were beautifully made with dark, spacious interiors, warm inside, while the air was still fresh. Two or three family fires burnt at intervals, and in one of the huts there was a large store-room and oven in the middle. In this one the rafters were blackened from the smoke of the oven. The women and children also wore no clothes, and yet there was no sense of shame or nakedness. Nor was there any embarrassment or worry about us taking photographs. Rather, we were often ignored while busily clicking away. None of them 'froze' or posed.

I gave the chief the small bag of presents I had brought with me. He immediately distributed them to everybody else. This was a practice which I had been advised to follow by others who had been to the Xingu, but I never found that the presents were either expected or demanded of me. Perhaps if I had been spending several days in each village filming and interfering with their lives it might have been a different story, but my small token bags of mixed useful things like razor blades, sweets, bars of soap and ·22 cartridges were always received more as surprising but acceptable presents than in any sense as a payment – rather in the same way as somebody coming to stay in your house might bring a box of chocolates.

In the centre of the village there was an enormous pottery bowl, about three or four feet across, in which a yellow rice-like mixture was being stirred. The bowl, I knew, was made by the Waura, a neighbouring tribe and the only one in the Upper Xingu to make pottery. The mixture was made from piqui fruit, which tastes and looks like a rather bitter apricot and grows wild in the Xingu, mixed with manioc, the staple Indian, and indeed Brazilian, diet. Manioc is a tuberous root, which has many varieties. Some of these contain prussic acid, a deadly poison, which has to be extracted by pulping the manioc and squeezing the juice out. Much of the domestic work in the Indian villages centres around this process.

Although we only spent an hour or two in the Yawalapiti village on this first visit we went back to the post with our heads reeling from the mass of impressions and the sheer beauty of what we had seen. The friendly relaxed atmosphere, and the complete lack of any pressure upon us to talk or take part in anything we did not wish to do was such an unusual feeling that it took some time to get used to. It was the sort of atmosphere that I have seldom felt in the civilized world except with very close friends or at home with my own family. And yet here we had walked straight into a world in which we were accepted as equals, neither superior nor inferior – again something which is very unusual in the Western world – and had been able to join in as much or as little as we pleased. We had walked around the village, stopping here and there to see what was going on beside a particular family fire or in a dark corner of a hut and, although our arrival had caused some excitement, once this had died down and we had been accepted, we had been completely free. Marika could hardly have had a better introduction to her first Indians.

In the early evening we visited the Txikao village which is a mere ten minutes walk from the post. This tribe is in a different position from the others in the upper Xingu. Orlando and Claudio rescued them only a few years ago from a situation in which they were being exploited outside the park at a prospector's camp. Many of the tribe had died and, with too few adult males left to support the remainder, their position looked hopeless. When they were first brought into the park they were in a state of despair and had almost given up the will to survive. As a result no children were born to the tribe for the first two years until they began to feel secure again. Now we learnt that from the twenty-five adults, nineteen children had already been produced in a very short time. This represents a major achievement of the Xingu Park. To rescue a tribe from the horrors of semi-slavery and prostitution, and to encourage them to restore their confidence and desire to live again must require tremendous patience.

The Txikao we met were small and wiry with sharp weasel-like faces and a bright inquisitive manner. Unlike the other groups in the area, most of them wore clothes, as a result of their prolonged contact with *civilizados*. Some of them still had a slightly aggressive and touchy manner, but this was offset by a lively sense of humour and quick laughs and smiles.

They were having a small party themselves when we arrived. A few women, two or three grown men, but for the most part, children, were doing a sort of conga in and out of the main hut. Stamping on every fourth beat with the right foot – around which bells made from pigs' trotters had been tied – the fifteen dancers wheeled merrily along, turning around to go backwards for a step or two, and then turning again and circling a pole stuck in the ground before chanting and dancing back into the hut from which the muffled sounds of the continued dance emerged. It was becoming dark and so we had to photograph with flash, but nobody worried when we did this inside the hut as well as outside. At first, all the adults were fully clothed, but when it became pitch-dark we suddenly noticed that the two women dancing in the procession had removed their dresses and that some of the men were also naked. This, I thought, showed an interesting consciousness of nudity, inspired presumably by their contact with the miners, and perhaps indicated that they wore clothes to avoid being laughed at and not because they were more comfortable in them. On the other hand, a couple of the teenage boys looked very smart in their brightly coloured shirts with scarves knotted at their necks and gave the impression that they would be at home in any company. Before we left, Marika was given a very pretty and well-made woven basket.

When we arrived back at the post we heard that the Yawalapiti were playing their famous flutes and, as they did not do this very often and it was a rare opportunity to be able to see them doing so, we immediately took the jeep again and drove to their village. As we drove into the circle of huts we saw in the headlights a group of men hurrying into the central hut carrying something. Women, *civilizado* or Indian, are never allowed to see or even listen to this ceremony under any circumstances. Someone had slipped up badly in failing to tell Marika this, so that as a result she was with us in the jeep. How the Yawalapiti suddenly knew this, I was never able to find out, but they did not bring the flutes out of the men's hut again until the jeep had left once more taking Marika with it. They then began to dance and play the flutes again and had no objection to my taking photographs. The music had a strange lilting monotony with one of the flutes playing a very musical theme over the top of the other two rather Tibetan-sounding bass ones. There was an intensely ritualistic and important feel to the scene as well as a deep sadness and nostalgia for the days when the tribe had been great. Around the village the little doors of the thatched communal huts were firmly closed and the women of the tribe were, I understood, burying their heads in their hands so as not to hear the music. One or two young boys stood in the shadows some distance away from the central group looking embarrassed, but the men in the middle merely listened intently, sitting in a row, and nodded their heads as the same theme was played four or five times.

In the morning we swam for the first time in the river below the post. Feeling very self-conscious of our pale bodies, the products of an English winter, but which drew neither comment nor laughter from the various Indians washing on the river bank, we plunged in and swam across to the other side. Immediately a group of a dozen small children, who had been playing in a natural sand-pit on the edge of the river, raced across the beach and into the water and began to dive and splash around us like a school of porpoises. The water was just cool enough to be refreshing and the current kept everything clean. Afterwards I went for a long walk through the jungle near the post following an Indian path which brought me back again after a couple of miles. I took my little hand tape-recorder with me and recorded as I went, which I found an excellent system for keeping a diary as it gave me some exercise at the same time. I finished off the tape walking up and down in the middle of the post while groups of Indians sat and watched me with interest as I talked to myself.

Claudio apologized very charmingly and unnecessarily for having gone to bed early the night before, explaining that he had had an attack of malaria. This is something from which he suffers a great deal most of the time. He also said very convincingly that, although he nearly always told visitors to Posto Leonardo to regard it as their home, he really meant it in our case and hoped that we would do so. He then arranged for the post's pilot to take us to the Waura village. This is the village which is famous for the very beautiful pots which they make and trade with the other tribes. They, almost alone in the Xingu, have the ability to work with pottery and are, I believe, the only tribe who can make the very large shallow pots which are used in the processing of manioc. The very ancient Cessna took quite a while to start, and it was explained to us how we had to hold the doors shut and to be careful not to drop our cameras through the hole in the floor. However, the elderly pilot, Hausen, although he made a point of saying how old the aircraft was – really much too old to fly – and how badly they needed a new one, was clearly exceedingly competent. We bumped and rattled down the pitted earth runway of the post and then sailed up over the jungle. We headed due west and flew for ten minutes, about twenty-five miles, before sighting the village near to a small lagoon. By the time we had circled once and landed, there were already some children from the village waiting for us on the strip. They chattered cheerfully and ran about playing in excitement, or walked beside us solemnly holding our hands as we went the few hundred yards up to the village. It consisted of two of the largest Indian communal huts I have seen, of a slightly different design from those in the Yawalapiti and Txikao villages, with a ridge along the roof; and a couple of smaller huts, one of which was made of mud, wattle and daub.

After a few moments the chief and some other men arrived back from the outskirts of the village where they had been working and we were warmly welcomed. Hausen had some things to give to the chief from Claudio and made a great ceremony of this, whispering behind his hand how important we were and how we were going to send marvellous presents after we got back to England. We then gave our small bag of presents and were invited inside the largest of the huts. This had an unusual fire area in the middle where the pots were made and baked in open fires. The atmosphere here was even better, I thought, than with the Yawalapiti. The cleanliness, airiness, lack of mosquitoes and general sense of prosperity, without a single visible 'Western' object, was very striking. The chief, said to be a most skilled potter and perhaps the last of the great Waura craftsmen, was a most impressive figure. He, being old-fashioned, refused to have any truck with Western ways, or even to learn Portuguese, although he understood some. Perhaps his strength had something to do with the health, charm and general sense of well-being which his people appeared to enjoy. With great dignity he showed us two magnificent pots about three foot high and beautifully decorated which he was making as a special present for Claudio. Then he presented us with two most attractive small zoomorphic pots, one depicting an armadillo and the other a tortoise. I was also given a brightly-coloured pair of earplugs made from wood and parrot feathers, which one of the young men was wearing and which I had admired.

We took some photographs and had some amiable talk and exchanged *abraços* – the name of Adrian Cowell, who has filmed all over the Xingu, always produced delighted hugs and messages to take to him. As we were about to leave, one of the Indians insisted on my accompanying him. Like all the other men of the village he wore only feathered arm bands and a liberal coating of red urucu paint. I suppose I should have felt embarrassed or apprehensive, walking off into the jungle beside a completely naked 'savage', unarmed, while he carried a bow and arrow. But somehow these kind of thoughts never even crossed my mind and, certainly in the Xingu, in the company of the Indians, I never felt anything except complete trust and friendship. He led me to a tall wigwam-like construction of long poles and, pulling one back, said that I could peer inside, indicating that there was something interesting that I should look at. I found myself practically nose-to-nose with a very regal and fierce-looking black and white harpy-eagle. They are called *'gavião real'* – royal eagle – in Portuguese and I could see why as it looked down on me from its perch. It gave an imperious squawk, appearing to command me to show more respect. Most of the Xingu tribes keep one of the eagles in the village and I was to see several more, but my first face-to-face confrontation with one made a strong impression. The bright, penetrating, yellow eyes and the sharp beak had a raw and pure savagery, while the tufts of upright feathers like ears on the top of its head, made the bird appear alert and watchful as though it were about to strike at any moment. Claudio later told me that ethnologists have often pontificated to him about the totemic significance of these birds, and how they are worshipped and held in the highest esteem by the tribes. He said that this was complete nonsense and they simply wanted the tail feathers for some of their head-dresses.

My greatest success with the Waura children was balloons. I had brought a pocketful. These they thought extremely funny and enjoyed playing with them. I always made a great performance with each balloon, blowing it up very large while everybody backed away in case it burst, and then letting it go so that it flew high into the air and they all scrambled for it. They always seemed to me the ideal presents for Indian children because they gave such tremendous pleasure and were quite unlike anything else that they had or could make, and yet practically vanished when they burst. On the way back to the airstrip we were accompanied by nearly all the village. The lithe, brown children ran and played and chased each other around us while the men and women, either brown like the children or bright red with a coating of urucu, walked in a more dignified way. Affectionate good-byes were said beside the aeroplane, many *abraços* sent to Adrian, and requests that we should come back soon. One last balloon released into the air to encourage the children away from the propeller and then the engine was started up and we took straight off. This was slightly unnerving as the runway was very short and I doubted whether we were going to make it over the bushes at the far end. However, we cleared them by about two feet and our pilot, who handled the aeroplane rather like a motor-bicycle on ice, made a tight turn and came back low over the watchers on the strip, and then on literally through the village, practically knocking the top off the tallest hut.

We made a detour over the very large lagoon on the edge of which is the Kamayura village. This was said to have the best situation of all the villages. Certainly the scene as we flew over was idyllic. One canoe broke the still surface of the water as a couple fished some distance from the shore. Others were washing clothes and mending nets on the edge of the lagoon while the inevitable troupe of children splashed in the shallows. Again we made a very low pass over the thatched huts to the obvious delight of the Indians underneath who waved happily.

After a late lunch, which included venison from the open stretch of *sertão* across the river from the post, and fish from the river as well as the inevitable rice, beans and farina, we rested in hammocks and talked for a while before going for an energetic swim. We allowed ourselves to drift a couple of hundred yards downstream to where the boats were tied up and then scrambled aboard them. I always find doing this a little frightening because I have a fixed idea that water-snakes prefer to live under these boats on Amazon rivers. I have in fact disturbed snakes from under boats in the past, and once from under a hovercraft, and although I have no great aversion to snakes on dry land, in the water they do rather tend to give me the horrors. We then swam back upstream against the current, which we suddenly realized was rather stronger than we had thought and it took quite a long time and a good deal of exercise before we were back below the post.

Claudio came with us in the late afternoon for a short

preliminary visit to the Kamayura village. This involved driving for about half-an-hour through the jungle, past their recently abandoned village and on to their well-made and clean new one right on the edge of the lagoon. It began to pour with rain and we sat in one of the huts talking to two Brazilian anthropologists who were living with the tribe. We ate with our fingers the delicious fish called *tucunaré*, which was presented to us fresh from the lagoon. Laid on a bed of coarse toasted manioc, it had been specially salted in our honour, as the Indians seldom use salt. The anthropologists, who had been with the Kamayura for some months and were obviously fully accepted by the tribe, said that they never locked or hid any of their food or possessions, and that nothing had ever been stolen from them. They greatly admired the park and said that there was no possible alternative system through which the Indians could survive.

As it went on raining and we learnt that the Kamayura were planning to have a feast and dance the following afternoon, we decided to return then. Our exit from the village was magnificent. Fifteen people piled into the open jeep, including two superb Kamayura warriors sitting on the front wings as outriders for the first mile or two. We also took back to the post with us a little Indian girl and her mother as the child was probably suffering from the after-effects of malaria. When we arrived back, we photographed her being treated in the operating theatre at the post, where she was made to take some nasty medicine and, like children everywhere, she objected. The doctor said that they would probably stay two or three days at the dispensary and then one morning he would wake up to find that they had walked back home.

Our longest flight from Posto Leonardo was to the Kuikuro village. This lay in the opposite direction to the Waura, in other words due south, and we crossed a lot of open country – *sertão* – which was said to be rich in game. When we landed, once again on a very short airstrip which seemed to run right into the middle of the village, a large crowd immediately gathered around the aircraft and more people kept running from the distant huts. They were very agitated and in a state of high excitement and nerves. Apparently the Kuikuro tend to be like this anyway, but there were extra reasons this time as there were two very sick people in the village. One of them was a man who was vomiting blood. They said he was about to die. We went and saw him first, but as it was very dark in the hut we could do nothing except say that the doctor would come shortly. The other was an older man who had been lost in the jungle, we were told, for a month. Entirely alone, he had had no hammock or means of getting food, and had staggered back to the village a couple of days before in an emaciated and desperate state. He, too, was just lying in his hammock gazing upwards. His eyes barely flickered in recognition when we bent over him and made reassuring noises. Beside each man – they were in different huts – sat his wife, holding a baby and beginning to cry in mourning and anticipation of his death. Once we had seen the invalids the atmosphere began to relax a little as we promised that we would send the doctor as soon as we returned to the post. The Kuikuro seemed to us less placid than the other tribes we had seen. The village, without being dirty, was rather untidy and everything seemed slightly disorganized. Even the chieftainship of the tribe was in dispute as there were two rival contenders. However, they are the largest and in some ways the most successful upper Xingu group, comfortably on the increase and living in an area rich in game. They were very generous with presents, showering us with mats, feather head-dresses and a set of feather arm bands which were tied on me by one of the men. They, too, had a large harpy-eagle in a cage similar to the Waura, this time in the middle of the circle of huts.

On the flight back to the post we flew low looking out

for game and almost immediately saw several small herds of three or four deer, *veado*, and then a couple of the larger variety called *cervo*. One of these was standing in the middle of a shallow, marshy lagoon. This gave us a marvellous opportunity to swoop low and photograph it as it bounded through the water. We then flew low over the Kalapalo village, related to the Kuikuro and the tribe which was probably responsible for the killing of Colonel Fawcett. Theirs was a large circular village of nine huts, once again set on the edge of a lagoon. We also flew over the Matipu village but did not land, although both of these villages have a small airstrip beside them. As we swooped past, the Indians ran out of their huts waving to us and encouraging us to land, but time was too short for us to do so. The proportion of those wearing shirts or other odds and ends of clothing appeared to be about the same as we had found in the villages we had visited. Between ten and twenty per cent might be wearing something and the rest nothing, except perhaps for some feathers on the arms, or bands around the arms or legs. The women of all the tribes wear a single strand of cord around their waist at all times.

We flew on down the Culuene River – the name for the early part of the Xingu River – which was exceptionally low with a lot of sandbanks. I wanted to show Marika her first crocodile (actually caimans here) but, although we flew low over the water, we did not see any.

As soon as we landed back at the post the pilot took off again with the doctor to go back to the Kuikuro. Shortly afterwards he returned with the emaciated Indian who had been lost and also one the Kuikuro chiefs. The patient was helped out of the plane and carried on a stretcher to the dispensary. Because the aircraft could only carry three people, the doctor had remained behind with the other patient and so the pilot took off once again to go and fetch him.

The Kamayura village, when we returned to it, had

completely dried out after the heavy rain of the day before and the palm thatch huts of the new village to which they had recently moved glistened in the sun. Everything had a fresh, pristine air. The men were about to dance, and most of the Indians and the children had decorated themselves elaborately with red urucu and feathers. The young men, muscular and handsome, were sitting in a row outside the men's hut in the middle of the village. On our previous visit, they had discovered Marika's name, which was the same as that of one of the elders of the tribe, and they took a delight in shouting 'Marika' with the accent heavily on the final *a*, and then roared with laughter when she responded and came across to them. The young chief was the best looking Indian I have seen anywhere with fine Grecian features and an intelligent and conscientious bearing. Unlike his contemporaries, who seemed to regard life pretty much as a joke and reminded me rather of an American football team waiting for the game to begin – only their shoulders were so well muscled that they needed no padding – he took life very seriously and spent most of the time we were there deep in discussion with Agnello Villas Boas, Claudio's nephew, who had come with us.

Three of the men were covered with particularly elaborate decorations. Apart from the heavy coating of red urucu, and the black lines and markings made with genipapo, a black dye, they also had bells made out of empty nut-shells around their ankles, grass skirts, elaborate feather head-dresses, arm bands and, most surprising of all, fishnet 'visors' over their faces. Green leaves were woven across their backs and down their arms; and with these spread out like wings they wheeled and swooped and stamped backwards and forwards in unison, heading off across the beaten earth on three points of the compass and then returning to the centre. There, one man sat beating out the rhythm on a small hollow log while another, older, Indian bent over him leaning on a stick and kept up a long and involved chant. This, combined with the intermittent, high-pitched singing of the drummer and the stamping of the dancers' feet, made an impressive volume of sound which dominated the village and focused everybody's attention on the dance. It was a fine and energetic sight and went on for a very long time until the sweat was pouring down the dancers' backs. They had no objection whatever to Marika and me photographing them from all angles and almost joining in the dance to do so.

The children who gathered around the jeep were delightful and very friendly. The two or three balloons I gave them were much appreciated and enjoyed. They also took great delight in covering us with urucu so that our white skins would stand out less glaringly. As they applied the red, greasy stuff to my face with deft professional fingers, standing back to admire their work and then adding more touches here and there, it felt exactly the same as being made up by the girl at the television studio in London where we had made an appearance before leaving England. One of the older girls, a very pretty and attractive child of about fourteen who, we were told, was recently married, took a great liking to Marika. Holding her firmly by the hand, she led her all around the village to show her everything. They made a charming pair. Almost exactly the same build and height, they somehow communicated extremely well without having a single word in common.

Later, in the early evening, we went down to the lagoon for a swim. The Indians who came with us warned us to be very careful as there were a lot of stingrays about. This meant that while walking out into the deeper water we had to shuffle our feet and stir up the sand so as not to step directly onto one of the rays which automatically flick their sharp, barbed tail over into the offending ankle, causing an extremely painful and slow-to-heal wound. I have seen the damage stingrays can do and always treat them with deep respect. The Indians sometimes use their 'stings' as heads for their arrows. The water was marvellously warm on top, refreshingly cool with currents underneath.

As we were drying ourselves on the shore, an Indian, bright with urucu, came down to collect some fishing pots from his canoe. With him was his small son. He gathered his things together and, putting them across his shoulder, set off back to the village again. This scene, which I photographed (opp. page 88), became fixed in my mind and has remained, despite all the subsequent sights and impressions of Indian life in Brazil, as the perfect image of pre-conquest America. The lagoon was quite rich in fish; he had a canoe and was a good fisherman. What more could anyone want?

Back in the men's hut in the village three of the elders had started practising their flutes – *jabui*. The same rule about women not being allowed to see this applied as with the Yawalapiti and Marika could no longer come near the hut. The rule did, though, seem less strictly observed here, as the women of the tribe continued to go about their business and did not shut themselves away. Perhaps it was just that this was a practice session and the full ritual playing would come later that night. I was allowed to go inside the hut and sit and watch them, and take photographs. The flutes were about three foot, six inches long and were dipped in a bowl of water each time they started playing. There were four small holes, about three-quarters of the way down, which meant that the players had to reach to the full extent of their arms in order to cover them. Feather head-dresses and other regalia from the dance were scattered about the hut, and the atmosphere inside, particularly while the flutes were being played, was very serious – in marked contrast to the joking and laughter which went on outside. I felt privileged to be there and that I was expected to behave with decorum. The three men played sitting down and leaning well back holding the flutes out in front of them, unlike the Yawalapiti who had stood up and danced outside the hut at the same time as playing. The tune, too, was different, being lower and more monotonous.

The scene we left behind us as we drove out of the village was perfectly relaxed and busy. Everybody was happy and enjoying himself, and the party mood was building up of its own volition. I found it hard to realize at first that our presence had had little or no effect on what was going on. It is this arrogant Western assumption that entertainment has been laid on for one's benefit that has led to accusations from some who have visited the Xingu that the Indians there 'dance for the tourists'. As far as I could see, they danced or held festivals according to the natural cycles which govern these things, or when they felt like it. If someone they liked and were pleased to see, like Claudio, visited them, they might dance to share their pleasure. But only if it fitted in with their own feelings.

On the track back to the post we saw first of all a large, black, hairy spider about five inches across, which scurried out of the way. We also saw a small wolf, about the size of a dog, which ran along the track ahead of us for some distance before leaping to one side into the jungle.

In between visiting the Indian villages by plane or jeep or on foot, there was plenty of time to relax and enjoy ourselves. It was Marika's first visit to the jungle. Naturally, the newness of it fascinated her. I had bought her a little Beretta ·22 and we walked some distance away from the post so that she could learn how to use this, practising shooting holes in a large leaf. On another occasion, we went for an hour's drive in the jeep, following the river downstream. There were a few open clearings where efforts were being made to grow rice, but for most of the way the jeep brushed the undergrowth on either side of the narrow, rough track. The trees met overhead and it was seldom possible to see any distance into the surrounding cover. On the way back we disturbed a flock of pigeons and I was handed the ·22 rifle belonging to the post to see if I could shoot one. Luckily I did so, killing, with the first shot, a bird perched on a branch about fifty yards away. Although I subsequently missed several, this helped to give me a reputation as a good shot, particularly as Mekarao, the Indian with us, had already failed a couple of times. He and I then ran off through the very thick undergrowth trying to get closer to the rest of the pigeons, but they kept moving further on as soon as we were nearly in range. Otherwise we saw little game near to the post.

I was able to borrow a face mask and snorkel and soon found that the little river below the post was very rich in fish. The most common were small ones of about six to eight inches with long whiskers, which fed busily on the bottom. There were also colourful, striped fish, which looked as though they would be more at home in an aquarium, and a few of the delicious and distinctive *tucunaré*, easily identified by the single dot halfway along their bodies. Having recently taken up skin-diving in Cornwall, I felt that snorkelling along the surface was child's play. This was only until, while investigating a little side creek in which I had seen a shoal of larger fish, I became entangled in some reeds and roots sticking out from the bank. I began to think about crocodiles and anacondas – which were said to be plentiful. Panicking, I floundered about, eventually arriving back at the beach below the post, very out of breath, not having dared to stop at any of the other sandy stretches along the bank for fear of stingrays.

Marika had integrated herself thoroughly into a group of Indian women washing clothes a short way downstream. I felt I couldn't give up so easily and so set off again. However, although the water was pleasantly cool and refreshing near the bottom of the river, and I dived several times to investigate the deeper parts, the visibility was not good and I never managed to make myself feel at home. I had much too vivid a picture of meeting a crocodile walking along the bottom, and although I saw none, the thought spoilt my enjoyment. I felt even less enthusiastic about under-water swimming in tributaries of the Amazon when I found that quite a lot of water had penetrated inside one of my ears and failed to leave in the usual way once I was on dry land again. After a couple of days, the young doctor at the post tried to extract it, but, instead, a painful ear infection developed which made me very deaf for several days. In fact, the large lump of wax which was causing the trouble was not removed until I returned to England.

Marika's friends, with whom she had been spending the afternoon, turned out to be the entire female population of the almost-extinct Trumai. There are only twenty-six sur-vivors of this tribe, a few of which have married into or live in other Indian villages. The rest, about fifteen, live at Posto Leonardo. They are a strange and gentle people who appear to be quite unrelated linguistically or racially to any other tribe in South America. The girls with whom Marika was now swimming had sensitive, delicate faces with very large eyes. They laughed and twittered like birds, reminding us both vividly of Rima in *Green Mansions*, which I had given Marika to read on the journey. They are the most recent of the tribes to have come into the Xingu area, and the culture they brought with them has had a strong influence on many of the other Xingu tribes. In recent years, before the park was formed, they were virtually exterminated. Those living at the post spent a lot of time washing and bathing in the river and they were always a delight to be with. They invited us to come and visit them later in their hut. But when we arrived, we found that they had all gone off to watch the Txikao dancing. Only the old chief of the tribe, called Matti, remained. He was crippled with rheumatism and in spite of having been to São Paulo for operations in hospital, it was not thought that he would ever walk again. He was a nice man, with his shrunken legs dangling over the side of his hammock, and a smiling moon-like face in a dis-proportionately large, round head. He spoke excellent

Portuguese and we chatted quietly, sitting on stools at his feet. He was keenly interested in what I was trying to do and surprisingly well-informed about the outside world. He showed no self-pity about not being able to move out of his hammock without being carried. We asked him if there was anything he needed and he admitted, in his gentle and modest way, that it really didn't matter a bit, but if we happened to have any spare torch batteries that would fit his wireless they would be most welcome as his own were flat and he did like to listen to what was going on in the world. Of course, we went and got some immediately, and returned to find the others back from the dance and all in a very cheerful mood.

The atmosphere inside the Trumai hut was delightful with different things going on under the large, domed roof where fires burnt in various areas and the smoke rose to the rafters and then passed out through the palm leaf thatch. There was a strange feeling of privacy and respect for other people's privacy, in spite of all living in one open area, as well as an almost forgotten sense of community living as a member of a tribe. I was able to go off into a corner and catch up on taping my diary. After a while a pretty little Trumai girl and a very small Trumai boy came and sat on either side of me, their arms around me, listening intently and watching the tape-recorder as I spoke into it, while other people bustled around chatting, laughing, cooking, making things and paying no attention to us at all. It is one of the most remarkable features of the Xingu Park that being different or doing something strange is not considered a cause for interference. Whenever I used my tape-recorder elsewhere in Brazil, someone would always sooner or later come up to me and ask what I was doing. On the whole this did not happen in the Xingu and perhaps the reason is partly that the different tribes have learnt, many of them long before they were contacted and the park was created, to tolerate each other and accept each other's customs. Also, due to the existence of the park, many strange and different people have visited the Indians and they are perhaps better used than others to coping with eccentrics. This was not, of course, only confined to the way in which my tape-recorder was received, but applied to the whole spirit of acceptance which I felt very strongly all the time in the Xingu. Most of the other Indians we were to meet in Brazil were friendly and hospitable, but we never met elsewhere the same level of calm acceptance and tolerance of our differences. It is these qualities which led me to feel most strongly that the Indians of Xingu stand the best chance of integrating eventually on equal terms with our culture, provided that what they have now is not taken away from them.

Through contact with each other over a long period, the ten tribes of the upper Xingu have developed many similar customs and beliefs. They come from several different racial origins, and each tribe still speaks its own language and preserves many of its own myths and individual characteristics. Yet through inter-marriage and proximity they have grown very alike in spite of their different origins. The Kamayura and Aweti are Tupi; the Mahinaku, Waura and Yawalapiti are Aruak; the Kuikuro, Kalapalo, Matipu and Nahukua are Carib, while the origins of the Trumai are unknown. They were the last to arrive in the area, probably about one hundred and fifty years ago. The Txikao, also Carib, only recently brought in from outside, do not strictly count as an upper Xingu tribe.

The villages we visited were broadly similar in their layout, consisting of five or more large, palm-thatched communal huts set in a circle around the wide, beaten-earth area with a smaller men's hut in the centre. Most of the tribes also kept a harpy-eagle and there were always dogs. The principal meat eaten was fish, which was fairly plentiful in the lagoons and rivers on the edge of which most of the villages were sited. Other game eaten was mostly monkey, and certain birds which were fairly scarce close to the villages and necessitated hunting journeys of several days' duration. Most of the Indians still used bows and arrows although each village had at least one ·22 rifle. Far the most valued items as presents or for exchange were ·22 bullets and fish hooks and line. I got the distinct impression that, although other presents were welcome, these items were really the only ones that the Indians needed.

Manioc and maize were grown in small clearings close to the villages. New clearings had to be made every few years as, due to the 'slash and burn' system of agriculture, they rapidly became exhausted. Some varieties of wild fruit and nuts, edible plants, roots and honey, gathered in the surrounding jungle, all play an important part in their diet. This was supplemented when necessary with rice provided by the post.

The reasoning of the park administration seemed to me to run as follows: The Indians' way of life is as near as possible perfect for them and certainly infinitely superior to anything we can offer them at the present time. Medical aid is imperative and hence the airstrips by all the villages any distance from the post. But this means that the villages must remain fixed, and this inevitably puts a strain on the food resources of the village because the game becomes scarce and the easiest spots to grow crops are used up. Therefore the Indian must be given every possible help to maintain his standard of living from his available and gradually diminishing resources. This means that, in order to make it easier for him to kill game, he should have a certain number of rifles, some ammunition and improved fishing tackle. Axes and machetes, to help him clear the ground and cut down trees more efficiently, are also permissible. But the imposition of alien ideas, which may change his culture and shake his confidence in his own abilities, are not.

If the Xingu Park did not exist there would have been many times in Brazil at which I would have despaired of there being any hope of salvation for the Indian. I think that this must also be in the minds of some of those who would like to see the park destroyed. If there is no satisfactory alternative to rapid integration for the Indian, with all its inevitable shocks and problems, then it is much harder to argue against schemes which will theoretically benefit the starving masses of the coastal cities at the expense of a few doomed tribesmen.

The most remarkable thing, I felt, about the Xingu Park, is that it works.

Xingu-Diauarum

�֍

THE other post in the Xingu Park is Diauarum, which is one hundred miles downstream from Posto Leonardo, at the very centre of the park. This is where Claudio spends most of his time caring for the four quite different tribes who live in the northern end of the park. I was very anxious to visit these and also to see something of the Xingu river, and so it was decided that we would all travel by the post's launch from Posto Leonardo to Diauarum, camping on the way.

The launch, driven by a vile-smelling and unreliable old diesel engine, leaked in several places and had quite a few rotten timbers. However, it did have a low roof built over the central section which was useful for keeping things dry and getting under when it rained – for as long as one could stand the fumes – but it also made it extremely top-heavy so that if two people stood on the same side it began to turn turtle.

We spent two full days and a night on the journey, travelling through dense jungle the entire time, broken only by occasional sand-banks, tributaries and marshy lagoons. There are no Indian villages along the river until shortly before Diauarum, although much of the territory is visited by hunting parties from the upper Xingu, who make temporary camps.

Our party consisted of Claudio Villas Boas, his nephew Agnello with his wife Cida, Edson Ramalho Jnr, our FUNAI-appointed companion, two Indians, Bejai and Mekarao, and us. The chug of the engine and the sun beating down made us all feel sleepy but it was an excellent chance to sit and exchange ideas with little chance of interruption. Every now and then the engine died or we touched a sand-bank and had to push ourselves off, or someone would spot a crocodile slithering into the water or an interesting bird perched in a tree, but on the whole there were few distractions.

Cida, Agnello's wife, was dark and attractive with a natural chic and a trace of Indian blood in her ancestry. Although she and Marika had few words of the other's languages they seemed to understand each other well enough and spent a lot of time cheerfully discussing the effect tropical heat was having on their hair and complexions, and describing their respective children to each other.

Agnello, the son of Orlando and Claudio's eldest brother who had died in 1943, was the same age as me. He had begun life working in a family business for a maternal uncle in São Paulo and then, two years before, had joined FUNAI and worked for a time on the Trans-Amazonica Road Programme and the 'pacification' and re-settlement of Indians arising from this. He had then come to Xingu where, on my arrival, I had been introduced to him by Claudio as his successor. I took an instant liking to him. He was fair-haired, well-built, bearded and spoke little, watching and listening to everything that Claudio did and said. I learnt that he had always had a great love for the jungle and had spent every available moment escaping from the cities where he had grown up and worked. Now he felt completely at home living in the Xingu, enjoying the life and work and getting on well with the Indians. His main problem was that Cida had grave reservations about living permanently in the jungle, not so much for herself as for their children who would inevitably get malaria and possibly other diseases which would permanently weaken them. I hoped very much that he would be able to resolve these problems, and told him so. Although, as he was the first to admit, he lacked the flair and genius of his uncles, he was after all a Villas Boas and a man of integrity and courage. Sooner or later someone would have to take up their mantle and I tried to strengthen his belief that this was a worthy ideal to which to devote his life.

One of the reasons he was liked by the Indians was his great skill as a woodsman and his active enjoyment of everything connected with life in the jungle. When we stopped to camp on the river bank that night I saw how skilfully he organized the slinging of hammocks and building of fires while at the same time joining me to fish for piranha which he then took off and cooked. He seldom expressed an opinion, but when Claudio and I talked he would often sit with us and listen attentively, his forehead creased in the effort to understand some of his uncle's more complicated theories.

Edson, our FUNAI escort, was the complete opposite. He disliked the jungle and I began to suspect that he also disliked Indians as he always treated them either with forced heartiness or with contempt. All the time he was with us in Brazil I never once saw him lift a finger to help either us or anybody else. He had recently become a macrobiotic and as a result had practically halved his weight so that he was thin and emaciated to the point of ill-health, a situation with which one might have sympathized had he not talked ceaselessly about how well he felt on his regimen and how he ate only the most rarefied and pure of foods and then only in small quantities, while in fact he gorged himself upon almost anything that appeared. This he did without any consideration for others, first demanding angrily whether any artificial or, in his book, 'unnatural' ingredients such as animal fat, had been used in preparation. Once satisfied that what we had been offered was wholesome he would tuck in with both hands, shovelling his mouth full of food and munching with deep concentration until long after everyone else had finished. In between meals he often took out his primus and cooked himself a special macrobiotic meal, explaining as he did so that this was his exclusive diet and that he felt much better for not eating the same food as the rest of us. He also gave the world at large the benefit of his opinions whenever the opportunity arose, laying down the law on every conceivable subject, on which he usually had rigid right-wing views. I derived a lot of pleasure on one occasion from telling him that macrobioticism was well-known in Europe as a cover for Communist ideals and activities, and was much encouraged by the Chinese. He almost gave it up until I weakened and admitted that it had been a joke.

Although he spoke excellent English, he really was a most unfortunate choice to be our travelling companion as he obstinately refused to accept that any problem over the Indian question existed or that what I was trying to do could be of any use. In fact he made it clear as time went on that he had grave doubts about my ante-cedents and suspected that I had some sinister ulterior motive for being in Brazil. This made travelling together difficult at times, particularly as I often heard him telling the people we were visiting to show me only the best side of the picture and to be very careful what they said to me as he would be listening. I was having trouble enough communicating and understanding in high-speed Portu-guese, and would often have been glad of some helpful translation and clarification. Edson, however, preferred to listen with a superior smile to my ungrammatical ramblings and then give his own views. I could have forgiven him all this, as it must have been irritating that I had travelled so much more in the interior of Brazil than he had, and usually knew exactly what I wanted to do next and where we were going, thereby making his presence unnecessary. What I could not forgive was his attitude towards Marika. He constantly tried to take out on her the frustrations my apparent self-confidence caused him. I never once saw him offer to carry her luggage or open a door for her and he was for ever telling me how well he would have got on had she not been in the party. But enough of Edson, with-out whom our journey would undoubtedly have been much pleasanter, but whom we very soon learnt to ignore except when absolutely necessary.

It was Claudio whom I had come to see in the Xingu and with whom I spent as much time as possible. For long periods he would either disappear alone into his room or, on the boat, sit silently musing. But when he spoke, his manner ranged from gentle humour and praise for the Indians, and those who work on their behalf, to powerful and impassioned oratory and fearless condemnation of wrong policies and mistaken attitudes. Behind his shy and weak manner, and the heavy glasses which he always wore, great charm and a sense of humour were always ready to emerge. When talking to Indians he would often accuse them of being extremely savage, wild, dangerous, wicked men emphasizing each word hard, yet without betraying a hint of paternalism. They seemed more at ease with him than with other men, very much aware of his presence and listening attentively when he spoke seriously. Little children ran to him and he would absentmindedly punch at them or tousle their hair as they toddled along beside him. His extreme humility, for example, in relation to the Nobel Peace Prize nomination or the high regard in which he is held internationally, appeared forced at first, until I realized that it was based on complete sincerity and a genuine lack of any sort of pride. One of the most gratifying things about him was the way in which he never said anything bad about any individual and always looked for the best in people and pointed it out. Of course, whenever he was talking about any aspect of Indian life, it was always good, fine and brave and worthy of respect but his attitude towards people with a Western outlook was just as laudatory. The doctors and nurses, for instance, who came to Posto Leonardo were, he said, extraordinarily dedicated to their jobs and showed this in the way they did not go home for Christmas or other holidays but stayed nursing the Indians. When speaking of the pilots, he praised their skill and courage when they flew in and out of small jungle airstrips. He spent a long time talking to Edson, who had left his normal job teaching two- to five-year-old children, to run FUNAI's education and recruitment programme for the training of young men to work with the Indians. Claudio praised this work saying how vital it was and that it was the most important of FUNAI's functions. Unfortunately, Edson refused to accept most of Claudio's ideas about the value of the Indian culture and the need to protect and respect it, arguing loudly that his programme was a means towards the rapid integration of the Indians. Edson, who was barely thirty to Claudio's fifty-four, tended to shout and lay down the law, calling the older man '*rapaz*' which means, literally, 'boy'. To be fair this was what he called almost everybody, but it contrasted badly with Claudio's polite and patient manner.

I was surprised at first to learn that this mild and very gentle man had in his time killed five jaguars single-handed. It surprised me less, however, when I saw the fearlessness with which he approached the whole problem of people's attitudes towards the Indians. He had no hesitation in stating emphatically that his own government, most Brazilians, and indeed most people in the world, were completely wrong in their approach to primitive societies. As a loyal Brazilian he said that of course he wanted his country to develop and raise the standard of living of its people. He applauded the efforts that were being made to do this but said that to extend the same ideals to the minute Indian population was madness. This was the foundation of his philosophy. The problem does not arise from the existence of the Indian but from the desire to change him and incorporate him in some vast gesture towards progress which will neither help him nor anybody else. Without this desire to interfere there really need be no problem. If Brazil would only wait until the rest of the population were sufficiently mature to understand the Indians' values, then they might well find that the problem no longer existed because the land on which the Indian lived was no longer needed, and the Indian himself, instead of being regarded as a liability, had come to be regarded as a national asset. It might then be possible for the Indian to take his rightful place in Brazilian society and play a useful part in its future. Claudio said,

'The Indians are our ancestors and we owe them honour.

Man is of much greater value than the moon. We have forgotten this and now we struggle with vast problems of our own making ignoring the things which make our lives worth living.

Why do we not solve this one human problem which it lies within our power to solve?

No man could integrate the Indian into our society. Into what sort of society could the Indian actually integrate? Into the frontiersmen and farmers and prospectors opening up the interior of Brazil? No! Into the *favelas* of Rio and São Paulo? They would come out even lower.

Trace any process of integration which has taken place and watch the destruction of the people concerned. You cannot integrate an Indian by modern technological means. It has never been done and must always fail.

At least give the problem time and let us try to learn. There is no need for hurry.

The Indian is happy, he is complete, he needs none of our culture for his happiness; only medicines to protect him against our ills.

In ten to fifteen years the Indians will vanish, not just as a culture but as human beings. They will physically die.

The Indian should never be involved in other development programmes. He should be left alone and only given the help he needs and wants.

The Parque Naçional do Xingu is the only place left where you will see Indians living as they did before and always have. Elsewhere they are changed or broken into little groups.

What good would it do to remove the Parque? It will turn into three or four large fazendas (farms) which will contribute nothing to the national economy.

The best that integration could offer the Indian would be to make him a small-time farmer farming his own property – a fine aspiration for our own poor people, but no step up for the Indian. Can anyone honestly say that the Indian would be any better off like this?

Let us wait ten or twenty more years until we have a society fit for the Indians to integrate into and ready to receive them. The Trans-Amazonica roads need put no pressure on the Indians if the Parque and other Indian areas are avoided.

To improve the Indians' lot beyond their wildest dreams would cost next to nothing. Give them all they need – isolation, medical help and all the clothes, fish hooks and tools they want. If there were three million Indians then Brazil might have a problem, but there are so few. It would not only be in their best interests but also much cheaper to leave them be and take care of them than to try and change them.'

Claudio sees a third world coming, after Capitalism and Communism have both failed. It will arrive out of an awareness that we have over-exploited our world and that further exploitation will only bring about our own destruction. A new respect for cultural diversity will create a world in which the ways of an individual or a group will be respected and it will not be necessary to conform to certain rigid principles. It will be a world in which the Suya people will have a place in society.

I asked him what sort of society this would be and he answered, 'You are the first sign of this society which I see coming.'

* * *

On the day after we camped on the Xingu it rained and we were glad of the small shelter on the launch into which we crowded. While it was still raining, we arrived at the first of the villages administered from Diauarum. This was a Kayabi village; Pripuri was the chief. I recognized him at once as he came down the bank to greet us – he was the one who smoked a short stubby pipe and looked like a pirate in Adrian Cowell's film. There were many Indians in the Xingu Park whom I recognized from having seen the film so many times, but none as instantly and certainly as Pripuri.

The Kayabi village was laid out completely differently from any we had seen in the upper Xingu. There was a large open house with no sides, under which some hammocks were slung and about four other thatched huts with wooden sides where the various family groups lived. The people, too, looked quite different and were much more acculturated than any others we saw in the Xingu. Although the scene was rather dispiriting because of the heavy rain, the Kayabi were clearly delighted to see Claudio and showered us with presents of fruit and eggs. Apparently the Kayabi are great workers and always produce a surplus which they either give to other tribes or send to the post. They were in intermittent contact for many years with prospectors and rubber gatherers and suffered terribly in the past from being massacred with carbines, and then driven out of their lands when they retaliated. Most of the tribe are now safely inside the park where they live in several widely scattered villages, but we were told of twenty-seven who were being kept as virtual slaves on the Teles Pires River where they were made to work for skin collectors. Pripuri himself had had terrible experiences, being made to work for nothing and having his women and children taken away from him. He had managed to escape and was now strongly opposed to civilization and its influences. I felt, as I handed over our small contribution of presents, that our reception would have been much less friendly had Claudio not been with us.

In Pripuri's hut there was a very fine hat made out of sloth skin which looked rather like badger, but was much softer. 'Ear-rings' made out of red feathers hung on either side and he put it on, indicating that it was his ceremonial chief's hat. The Portuguese word for sloth is literally 'lazy beast', which amused me as it was the first time I had met the word. We all laughed and made a joke about the inappropriateness of Pripuri, who was clearly anything but lazy, wearing this animal on his head. After talking for a time, and visiting the rest of the village which seemed to be relatively prosperous, the rain stopped and we all went back down to the boat again. Just as we were pushing off from the bank, Pripuri impulsively took off his hat and gave it to me, which pleased me very much. I wore it for the rest of the boat journey and later brought it safely back to England.

Our arrival at Diauarum was greeted with great joy from the small crowd on the bank, most of whom were Txukarramai who were visiting the post. One of them was Mekarao's mother who made an extraordinary high-pitched keening lament as soon as she saw him, and for some time afterwards. This happens in several Indian tribes when women see a friend or relation after they had been separated for some time. I had always understood that the weeping was for someone who had died during the interval but was told on this occasion that it was to signify how much she had missed her son while he had been away at Posto Leonardo for the previous year.

All the houses at Diauarum were thatched and made of wood and it was a very pretty and delightful place. There were about five canoes moored to the bank, two of them with outboard motors, and the river was four or five hundred yards wide and glassy smooth. We carried our things up to a dry house on stilts and slung our hammocks. The Txukarramai at the post, members of the largest tribe in the area which occupies much of the land north of

Diauarum, then danced to celebrate Claudio's return. More than half of the men had the large and at first sight frightening and grotesque discs in their lower lips. First they sang a legendary song about planting maize. This was accompanied by a deep resonant chant and slow shuffling dance. Then came a more impressive and noisy dance which is the one they perform to get themselves in a war-like mood before going into battle. This we were told was how they would have danced in recent years before attack-ing the Kreen Akrore, the still uncontacted tribe which is the subject of the film *The Tribe That Hides From Man*. Claudio asked them to sing a very beautiful song for us which is performed when a child of the tribe has died, but they said it would make them too unhappy.

Over two hundred and eighty Txukarramai live in the park and about the same number outside. Neither of the chiefs was at Diauarum but the leader of the small group there sat up until late that night talking to Claudio. He told him that Krumare, one of the chiefs, was away at one of the new fazendas being built near to the new road and that the road had now reached the Xingu river about forty miles north of Diauarum. Most of the tribe had, we were told, left the Txukarramai village with Rauni, the other chief, and gone off on a hunting expedition, making a temporary camp in the jungle. This meant that we would not be able to visit them as the camp was some distance from the river and would be difficult to find. They were extremely disturbed and upset by the road and I watched Claudio explaining how very sad he and Orlando were about what had happened and discussing what the Txukarramai should do. They were angry that their land was being taken from them and reluctant to leave, but at the same time frightened of staying where they would progressively find themselves more and more threatened as development took place along the road. A two thousand yard airstrip had been constructed on the edge of the river, long enough to take large aircraft and there was a lot of activity in the area with construction crews and heavy machinery setting up camps. Claudio looked desperately tired and worried as he heard more news of internal problems and rivalries within the Txukarramai who were clearly uncertain as to their best course of action and in danger of fragmenting into smaller groups.

What seemed almost incredible to me was that the whole situation was unnecessary and mistaken, even economically. The original route planned for the road would have taken it through largely open country to the north of the park which would have presented less logistic difficulties and would have opened up an area of potentially valuable farmland. It had been routed to go below the Von Martius Falls and would not have cut into any National Park land. The new road, however, had virtually bisected the park and would, on the far bank, encounter very difficult country with high rocky ridges and many rivers which the constructors would not otherwise have had to face. The new route was no shorter and would cost more to construct. Why had it been chosen and why had the supposedly protected land of the National Park been violated?

The only answer seemed to be that either it was part of a deliberate plan to destroy the Xingu National Park or else the commercial interests owning the presidentially revoked titles to land inside the park had been able to bring pressure to bear. I found it hard to believe that this practically virgin and exceedingly valuable area, both ecologically and from the Indians' point of view (although of doubtful economic value), should have been allowed to be destroyed simply because of the powers of persuasion of some property developers in São Paulo. This only left one with the conclusion that it was a deliberate policy to destroy the park and with it the Villas Boas brothers.

Shortly before leaving England I had been given an official document written barely a year before by the then President of FUNAI in which conditions in the Xingu Park were hailed as being the best in the whole country and it was stated that others would be set up on the same model. In the park the Indians were thriving and increasing in numbers, as I had seen for myself, and throughout the world the park was recognized as an excellent example of what could be done. Had the official policy really changed so rapidly and so completely? It was all very confusing.

During these talks I heard it suggested that Diauarum itself might be given to the Txukarramai and a new post then created further upstream. This would mean that the Txukarramai, already pacified, already receiving proper medical care and the recipients of everything which an Indian park should give to the Indians, and resident inside such a park, would have to be persuaded at great difficulty and emotional upset to move once again further into the park so as to be safe from exploitation. These Indians did not understand boundaries and limitations, only freedom of movement. The nearer frontier settlement came to them the more often would contact take place – unfortunate contacts out of which only prostitution and degeneration would develop. This would be inevitable because those with whom they would come into contact would not be developed, sensitive, intelligent people who could understand the virtues of the Indians and appreciate that they were no less human beings and heirs to a valuable culture than the uneducated frontiersmen with their cheap guns and cheap liquor. Inevitably, such contact must destroy the Indians either by disease or by degeneration and, just as inevitably, I was forced to the conclusion that there must be those who desired this to happen.

The next day we visited the Suya in two canoes, going about an hour's journey up the Suiá Missu River and passing an abandoned Suya village on the right bank. When we arrived, we found a broadly similar village to the Kayabi one we had visited the day before with an open 'house' and some other closed ones. As they belong to the same racial group as the Txukarramai, many of the men also had large lip discs. We were given a cheerful welcome to the village which seemed to be thriving. But most of the inhabitants were away fishing and, as Diauarum was only two hours away on foot, it was arranged that a large party would come and visit the post the next day.

The Suya were only contacted in 1960 by the Villas Boas who found them living in a completely virgin and isolated state but dying in great numbers from 'flu which had recently been introduced to the tribe. Now they were strong and on the increase again. Recently forty Beiço de Pau, the remnants of a related group from the upper Tapajós River, had been brought to the village and had integrated into the tribe.

Von den Steinen, the first man to go down the Xingu, had had a brief encounter with the Suya in 1884. A few days after their next contact in 1960 had been established, forty-two members of the tribe were given a tuberculin test. Eight of them reacted positively, an infection rate of nineteen per cent. It has been suggested that, as there was no record of contact during the interim seventy-five years, the presence of tuberculosis in the tribe was a legacy of that one contact. The possibility that this might be true paints a frightening picture of the dangers of accidental or deliberate first contact with a tribe which is not followed by careful medical protection.

The next morning I was sitting in Claudio's hut talking when the party of Suya arrived. I was reading aloud, with occasional help from Edson, the letter which we had sent to the Nobel committee with Orlando and Claudio's nomination. I should probably have done this sooner, to check the facts and ideas expressed in the letter with him. He listened with deep concentration and his only comment at the end was that it was all more than accurate, except that he was much too unworthy to receive such praise. I also read him some of the Survival International literature which we both found very moving as, rather to my surprise, it struck exactly the right note in the setting of Diauarum.

This reassured me a lot and strengthened my resolve to do everything possible to make Survival International a success. Inevitably, I had had doubts about whether what we were trying to do was valid or even right and proper in a rapidly developing modern world, and whether we were not perhaps indulging in a nostalgic exercise, trying to recreate something which was vanishing and must continue to vanish. Many people seemed to think so; could it be they were right?

Here in the Xingu, surrounded by 'ignorant, naked savages', who were among some of the best and sanest people I have ever met, I knew that they were not right and that I must do everything I could to help prevent their extermination, and try to make the rest of the world stop wanting to change them.

When the Suya arrived, everything else stopped for a time as they crowded around Claudio's hut greeting him and making a cheerful commotion. There were three huts on the edge of the village which belonged to the Suya and these were soon a scene of tremendous activity as men, women and children in different groups prepared themselves and each other with red urucu, black genipapo, a blue preparation and an orange one, and then drew strange designs over their bodies, ranging from butterfly wings on the chest to leopard spots all over the body. Cords were tied around their arms and legs to make the muscles bulge; and their hair was combed out and sometimes tied up with head-dresses or ropes of palm leaves. Altogether the atmosphere was rather like a troupe of circus artistes getting ready to enter the big top. Every now and then someone would leap up and run across the open area in front of the huts, chanting and stamping his feet. There was a general air of anticipation and excitement and one of the noticeable differences from a circus was that the whole performance was quite clearly being done for their own personal satisfaction and amusement and in no way for the two or three Europeans present who were going to watch. They were dancing because they were glad that Claudio was home and wanted to show it, and for no other reason.

About half the adult men had discs in their lower lips. These were up to four inches across and often stretched the end of the low lip as thin as an elastic band. I could never understand how, in the rough and often hostile world they lived in, they could manage to go through life without splitting this thin band. Various theories are put forward as to why the men do this but I don't think anyone, not even themselves, really knows why it is done. The reason I like best, and which seems most right to me, is that it makes them look frightening and fierce to their enemies. Certainly, the first time one comes face to face with a member of one of the tribes which wear lip discs is an alarming experience which one does not forget easily. We found, however, that we very soon grew used to the idea and hardly noticed the discs. One of the Txukarramai men, a tall smiling man called Renieú, whom Marika called 'Laughing Boy', had adopted her and made it his personal responsibility to keep an eye on her. He used to sit for hours on the floor beside her hammock while she wrote and he was always at hand when she needed help. Although it is impossible to smile with one's face distorted by a large disc, we could tell that he was always laughing by the twinkle in his eyes and the way his face creased up.

The Suya danced on and off all the rest of that afternoon and quite late into the evening. The chief, an extremely strong and well-built man, danced bent low, with his five-year-old son gently held in one large hand at his side trying hard to learn the steps as well. It was a picture of conscientious parental care and concern which I found very touching.

Later in the evening they all squeezed into Claudio's hut and danced again, keeping up a very energetic stamp-

ing rhythm for over an hour until the sweat poured off
their backs.

One of the most interesting things I found the Suya
using and which I was subsequently given, was a set of
bow and arrows for shooting birds. The arrows had circular
nuts attached part way up the shaft with a hole cut in
them which caused the arrow to whistle when it was fired
into the air. This supposedly hypnotized the bird into
remaining on its perch instead of flying away as it might
have done had it heard the usual swish of an arrow. The
arrows, instead of having points, simply had a lump of
beeswax on the end which would stun the bird and make
it fall to the ground. When I expressed an interest in these
and asked what the lumps on the shafts were for, the Indian
who was carrying them immediately demonstrated for me
by firing the arrow high into the air. It made a strange
fluty whistle before turning at the top of its arc and plum-
meting to earth, scattering a crowd of small children. He
then retrieved it and put it with the other arrows and the
bow, and handed them to me.

Diauarum, which means black jaguar in Suya, is a
beautiful place with all the buildings made of palm thatch.
Unlike at Posto Leonardo, where a FAB plane calls once
a week, there is little coming and going and the only engine
heard is an occasional outboard motor setting out from the
river bank, and from time to time the pump lifting water
from the Xingu. There is an electric generator, but it is
seldom used except to operate the post's radio. Claudio
spends most of his time there, and there is a resident nurse
and occasional visits from the current doctor at Posto
Leonardo.

Nearly all the medical work in the Xingu has, for the
last five years, been managed by the São Paulo School of
Medicine which provides most of the medicines and sends
volunteer doctors and nurses during their holidays and
as part of their training. Claudio says that they nearly
always ask to come back again and that their work with

the Indians is the most useful and valuable part of their education. Some of the medicines are paid for by FUNAI and help is also given by the LBA (Brazilian Legion of Assistance), a charitable organization. All the Indians in the Xingu are vaccinated against smallpox and most of them are now also inoculated against measles, since there have been several epidemics. The worst of these was in 1954 when a considerable number of Indians died. An indication of the improvement in medical assistance is that during the most recent outbreak, in early 1968, no lives were lost at all. The worst calamity of all was on the original first contact between the Roncador–Xingu Expedition of 1946 and the tribes of the upper Xingu. Then, out of six hundred and fifty-four Indians, one hundred and fourteen died of 'flu.

Apart from the medical help, the whole Xingu Park of eight thousand five hundred square miles and over fifteen hundred Indians was administered by six FUNAI employees. These were, at the time of our visit, Orlando and Claudio Villas Boas; Agnello, their nephew; two nurses, Orlando's wife Marina and her sister Maria; and the pilot, Captain Hausen. There was also an Indian at each post responsible for day-to-day administration, who received a small wage. Pionim, at Posto Leonardo, was a capable, outstanding character who drove the jeep, operated the radio and always seemed to have the situation well under control. He also had that remarkable talent, for an administrator, of being completely approachable and able to solve any petty problem which cropped up. Mairewe, his opposite number at Diauarum, was small and more shy but appeared equally capable. Both Pionim and Mairewe were Kayabi Indians and an interesting situation existed between them, as the result of a complicated blood feud. Although they spoke to each other daily on the radio in the most friendly and efficient way, they could never meet as it would then be incumbent upon one to kill the other.

Also at Posto Leonardo were three young Txukarramai

men who had been reared at the post by Orlando and Claudio since they were small children. Bejai, Mekarao and Cocti were handsome and romantic characters with straight black hair down to their shoulders, who enjoyed life to the full, took part in whatever was going on, particularly hunting and fishing expeditions, and made themselves useful about the post. Bejai, who had lost an eye as a child, had come with us on the boat journey to Diauarum and proved himself the ideal travelling companion, leaping energetically into the water when we stuck on a sandbank and always remaining cheerful.

There was so much activity at Diauarum, and so many people wanted to come and talk to Claudio all the time, that it was very difficult for us to talk for long without interruption. Our days in the Xingu were slipping away and so I was glad when it was decided that we would go once more in the launch further downstream to visit the Juruna.

During the journey I asked Claudio how he saw the future of the park. He drew me a rough map of the park and the surrounding area and on it marked seven uncontacted tribes or isolated groups. He said that these were known to exist and that their numbers might come to fifteen hundred. If they could be persuaded, once pacified, to move into the park, this would effectively double the park's population and provide a balanced occupation, filling the large empty territory in the middle. The Kreen Akrore were, he said, the first priority because the new road would run straight through their territory. The Apiaka, too, were in considerable danger as the new Cuiabá/Santarém road went through their territory. Their location on the Rio Tapiama was well-known and they were thought to be closely related to the Kayabi. To persuade them to come to the park should not be too difficult. The Awaika, on the other hand, who lived on the very borders of the park, on the upper Suiá Missu, and might comprise quite a large group, were very secretive and had recently (within the

Kamayura Indian with fish trap

Yawalapiti Indians playing Jabui flutes

Harpy-eagle

An Indian village in
Xingu from th

Claudio Villas
and the author (*right*)
two Suya Indian C

The Waura Chief
with the pots he made
for the Villas
Boas brothers

Juruna girl

The young Yawalapiti Chief

Suya Indian

Suya Indian

Kamayura Indians

An old Terena Indian woman drinking maté tea

Bororo woman with monkey-tooth necklace

Young Paresi girl

Renieu, Marika Hanbury Tenison's
Txukarramai friend

The masked witch doctors of
the Karaja on Bananal

Karaja girl undergoing
initiation rites

Karaja Indian making
arrows. Behind him
stands an Indian guard

A Kadiweu dog. It is alive

The Bororo village at São Lourenço

last two or three weeks) had a brush with workers on the new road. As fazendas were springing up not far from their land, there was imminent danger that reprisals would be taken upon them before long and that they would be liquidated. The existence of some of the other groups was only known of through Indians who had come in contact with them. But in all cases Claudio emphasized that, since their isolation could not be guaranteed due to the road programmes, it was vital that first contact should be made in the proper way by people who would not shoot them on sight, but would instead attempt to give them the proper medical care and, if necessary, move them to a safer area.

On the question of the new Indian Statute, my copy of which he had been reading, Claudio said that the most important aspect was not the collection of high-sounding sentiments about giving the Indian his full rights as a citizen of Brazil, but how the Indians' land rights would be affected. Giving the Indian his full rights as a Brazilian citizen was not going to improve his lot. The right to elect representatives to Parliament, even if they could in time be taught to appreciate and make use of this right, was not going to be of any great value to the Indians because they comprised such a tiny minority of the Brazilian people and their voice would never be heard. What was much more important was to understand the particular situation of the Indians, isolated in small groups in the middle of a country of whose very existence and name they are not aware, and the possessors of nominal rights which they do not understand. It was not the laws pertaining to the Indians which needed changing, but the attitudes of the surrounding population. This would take time. The most disturbing aspect of the proposed law was that it appeared to undermine the existing 'inalienable rights of the Indian to his lands permanently and his exclusive enjoyment of the natural resources therein', and to substitute the idea that some specified person could decide on his behalf what would be in his and the *nation's* best interests.

We visited another Kayabi village on the way downstream, whose chief was known as Cuiabano. This time even more of the villagers were out hunting and fishing than when we had visited the Suya, and so we stayed only a short time before setting off again. After an hour or so we reached the junction of the Manitsauá Missu River and, turning left, went up it for another hour before reaching the Juruna village.

These Juruna, who have a reputation for being an extremely tough and independent people, were first contacted in 1760 more than a thousand miles to the north at the junction of the Xingu and the Amazon. There were then about three thousand of them but they were massacred in great numbers. As a result of this, and subsequent encounters with settlers and prospectors, they gradually moved further up the Xingu, retaining a deep mistrust and distaste for the white man. Having moved into the territory of the Suya and the Txukarramai, a series of long drawn-out battles ensued, in which their numbers were further reduced. Although still retaining their reputation and respect as warriors, the fighting did not cease until the Villas Boas brothers arrived on the scene, by which time their numbers were down to less than sixty. Now at last the tribe was increasing again as we could see from the large number of small children in the crowd waiting to greet us on the bank. However, they were now faced with a new threat, this time from the road. They had recently abandoned their village on the main stream of the Xingu, which had been only about twenty miles upstream of where the road met the river, and had moved to a temporary camp up the Manitsauá Missu. They had done this quite spontaneously and without any encouragement from the park's administration, simply as a result of their own fear and mistrust of the effect contact with the road workers would have on them. In fact, it was the first time anyone from the post had visited them at their camp. Claudio was interested to see how they were getting on with building their new village.

We found great bustle and activity in the clearing about one hundred yards in from the bank where there were two half-completed huts and several temporary shelters. Although our initial reception had been grim-faced and suspicious, as soon as they recognized Claudio the atmosphere began to relax and they turned out to be some of the friendliest Indians we had met in the Xingu. I was presented with a splendid head-dress of red parrot and wild turkey feathers, and later Marika was given a very pretty zoomorphic pot in the shape of a deer. They are the only other people apart from the Waura to make ceramics in the Xingu area but, unlike the Waura, they make them only for their own use and do not trade with other tribes. The women and girls of the tribe wore very pretty sarongs woven in traditional Juruna designs which looked rather like faded Scottish tartans. The children were enchanting and became particularly excited by the couple of balloons I had with me.

We were brought fried manioc and water-melon to eat, and while Claudio sat and talked to the chief, two of the men played on small flutes lying back in their hammocks and holding them horizontally. They made a strange lilting melody, repeating the same rather complicated tune again and again. I found it almost familiar, reminding me of the music played by shepherd boys in the mountains of Greece.

There was a particularly fine stool carved out of a solid piece of wood in the shape of a jaguar. I thought it was safe to admire this as it was clearly out of the question for us to take away something so large and heavy, but as soon as I did so it was presented to me. I tried to explain how we would never get it into the aeroplane and that it was impossible for me to accept it, but they were all very insistent. I was finally persuaded by Edson who said that if I didn't want it he'd have it. It was eventually air-freighted at vast expense to our house in Cornwall. It is one of the few things that I have collected in my travels which is regularly used – it stands in front of the fire and is very comfortable to sit on.

Time went by quickly with the Juruna, a remarkable people of whom Claudio admitted to being particularly fond. We left rather later than we had intended and it was soon pitch dark, with no moon and light showers of rain from time to time. However, Bejai, with his one eye, who was driving, seemed to know by instinct where the sandbanks were, but we made slow progress against the current and the motor kept breaking down. Passing Cuiabano's village we saw several fires burning and even one out on a sandbank with someone signalling beside it. Thinking that someone might be ill and wanting a lift back to the post, we nosed our way into the bank to find that a feast had been prepared in our honour. There were sweet roasted potatoes, manioc and corn-on-the-cob toasted in the fire, as well as tapir meat to eat. A row of ten women and girls, regularly graded from the highest to the shortest – a small child – were dancing. They would swing in a semi-circle and walk up towards one of the men of the tribe and stare at him until he began to chant one of their legends. Then he would be brought a bow and arrow by another of the men and begin to dance as well. Stamping hard on the ground he would go forwards and then back-wards for thirty or forty feet across the beaten earth, while the women floated behind him, like a train, going in a semi-circle and curving behind him when he stepped back. Their feet moved together in perfect unison creating a strange and hypnotic impression. This was repeated a dozen or more times with different men, and each time that the man stopped the women would just move around the crowd until they faced another man talking to his friends, and stare him into joining them.

Then there came a moment for which I was quite unprepared, considering that this village had not been particularly friendly when we had visited them on our way downstream during the morning. Presumably Claudio had said something about the importance of my visit because I suddenly found myself being given presents of all sorts, as one member of the tribe after another, from warriors to little children and old women, came and presented me with things. I began to feel like an African king receiving tribute, as they brought sheaves of bows and arrows, feather head-dresses, woven baskets, necklaces and fans, and handed them to me. Slipping into my royal rôle with revolting ease, I received each one graciously, and admired the fine workmanship enthusiastically before handing it to a helpful acolyte and accepting the next gift. The head-dresses were particularly fine and the most welcome as they were light and easy to send home. In fact, they tend to be rather disappointing away from their natural setting as the colours fade and the feathers go limp and dirty in time.

Everyone was in a very cheerful mood by the time we left, and the whole village clustered down onto the slippery mudbank to wave us good-bye. Their figures were silhouetted by the row of bonfires behind and their shadows leapt and danced across the water. It was the last village we were able to visit in Xingu and the send-off we were given made a memorable farewell.

It was midnight before we arrived back at the post, tired and cold, to find food waiting for us and several Suya, who had been dancing in our absence during the evening, still up and about. We packed our things together early in the morning, tied all the bows and arrows in a large bundle, and carefully rolled up the feather head-dresses. Carrying these out to the small airstrip a hundred yards from the edge of the post, we passed Claudio's hut, and he shyly invited us in, saying that he, too, had prepared presents for us. He gave me a magnificent Kukanga – a Txukarramai war club, which had been used in battles against the Kreen Akrore, and for killing wild boar and other animals. It was made of iron-hard wood and was a formidable well-balanced weapon with an elegant decorated handle and carved ends. To Marika he gave a Mura Pehi made by the Kamayura – a beautiful mother-of-pearl necklace – the most valued of all the ornaments worn by the upper Xingu tribes. It was, by general agreement, the finest one that anybody had seen. This was proved again and again during the next hour because Marika wore it waiting for the plane and numerous people came up to admire it and comment on its beauty. The Indians had not admired anything else that we had been given but this necklace was extraordinarily special. They are said to take about five hundred hours to make, shaping and grading small pieces of mother-of-pearl from the inside of Xingu river-oysters and then stringing them together. The carving is done with piranha teeth and the holes for stringing the pieces together drilled with dog-fish teeth.

Suddenly one of the Indians pointed towards the east and soon the rest of us could hear the sound of the approaching Beechcraft. Our luggage and presents were quickly loaded on board and it was time to say good-bye.

At that moment in Diauarum, I realized how deeply I had grown to feel about the Xingu National Park. I had already said earlier during the morning that I was sad to leave and wished I could stay longer. I have said this a thousand times before, all over the world, and meant it. People have been kind, sometimes exceptionally generous and hospitable. Places have been beautiful and I have wanted to stay forever – or at least for a few more days. But when it came to leave I always looked ahead with interest, if not eager anticipation, to the next place I would be visiting. But as we all walked across the rough, dusty ground towards the aeroplane I felt such an overpowering emotion of affection for those we were about to leave, and regret at having to do so, that I had to struggle to hold back tears.

Marika was weeping openly.

The Brazilians have a habit of giving each other *abraços* – to which foreigners, and particularly the British, always react a little awkwardly – that is embracing each other warmly when good friends meet or separate. Or one can deliver an *abraço* in the name of a mutual friend. This is not the Russian kiss on the cheek, or indeed a jolly bear hug, but simply an arm momentarily laid around the shoulders in a gesture of affection. Performing this simple gesture with these people, whom I had grown to love and respect, required an effort of self-control and detachment such as I have seldom had to muster.

As we took off I could only see a blur of upturned faces and waving arms. I felt a terrible sense of loss – of paradise lost – and an intense determination to fight for those whom we had left behind.

PART THREE

❧

Bananal

Southern Mato Grosso

The Kadiweu

Cuiabá

The Bororo

The Paresi

The Nambiquara

The Cinta Larga

The Seringal do Faustinho

Pôrto Velho

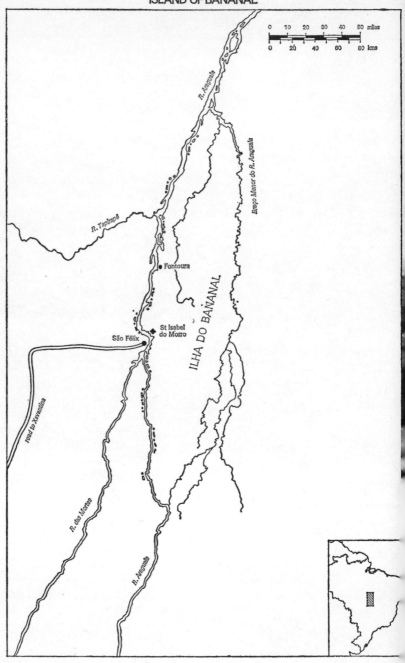

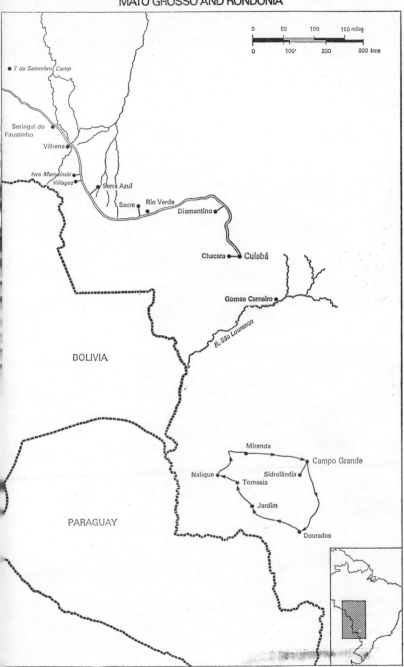

MATO GROSSO AND RONDÔNIA

0   50   100   150 miles

0   100·   200   300 kms

7 de Setembro Camp

Seringal do
Faustinho

Vilhena

two Mamaindé
Villages

Serra Azul

Sacre   Rio Verde

Diamantino

Chacara   Cuiabá

Gomes Carneiro

R. São Lourenço

BOLIVIA

Miranda

Campo Grande

Nalique

Sidrolândia

Tomasia

Jardim

Dourados

PARAGUAY

Bananal

❧

THE two hour flight eastwards from Xingu to Bananal was bumpy due to turbulence over the jungle. We arrived at the administrative centre of Santa Isabel do Morro feeling rather sick. We were taken to the so-called super-luxury hotel on the river bank which turned out to be practically deserted and very run down, but still charging higher prices than the Nacional in Brasilia. It had been built by Juscelino Kubischek, the President who built Brasilia, as another part of his dream of opening up the interior of Brazil. Originally named after him, this had been cleverly changed, when he fell out of power and favour, into the *John Kennedy Hotel*, thereby retaining the same initials on the silver and linen.

We wanted to visit the Karaja village at once but were informed that it was 'not yet ready for us'. Later, a torrential cloudburst and thunderstorm prevented us from leaving the hotel.

As we were told again the next morning, 'that it would not be convenient' for us to visit the Indians, I arranged for horses to be brought to the hotel early. We went for a pleasant, unexciting ride for ten or fifteen miles into the middle of the island. The man who came with us said that since all shooting had been prohibited on the island, crocodiles, deer and emu were beginning to increase again, but we saw none.

On the way back I suggested that we should ride through the Karaja village but was told that this was forbidden. Instead, we stopped at the FUNAI *cantina* where a group of Karaja were leaning on the counter and looking at the goods on display. I could see soap, tins of sardines, razor blades, spaghetti, bags of farina, salt and a pile of lavatory paper. Trade was not brisk and most of the men were simply squatting on the ground or lounging against the wall of the hut. They were all fully-dressed in rather ragged clothes, although one or two were very smartly dressed in blue silk jeans with wide belts and cowboy hats. All had the tribal circles like a second pair of eyes incised on their cheek bones. Some women arrived who were much more cheerful and garrulous, and with them was one small boy who looked very fine with black tasselled leg bands and feathers round his arms.

The village lay just beyond, but we were separated from it by a strong barbed-wire fence. Although it was clearly to keep cattle out of the village rather than to keep the Indians in, it did not give a good impression. Nor did the fact that there was only one narrow entrance through which the Indians could pass (guarded by a uniformed guard) help to dispel the idea of a concentration camp. I was anxious to visit the village as soon as possible, but on our return from our ride we were told that the Indians were still not ready for us and that we must visit the administration and hospital buildings during the rest of the morning.

The Indian hospital was a long, low, modern building around which we were taken by a silent nurse. The resident doctor was away and the place had a rather dead and unused feeling about it. Everything was clean and there was quite a lot of modern equipment, an impressive dentist's chair (but no dentist), a modern operating room (but no surgeon) and an X-ray machine which was not working. There were only four patients – all Karaja. Two of these were men, one of whom had broken an arm and the other four ribs in fights. Another man had stomach trouble which the nurse said was thought to be cirrhosis of the liver (caused by drink?). Finally, there was a very old woman with bad arthritis who had come to the hospital to die. The nurse told us that the Indians preferred to be treated in their own villages rather than go to the hospital and that serious cases were sent to Brasilia or Belo Horizonte, which accounted for the small number of patients. However, as the hospital was the centre for several tribes and was well equipped, it seemed strange that so little use should be being made of it.

The FUNAI executive offices and administration buildings were close to the hospital. Santa Isabel do Morro is the base of the Seventh Regional Delegacy of FUNAI, from which the Xerente, Kraho and Xavante tribes are administered as well as the Karaja. In spite of a considerable administration and clerical staff working in these offices, I found an alarming lack of information about numbers, conditions and the location of the Indians under their care. For instance, there was a large wall-map in one of the offices with several coloured pins stuck in it marking Indian villages and posts of the island of Bananal. I was interested in the numbers of Karaja at each of these places and several people, from the FUNAI delegates downwards, gave their opinion. The totals arrived at ranged from fifteen hundred (the delegate) down to seven hundred and it seems likely, on further investigations, that eight hundred is approximately the right figure. However, a considerable argument developed on the subject between the members of the FUNAI staff. There appeared to be an equal disagreement over the numbers of the other tribes in the Delegacy. On the other hand, everyone was agreed that there were about eight thousand Brazilian settlers on the island, mostly cattle ranchers.

The island of Bananal, which is eight thousand square miles, is known as an 'open' reserve and is sometimes referred to as the National Indian Park of Araguaia. It is also a nature reserve, and the flora and fauna on it are supposed to be protected. Tourists, who had, for a time, been encouraged to visit the island, were now banned, which accounted for the run-down condition of the hotel. But the small town of São Félix on the west bank of the

Araguaia river, opposite Santa Isabel, was growing fast. There seemed to be some doubt as to where the Indians fitted into this picture for, although there was general agreement that the land belonged to the Indians, the schemes for its exploitation seemed to have little to do with the Indians' welfare. There was talk of a cheese and butter factory to make use of the milk produced by the settlers' cattle, and also of a possible fish processing plant. These were to be administered by FUNAI and, although some Indians might be employed at the factories and some of the profits might be used for their welfare, there seemed to me little likelihood that it would do the Indians much good. I tried to suggest that what the Indians needed might be help in finding ways for them to work and exploit their own land rather than to impose alien systems, but I made little headway.

At last, the moment came for us to visit the Indian village. We walked across to the gap in the barbed wire fence where a detachment of the Indian Guard were lined up for inspection. There were nine of them, in uniform, under the command of a very smooth-looking Indian corporal in dark glasses who called them to attention as we approached. The Guarda Rural Indigena, GRIN for short, were created in 1969 with the aim of 'maintaining order in the Indian communities, defending their territorial integrity and defending the fauna and flora'. To this end eighty-four Indian youths from the Karaja, Xerente and Kraho tribes had been taken to Belo Horizonte and given certain training as well as 'moral and civic instruction'. They were then returned to their own tribes as a native police force. Paid a small government salary, which in some cases represented the only outside income of a tribe, their position seemed difficult and anomalous and it was hard to see what function they performed. Originally they had been armed but now their holsters were empty. Their job was to maintain law and order but it seemed unlikely that the non-Indian population on Bananal would pay much attention to them, and inside the tribe more authority was vested in the tribal chiefs. The sixteen GRIN were the only police on the island of Bananal and, in theory at least, if two white farmers should have a fight and one should kill the other – and in a community where everybody carries guns this must happen from time to time – it would be the duty of one of these unarmed Indian boys to arrest the survivor. An alarming prospect!

The eight Indian guards waiting for us at the entrance to the *aldeia* Santa Isabel were all Karaja. After talking to them for a while, they escorted us into the village. Two rows of almost identical rectangular huts faced us. Most were made of palm thatch, mud and wattle, but two or three in the middle had been built of brick and all were on raised brick platforms. We began to wander off to visit some of the huts informally, but were called back and made to begin at the first house in the row and work through all thirty which made up the village. This gave a ridiculous sense of formality to the occasion, as though the Indians were being inspected, and must have contributed to the rather sullen reception that we received. The interiors of the huts were dirty, dark and uncomfortable, and bare of the usual clutter of possessions and crowds of overlapping families which we had grown used to in the Xingu. A lot of work was going on, however, and artifacts of quite a high standard, which are sold through FUNAI, were being produced in large numbers. In every hut there was a simple frame for weaving belts in the attractive Karaja designs, and in several huts men and women were busy making feather head-dresses, baskets and bows and arrows. In some, pottery was being produced. Clay figurines, zoomorphic pots and even ashtrays were drying outside in rows in the sun.

The Indians were about to dance 'in our honour'. In several of the huts rather glum young men were being painted by their mothers and having feathers and arm bands tied on to their bodies. Also, surprisingly, as none of them took part in the general dancing, several of the girls and young women of the tribe were painting their own and each others' bodies with careful designs in urucu. It looked like rain and so, as we neared the end of our tour of the village, we spent less and less time in each hut, merely popping in the front door and saying 'hello' and dashing out the back one. We and our escort of guards were all in a group and almost trotting. We then walked across the open area behind the village to the men's hut. This was made in the old style of palm leaf fronds. Near it were a couple of benches, around which a group of thirty or forty of the Brazilian settlers and farmers on Bananal had gathered to watch the performance. Most of the Indian men and boys of the tribe stood or sat a little way apart, awkward in their finery.

The dance began. The younger men had embarrassed grins on their faces and were either glancing sideways to see how the audience was reacting or giggling over private jokes, while the older men gritted their teeth and half closed their eyes in an effort to create the right mood. The crowd laughed tolerantly and scratched and fidgeted.

After a short rest, they danced again, this time taunting each other in two teams before wrestling together in pairs. It was perfectly clear that none of them were trying at all. They were simply going through the motions. However, they ended more enthusiastically, with some amusing performances by two Indians dancing arm-in-arm around the area chanting in an aggressive way, as though crowing over the defeat of their enemies. The crowd of local farmers and cowboys began to take more interest and hooted and jeered, to encourage the performers.

Later, the witch doctors appeared. There were eight of them in straw costumes reaching to the ground. Six were dressed in pale natural colour and two in black. At first glance they seemed exactly the same as those I had filmed on the same spot in 1958. But then Richard Mason and I had been the only outsiders and the whole village had been gathered to watch with deep attention. Now most of the tribe remained in their huts, while the pairs of men, invisible behind their ceremonial thatch, shuffled uncertainly up and down, and the group of settlers laughed. An interesting, short, straw-robed figure, wearing a big wooden mask with white staring eyes painted on it, appeared briefly but vanished back inside the hut as soon as I took a photograph. I had not seen this figure before and was anxious to have a closer look. But one of the Indians stopped me from going into the hut. This rather pleased me as it showed that they still cared enough to want to keep something secret. Far the most unsatisfactory aspect of the whole dance was the way in which the Karaja themselves, and their audience of settlers, ridiculed and laughed at the whole performance. Both sides regarded it as a rather poor piece of amateur dramatics without much cultural significance, and with little sense of spontaneous enjoyment about it. It was also interesting that here, unlike in the Xingu, I was conscious of there being 'sides'.

And yet I also had a feeling that perhaps the Karaja knew exactly what they were doing. This was, after all, a command performance laid on for our benefit, probably at the wrong time of day and in quite the wrong season. It might well be that the atmosphere would be completely different when they danced in their own good time and for their own purposes. If this was so it could mean that the Karaja had adapted rather well and were managing to get the best of both worlds, laying on performances for the 'tourists' when necessary, without allowing that to cheapen and destroy the significance of the ritual. The possibility that this might, at least in part, be true was strengthened for me by an incident that took place right at the end of the dancing. An Indian beckoned to Marika and me, indicating that there was something we should see at the other end of the village. We followed him and found a beautiful, naked Karaja girl, wearing only a narrow leather apron, beads, arm and leg bands and some rather elaborate painted designs. She was standing at the end of an open area between two huts and, as we watched, two of the witch doctors danced towards her, while she made circular motions over her stomach with her hands, and backed away from them. This went on for some time and was clearly an important and serious ritual, performed well out of sight of the jeering cowboys. A few of the women from the village watched with us in silence and the girl herself, with head bowed, seemed almost in a trance before the two frightened figures whose faces were hidden behind the tall mantle of straw.

When we returned to the central area, we found that the dancing had finished and the Indians were being made to demonstrate their prowess with bow and arrow, by shooting at a tin can. At first they were hopelessly bad, missing by two or three yards, until a couple who were rather better arrived from the village. Suddenly the whole atmosphere of the afternoon changed as two fat black ducks appeared from the direction of the river, flying at about sixty feet directly over the village. Immediately a hail of arrows were discharged straight up into the air, one of which passed between the two ducks, causing them to separate. The whole crowd collapsed in laughter, and we all dodged about avoiding the arrows as they returned to earth. Luckily nobody was hurt and we left after being presented with a pottery duck and some small figurines, as well as a bow, three arrows and a large turtle which was very badly cooked for us in the hotel that evening.

Fontoura, thirty odd miles down the Araguaia River and also on Bananal, is the other main Karaja village. There are other settlements dotted about the island, notably at Macauba in the north and Canoana in the east, and there was talk of an uncontacted group of Indians at the very north of the island. I had slept at Fontoura in 1958 and filmed the Indians dancing in the evening. I remembered it as an attractive, haphazard collection of Indian huts on a bank high above the river. There had been a Seventh Day

Adventist Mission houseboat moored next to the village with an American missionary on board.

As we arrived by river after travelling for three hours downstream from Santa Isabel, I saw that everything had changed. A collection of modern buildings with a comfortable white house in the middle stood at the top of a flight of concrete steps. Further along the bank, and separated from the European dwellings by a substantial barbed wire fence, was the Indian village. This reminded me of prints I had seen of nineteenth-century slave settlements, with identical rectangular thatched houses on raised concrete platforms standing in rows. There were twenty-nine of these houses and each one contained one or two families.

We were greeted by the young Brazilian missionary who was in charge of the post. He told us that it was FUNAI's policy not to send their own man to villages which were already being looked after by a missionary. In spite of his and Edson's presence, we had some difficulty persuading the surly Indian guard to allow us through the barbed wire into the village. There was a tremendous amount of litter between the front row of houses and the edge of the river. The missionary agreed that this was one of the biggest problems in getting the Karaja acculturated. Presumably this stems in part from the fact that the Karaja were originally nomadic river people who did not spend very much time in their villages, and so were not used to coping with this problem. I remembered from my previous visit that many of the Karaja had then preferred to go down onto the sandbanks to sleep at night rather than to stay on dry land and sleep in their houses.

The atmosphere at Fontoura was much less energetic than at Santa Isabel, with little work of any sort being done either in the manufacture of artifacts or general household chores. Health was poor and in many of the huts people suffering from malaria lay in their hammocks. The rest of the village sat around lethargically. They either objected angrily if we took photographs, or demanded to be paid.

In only two places was there any sign of energetic activity. Near to the entrance to the village was a mechanical plant for grinding manioc which was being operated by two Brazilian men and a woman. None of the Indians were helping. It seemed that the people who were making use of the equipment were settlers from near-by. At the far end of the village, in the men's hut, which was once again the only building built in the old style, we found the other six Indian guards with a dozen or so men of the village busily making new heads for the witch doctors' ceremonial outfits. The missionary said that this was how they occupied most of their time. There were also two teenage boys of the village who were completely covered in black genipapo and preparing to be initiated into the tribe. Some of the smallest children were also painted and wearing Karaja arm and leg bands, but most of the people in the village were simply dressed in European rags. In the middle of the open area at the back of the village was a new well which the Seventh Day Adventists had dug. There was water about thirty feet down which looked fairly clean, although there were some empty tins visible at the bottom. The missionary complained that he was having considerable difficulty persuading the Karaja to drink out of the well rather than from the river.

He said that there was quite a lot of disease in the village, particularly malaria, and that he was desperately short of medicines. He had established a system of barter with the Indians, whereby they paid for the clothes, sugar and food which he gave them out of the store, in Indian artifacts which he subsequently sold in their names. I am sure he was an honest and dedicated man who operated this system fairly, although it is one which is very open to abuse, but I could not help feeling that the Indians would have been better served had their adviser and protector not been bound by the very rigid restrictions of his sect on what does and does not constitute permissible food. The subtle distinction between 'clean and unclean foods' was one which the Indians, often living on the borderline of starvation, can ill afford to observe.

When religious principles begin to interfere with and break down the culture and tribal patterns of a people, it is often easy to say that the Indians would be better off without the help of the missionary. There are cases when this is so and the destructive and prohibitive influence of a fanatical missionary does do more harm than good. However, before recommending his removal, one must remember that the missionary may represent the only assistance which the Indian is receiving. If that is removed there may be nothing to take its place. In the case of the Karaja at Fontoura it was difficult to see what to recommend. The Indians were in a bad state and seemed to be deteriorating rapidly. On the other hand, the missionary was young and energetic and obviously anxious to do what he could to help. He was the first to admit that the situation was grave and that help of all sorts was badly needed, help which he himself was unable to provide with limited resources. His comfortable and almost elegant house and garden contrasted badly with the almost slum dwellings of the Indians, and yet I was forced to wonder whether FUNAI would have been able to provide the same standard of accommodation for an employee of theirs, and whether without it they would be able to recruit men of sufficiently high calibre to cope with the very complicated problem of trying to help these Indians.

I gave a lot of thought to the problem of the Karaja on Bananal and it is one to which I could find no easy solutions. Certainly the medical facilities left a lot to be desired, and there is a golden opportunity, with the existing basic hospital at Santa Isabel, to establish a really first-class Indian hospital and mobile doctor service to take good medical care of the Indians, not only on Bananal but for a much larger area. This was suggested by the Red Cross and I endorsed the recommendation in my subsequent report. I also suggested that the Karaja should be encouraged in the manufacture of their artifacts as they undoubtedly have a great talent for this, and their tribal designs are varied and pleasing. Improved outlets for the sale of these could go some way towards boosting the economy of the tribe but it could never solve their basic problem. This is that they are being gradually swamped by a competing and growing population of settlers. As a result, they can no longer wander over the large areas of land and river from which they previously extracted their living. They now find themselves forcibly settled on small areas of poor land which they are not by nature inclined to cultivate efficiently. The Karaja are basically fishermen and river people. If all the fishing rights on the Araguaia and its tributaries on and around Bananal could be reserved for the exclusive use of the Karaja, and an honest and encouraging agency set up to buy the fish from them, then perhaps they might be able to develop their own niche in the industrial world which is about to smother them. Such a law would not be too difficult to enforce and would not impede the development of the region, which is clearly going ahead at full speed. Nor would it interfere seriously with the basic rights of the settlers. A fish-processing factory operated by FUNAI or private enterprise, in which some Karaja were allowed to work and earn a wage, would not solve the problem or go any way towards helping the Karaja.

I left Bananal feeling that I knew the Karaja little better than I had when I arrived. Although they were a resilient and tough people, they would continue to go downhill unless some way was found soon of reinforcing their pride in their own culture and tribe.

Southern Mato Grosso

❧

OUR Beechcraft failed to rendezvous with us again as planned in Brasilia, where we spent a couple of days after leaving Bananal, and so we were provided with a DC3. This we shared for the first leg of our onward journey, as far as Uberlândia, with a farouche collection of heavily armed officers who were on their way to 'sort out a little trouble'. They sat silently together during the flight, fingering and cleaning their weapons, and we were unable to find out what the 'trouble' was.

We were then taken on to Campo Grande in the southern part of Mato Grosso State, where we were hoping to see some of the more acculturated Indians, the descendants of tribes which had been in contact with civilization for a long time.

No one met us. When we made our way to the FUNAI office in the town, we found that the delegate for the region, Helio Bucker, had not been warned of our impending arrival. This I found annoying as it had been constantly emphasized in the FUNAI offices in Brasilia that we must stick as strictly as possible to our official time-table so that all those along our route who had been alerted to assist us would not be inconvenienced. It was unfortunate, too, that we had arrived at a moment when Snr Bucker was intensely busy. However, I was highly impressed by the way in which he immediately grasped the situation and set about making all the necessary arrangements for us to visit as many different groups as possible. A map of the region was produced and, in marked contrast to Bananal, I was given accurate and concise information by Helio Bucker and his staff about numbers and conditions of the Indians under their charge.

Three hours after our arrival, Marika and I were being taken by Snr Bucker's son in a jeep to visit a group of Terena Indians about fifty miles south of Campo Grande near Sidrolândia. Snr Bucker himself had to clear up some pressing matters in his office, as well as prepare for the longer tour which we were to make the next morning. Edson preferred to rest after the flight.

Over seven hundred Terena Indians live on the Buriti reservation, four thousand nine hundred acres of fairly fertile land. They are divided into two more-or-less equal groups, looked after by Evangelist and Catholic missionaries respectively. We visited the former, which is also the FUNAI post. It was pouring with torrential rain when we arrived, and the missionary who greeted us and in whose house we sheltered, had frightening, staring eyes and an apparent obsession with his collection of sharp knives. The rain continued and we sloshed through the mud from one Indian household to another discussing their problems. The Terena were very articulate and quite definite about the assistance they required and the priorities involved. First of all there was a lot of tuberculosis and many of them were suffering from colds. The medical supplies at the post had run out and more were urgently needed, as well as a trained nurse to administer them. In the meanwhile, they were having to buy patent medicines with their own money, which meant that they went without food, which in turn only aggravated the situation.

Secondly, they needed expert agricultural assistance so as to be able to work their own land efficiently, and to live off it. They were unanimous in agreeing that a communally-owned tractor would make all the difference in bringing this situation about. At the moment they were caught in a vicious circle in which they had to go out and work long hours for next to no pay, which was barely enough to buy food to feed themselves, and as a result their own land was neglected. If they were helped to break out of this dependent state and become self-supporting, it would alleviate the depression and despair which was causing widespread drunkenness.

Finally, as part of the process of becoming independent of the local population, they wished that traffic could be banned from the rough road which ran through the middle of their territory. It was in fact illegal for the local population to use this road, but they did so, and it led to the Indians and their women being abused, and encouraged prostitution and drunkenness.

The post was able to give them very little help as it suffered from a complaint which we encountered on several subsequent occasions.

This is that its meagre budget is barely sufficient to support the administration of the post and leaves nothing over to spend on the Indians' behalf. The post maintains a small herd of cows and employs two Indians full time, but the milk from the cows is consumed by the post, leaving none over for the Indians or for their tubercular children. The two Indians are kept busy looking after the post's own needs, milking the cows, working on the post's vegetable garden and keeping the electric light plant, which only provides light for the post, going. The result of all this is that, far from being of any help to the Indians of the reservation, the post is a positive burden on them. In other words, the system is not working and the Indians, who are forced to live on their reservation because it is the only asset they have, cannot complete the final stage of integration into the local community. Their land is fairly rich and should be enough to support them so that any work they chose to do outside the reservation would represent a profit, and money with which to buy the things they could not produce themselves. If this were to happen they would also then be in a position to command higher wages than the bare subsistence pay of about three pounds a week, which they told us they were receiving, and which in itself seems to represent a case of discrimination against them.

Due to the rain we were unable to take any photographs of this group of Terena, but they were very articulate and their desire to compete impressed me. Here were Indians who, through prolonged contact, had become acculturated and had to a very large extent overcome the difficulties of adapting from an Indian way of life to a so-called 'civilized' one. The desire and potential were there for them to become fully productive and competent members of a modern society and they were only being held back from achieving this by circumstances largely beyond their control. Their situation was quite different from that of the more recently contacted Indians that we had been seeing and, while it was still necessary to preserve and reinforce their pride in their ethnic origins, a very small amount of properly administered practical aid would improve their lot out of all proportion to the cost. Since this was not forthcoming they were in a depressed state and were being exploited. There was a danger that they might remain an under-privileged minority, living in ghettoes and useful only as a source of cheap labour. But there was also hope that with a little help and by their own efforts they might become a real and respected force in the community.

After a night in the hotel in Campo Grande, we were up and ready to leave again early the next morning. I was most impressed when the FUNAI jeep with Helio Bucker, his son and a driver, arrived on the dot of five o'clock, as planned, to collect us. Four hours fast driving south over good roads brought us to Dourados, close to which is another Indian reserve. The Indians were mostly Kaiwa with some Guarani and Terena. There are nearly two thousand of them living on eight thousand nine hundred acres.

Instead of living in villages or even small groups of houses, the Indians here are spread over the whole area farming their own small-holdings. We called in at the post and then drove through the reserve visiting Indian families.

The land is said to be some of the richest in the whole of Brazil and certainly the crops of maize, manioc, bananas and cotton were tall and strong, growing from deep, red earth.

Here again the problem is one of under-exploitation of the Indians' own land. Broken into small family units, with simple tools, they are only able to cultivate small areas and much of the reserve is wasted land. If there were any game left in this, or any valuable timber, there might be a case for preserving it. Since there is not, the Indians would clearly be much better off if they could raise the necessary finance to buy more efficient machinery such as tractors and, perhaps working as co-operatives, extract the maximum from their land. But, being Indians, the banks would laugh at the idea of lending them money and they lack the organization to set up co-operatives. This is a job which FUNAI should do, but here, as was the case at Buriti, the post appeared to be having trouble enough maintaining itself without having anything left over for the Indians. Also, as at Buriti, the reserve is cut by a road much used by local farmers and causing the same problems. In addition a giant power cable had recently crossed the reserve, cutting a swathe two hundred yards wide. Although compensation for the land thus lost had been negotiated, it looked as though none was going to be received and there was still no electricity in the reserve.

The families we visited were poor in spite of the lush crops growing about their houses. They had difficulty selling any surplus they were able to grow, as they had to take this into the local town where they were often cheated or encouraged to spend the money they received on drink. As a result, they seemed in many ways to be getting the worst of both worlds in that they had lost the art of making their own pottery, and had no money to buy any other, so that almost all of those we saw were using empty tins as cooking utensils.

One of the Indians, a Terena, who had done better for

himself than most, by having overcome considerable difficulties to get his children educated, poured out a series of
troubles to us. Like all the Terena we had met he was
extravert and friendly but seemed very vulnerable in his
anxiety to better himself. He said that one of his biggest
problems was that, as an Indian, he did not need to carry
papers, but as the reserve was quite near the Paraguayan
border he was often asked to produce them when he went
into the town. If unable to prove that he came from the
reserve he would be thrown in jail. This fear lay at the root
of many of the troubles these Indians were facing; they
needed to go into the towns in order to work, trade or buy
things, and yet they often got into trouble or came up
against prejudice when they did so.

The scattering of the Indians into small-holdings had
created a water problem – most of them no longer lived on
the edge of the small stream running through the reserve
in which they had been used to wash themselves and their
clothes daily. Now, although some had wells, none had
pumps to provide running water. As a result it was very
noticeable that the children, in particular, were often caked
in dirt. This in turn must have contributed to the health
problem and one of the forms which outside aid could
take, and which I recommended in my report, would be
the supply of water pumps.

Just off the Indian land we saw but did not have time to
visit there was, we were told, a very good missionary hospital which specialized in tuberculosis. FUNAI pays for
Indians to be sent there, from as far away as the Xavantes,
at a cost of about £1 per day. As tuberculosis appears to be
the biggest health problem with the Indians, and one to
which they are all susceptible, from the most isolated to
the most acculturated, the hospital undoubtedly serves a
most valuable function. However, we were told it is almost
the only good one where Indians are accepted in any
quantity, and there was a long waiting list. Also, they were
usually discharged after three months, but if the cure were

to be effective they should have another year of rest and treatment. Instead they would have to go back to work, and tended to fail to take their medicines or look after themselves properly, which meant that by the end of the year the disease had simply developed a resistance and they were back again iller than ever. A very good plan which was talked about (but seemed unlikely to materialize without substantial help from outside) was that a piece of unused Indian land should be made into an isolation hospital and farm. Indians could then go there on discharge from the main hospital, their families could join them and they could work according to their abilities on the farm.

Although the problems at Dourados were slightly different from Buriti, the first steps towards solving them seemed to me to be much the same. The Indians needed a resident agricultural adviser with adequate resources, who could develop a viable farming programme and so make the reserve self-supporting; and a nurse to get on top of the health problem and make sure that proper after-care treatment was observed in tuberculosis cases.

The Kadiweu

❧

AFTER lunch at the post we set out on the long journey west towards the Bolivian border to visit the Kadiweu Indians. The last remnants of this once powerful and mighty tribe now live in the middle of a vast area of grassland, forest and swamp known as the Pantanal. To reach them we had to drive for most of the next twenty-four hours, stopping only briefly to sleep at a scruffy roadside hotel in the small town of Jardim. Due to heavy rain the roads were in a very bad state, with mud up to three or four feet deep churned into great ruts. To begin with we passed through endless rolling plains where cattle grazed. Occasionally we passed great herds of beautiful white beasts with long curving horns, driven by their tough and romantic gauchos. Then the road deteriorated into a rough and little used track as we climbed into the Serra da Bodoquena.

For the next two days we were constantly passing fences marking farm boundaries or divisions within large farms. The 'gates' consisted of three or four parallel poles which had to be removed and replaced as we passed through. Helio Bucker's son, also called Helio, and I rode on the back of the jeep so as to do this, and also to clear any branches, stones or other obstructions out of its way. This was marvellously exhilarating as every now and then the skies opened and released sheets of torrential rain which soaked us to the skin. However, clinging onto the outside of the wildly-bucking jeep kept us warm and, as we always rewarded ourselves after these stops with a long draught from a bottle of *Cachaça* (raw cane alcohol), we also kept cheerful.

The road became worse and worse, until much of the time the jeep was in the lowest of low gears, struggling through deep ravines, river beds and thick mud. Once over the first ridges of the Serra, we found ourselves passing through more stretches of open grassland interspersed with rocky outcrops and jungle. This was now the territory of the Kadiweu, where the grazing is said to be among the best in Brazil. Certainly the cattle we saw looked extremely healthy and we were told that they suffered from few diseases and kept free of ticks through spending a lot of time in the waters of the swamps and so staying clean.

The Kadiweu are the remaining descendants of one of the few South American tribes to make use of horses for hunting and fighting. Horses were introduced by the Spanish in the first half of the sixteenth century and wild herds became extremely common on the plains of the southern Mato Grosso. The other Indian tribes simply re-garded these as a new form of game to be hunted and eaten, but the Kadiweu's ancestors learnt to ride the horses and with their help were able to become very powerful and conquer most of the other tribes in the region. They also effectively prevented Spanish and Portuguese penetration of their lands for many years, and in fact allied themselves with one side after another during the long struggle for ascendancy over the river Paraguay.

It was only in the second half of the last century that disease, drink and determined penetration by cattle ranchers into their territory began to have the effect of reducing their power and numbers. By the early part of this century, only the Kadiweu in the Pantanal retained any relative independence, but their land, too, was gradu-ally invaded by settlers with herds of cattle. Even a *Cachaça* factory was built. Many Indians were corrupted by the drink, but others fought back and official troops were called in who attacked and burnt down many of the Kadiweu villages.

After years of trouble during which the settlers lost

many of their cattle and the Indians were brutally ill-treated, the government intervened and established large and well-defined lands as being the inalienable property of the Kadiweu. These amounted to nine hundred thousand acres, and were administered on the Indians' behalf by the Indian Protection Service.

Although little was done for the Indians, due to inefficiency and corruption, they were well provided with land and enlightened administration might at any moment have achieved great things for them. Then about five years ago, shortly before the SPI was to be discredited and abolished, an Act was hurried through the Mato Grosso State Parliament putting up most of the Kadiweu land for sale at auction. The day after the Act was passed, the auction was held and the land was sold off to several large land-owners. The title deeds were drawn up surprisingly quickly (they usually take six months) and when, twenty-four hours after the auction, the Cuiabá Indian Protection Service Delegate then responsible for the Kadiweu heard about it, the whole thing appeared to be a *fait accompli*. The delegate, who happened at the time to be Helio Bucker, made the Indian Protection Service appeal officially to the High Court against the Act and it was eventually declared invalid.

However, it was put to the then Governor of the State of Mato Grosso to set the matter right and he pointed out that between the passing of the Act and its invalidation the land had been occupied and settled and that it would cause a great deal of hardship and upset to have to move everybody out again. Finally a compromise solution was arrived at, whereby the settlers or their proprietors paid a rent of half a cruzeiro (about 2p) per acre to the Indians for their land. This money, amounting to about £30 000 a year, had been paid regularly to the SPI and more recently to FUNAI but only in the first year was a small part of it used on the Kadiweu Indians' behalf. It has all gone into central funds and the amount spent on aid and assistance to the

Kadiweu has only represented a small fraction of this sum.

The ironic situation therefore exists that the Kadiweu, who should be among the best provided-for Indians in Brazil due to the large amount of excellent land which they own and the rent paid for much of it, in fact live in virtual penury. Certainly those we saw were far from prosperous.

Once across the Serrada Bodoquena we were in Kadiweu country. The boundary of their territory was marked by a small stream. About an hour after we had crossed this we met an Indian coming towards us leading a woman on a horse. She had a cloth covering her head and shoulders and pulled across her face, which made her seem more Middle Eastern than Indian. He told us that the woman was his sister and that some time before – he said three months, but we found this hard to believe – a spider had fallen on her face during the night and in brushing it away some of the poisonous hairs from its body had come off in her eyes. She had been practically blind and delirious with pain most of the time since this had happened. They were now on their way to see a local Brazilian settler who was said to have a certain talent for curing things if he was paid well enough, using some western medicine and some magic. The girl was obviously in terrible pain and very frightened. Fortunately I had with me some eyedrops containing cocaine for killing pain and also some very effective ones for clearing up infections. We carried these things because Marika had in the past scratched both her pupils with a broken finger nail and her eyes were liable to become infected and very painful from time to time. I put both sorts of drops into the Indian girl's eyes and we all agreed that she should come with us and so end up eventually at Campo Grande where she could go to the hospital, rather than continue on her dubious journey. Almost immediately her eyes began to improve, particularly when we persuaded her to stop rubbing them. She remained with us for the rest of the journey, a silent, hunched figure in the back of the jeep. Continued treatment had practically cleared up her eye trouble by the time we delivered her to the hospital in Campo Grande but, whether through the prolonged pain or for some other reason, her brain appeared to have been affected.

The first Kadiweu post that we reached was in ruins. There was only a Terena Indian who had been brought in by FUNAI as a cowboy to help look after some of the Kadiweu cattle. Some time after this we reached the first of their villages, called Tomasia. Here we had our first proper sight of the Kadiweu horsemen, as a man and a boy galloped past the jeep and lassoed a horse before dragging it off to the corral. They were fine, big and splendid-looking people, quite unlike the other Indians we had been seeing and reminding me more of the North American Indian.

The old men who were sitting in an open-sided, thatched hut greeted us solemnly and with dignity, their angular, weather-beaten faces betraying no emotions. The young women and girls, in marked contrast, were very buxom and coy. Soon after we arrived they disappeared for a moment and came back dressed in their best party clothes with heavy applications of lipstick and rouge, which made them look like the re-touched photographs they hoped we would take of them. One after another they came and stood rigidly to attention in front of the camera. The children were charming and friendly and, as we nearly always found with Indian children, they came cheerfully, and with no shyness, to play with and examine us.

There were one or two pieces of quite fine pottery, in particular a large jar for holding water, with good painted designs. But most of the pieces were old and it did not look as though they were making any more; all the cooking was being done in old tins. There were about forty Indians living in the half-dozen dilapidated huts at Tomasia and more lived in small groups or isolated families near by.

We carried on through the rain, the mud and the steep rocky stretches, heading further into the Pantanal. The game in this region is particularly rich and Marika was able to have her first look at several wild animals and birds. Deer were said to be common but we had only one or two fleeting glimpses. Emus, on the other hand, appeared again and again, often running along in front of or beside the jeep in their ungainly but fast way, as though they had their hands clasped behind their backs. Crocodiles lay in broad daylight in shallow lagoons beside the track, something they have learnt not to do on the rivers, and once we saw a water-snake. Seriemas or secretary birds also ran through the long grass, pairs of red and blue macaws flew overhead as well as flocks of green parrots and white egrets in the marshes. From time to time we stopped and tried to shoot duck with the ·22 rifle we carried. Once or twice we were successful. The country was much more beautiful and varied than I had expected; the endless, flat swamps and marshes through the edge of which I had travelled on my river journey down the Paraguay in 1965 lay forty miles further to the west and we were still in the spurs and outcrops of the Bodoquena range.

Just as night was falling we came to a large river which was in spate due to the heavy rain. At first it was suggested that we should stop and camp for the night on the bank, and hope that the water level would have dropped by morning. But after wading through it we found that it was on average only between waist and knee deep, with a stony bottom. As the water level seemed to be rising rather than falling we decided to have a go. Dijamo, the driver, wrapped a cloth around the distributor and I forgot to suggest that the fan-belt should be taken off, which is a good idea on these occasions, as it prevents water being thrown up on to the engine and wetting the plugs.

Edson was at his very worst, getting under everybody's feet and, without ever having actually driven a jeep through a river before, shouting advice and instructions at us all and saying over and over again, 'You must drive slowly'. Just as we were about to drive into the river – all the rest of the party were in the water moving stones out of the way and ready to push if the jeep got stuck – I went round to the back and looked in. On the floor of the jeep was my large camera case with about three hundred pounds' worth of equipment and film. Squatting on top of it was Edson, holding his own precious belongings high above his head so that they would be kept dry when the water came in. Had we not all been so busy, an ugly scene might have developed as this was only the latest of a series of irritations and it made me angrier than was wise. However, I persuaded him to move into the cab, saying that he would be safer there from the crocodiles, hung my camera case from a hook in the roof and jumped out as the jeep ploughed into the river.

The engine stalled and died in the deepest part where the water was between three and four feet, and it looked for a time as though we might have to spend the night there with every chance of the river rising and sweeping everything away. However, after drying the plugs and removing the exhaust manifold and fan-belt, the engine fired and we were able to drive out with everyone, except Edson, pushing. By now it was pitch-dark and for another two hours we drove fast along the overgrown track.

We finally arrived at the cattle station at Nalique, where a man employed by FUNAI looks after about one hundred head of cattle. There was just one house and no Indians lived there, so we all slung our hammocks in an open shed and were fairly comfortable in spite of more rain during the night.

The FUNAI employee, whom we met in the morning, did not impress me. He was simply a cattle man and he resented the presence of the Indians. He spent a long time telling us how stupid and lazy they were and admitted to being frightened of them, saying that he carried a gun at all times and even slept with it under his pillow because the Indians were dangerous, wild animals. Clearly this is not the sort of man who should ever be allowed near Indians, let alone have any responsibility for their welfare.

All too often in the past the Kadiweu have been exploited and their cattle sold off until the man employed to look after them for the Indians had made enough money to retire and set up a business in Campo Grande or elsewhere. Meanwhile, the Indians have seldom been allowed to kill any cattle for their own use and consequently almost never eat meat. Of course, there is a problem in teaching the Indians to run their own herds of cattle, in that they are liable to kill and eat them all one after another, keeping none as breeding stock. There are various stories in Brazil of tribes, including the Kadiweu, who when given their own herds of cattle release them into the wild and then hunt them down like wild animals. One rather delightful, but I fear impracticable, suggestion put forward for the Kadiweu was that if they were only given enough cattle in the first instance they would not eliminate them but would maintain a balance. All things being equal, this might well be so but, unfortunately, where the Indians are concerned today things are not equal, and others would soon take their cattle from them. The difficulty is to find the right type of man to work with the Indians.

At Nalique we were shown a particularly beautiful pot which the Kadiweu had recently brought as a present. It was finely painted and engraved with elegant designs, but the cattle man only complained that the Indians would keep bothering him with things and he was expected to reward them with a bar of soap. The whole situation of the Kadiweu made me feel frustrated and miserable.

A few hours' drive on from Nalique we reached the main Kadiweu Post, called Bodoquena, where there is an airstrip usable only during the dry season. Over two hundred Kadiweu live in scattered groups around the post where another untrained FUNAI employee lives in quite a pretty small house. The best feature of this, which we took advantage of on arrival, was a natural bath house formed where a spring full of small fishes bubbled into a deep pool. There were also fruit trees, and the setting, in a valley surrounded by round, wooded hills, was spectacular.

The Indians, in contrast, were in a miserable way. The worst part of their situation, they told me, arose from the fact that they were not allowed to carry weapons. The countryside was rich in game, ranging from deer to wild boar, and they were not only unable to kill this for food but the animals came into their cultivated patches and destroyed their crops. Through prolonged contact and acculturation they had lost the ability to make and use bows and arrows, although they said that one or two of the old men still knew how to do this. They are therefore caught between the two cultures and are getting the worst of each, regarded as sub-human for being Indian but lacking most of the talents of their own culture.

Some of the Indians had pottery which they had made and encouraged us to buy. It was not of particularly good quality or very well made but the Indian patterns were attractive and the crude workmanship had some charm. In particular there was one voluble and intelligent old lady who spoke very good Portuguese and explained to me at length how she would like to make more pottery and be able to sell it so as to be able to support herself, and not be dependent upon her daughter who had her own family, while her son lived a long way away. Her problem was that she had no way of getting the pots she made to market and almost no one ever came to Bodoquena. She was an unusually forceful and bright old grandmother and we found ourselves in complete agreement that the Kadiweu should be rich and strong again and that it was a terrible thing that they should be reduced to their present plight. Like all the Kadiweu, she had great dignity and was not in the least ashamed of discussing their poverty and the wrongness of it. With an endearing simplicity she put a price of one cruzeiro on all her pots both large and small, and so we chose the best one and gave her five saying that it was better than the others and therefore worth it.

At another house we visited there was a woman suffering from the disease called *fogo selvagem*, or jungle fire (*penfigo foliaceous*), which we had heard was increasing amongst Indians in South Brazil. Her body was bloated and covered in sores that looked like smallpox, but she claimed to have been cured. She showed us a photograph of what she had looked like seven years previously, in hospital. Then, she had been infinitely worse with the flesh peeling off her body. Little is known about this disease, what causes it and how it is communicated, and there are only two hospitals in Brazil where treatment can be received. One of these is in Campo Grande and the other in Minas Gerais.

We heard that there was a German Evangelist missionary living not far away who brought medicines to the Kadiweu, but there was no time to visit his house. The post itself had no medicines, radio or electricity and it was hard to see what one untrained man could, with the best will in the world, do for the Indians. He was only being paid half the minimum FUNAI salary and he had not received that for nine months – a situation which he did not appear to regard as particularly abnormal but which would not, I felt, encourage the best calibre of man to work for the department.

If someone were prepared to adopt the cause of the Kadiweu, fight for them to receive their legal rights and the income from their land, and then help them to spend that money on a wise programme of development for the whole tribe, they could very quickly become a healthy thriving people again. What is needed is proper organization and a few small successes which would begin to improve their situation and give them confidence in the people who are helping them. Once this happened and they no longer felt that they were constantly being oppressed and robbed of their rightful heritage, their own self-confidence would be restored. Provided the tenure of their land was insured and perhaps some of their leased properties returned to them in due course, they would gradually become self-supporting.

To put it another way: until they become successful Kadiweu who are proud of being Kadiweu, they will not become successful Brazilians who are proud of being Brazilian.

The road out of the Pantanal over the north-western end of the Serra da Bodoquena was even worse than the road in. We passed two or three small groups of Kadiweu on horses and visited another collection of huts near the track before turning up into the hills again. We then had to creep slowly for mile after mile through washed-out sections where the track wound through deep gullies and ravines and, worst of all, a long muddy stretch of perhaps thirty miles where the track had become deeply rutted and the jeep's wheels were not wide enough to straddle the ridge in the middle. Eventually the inevitable happened and we became wedged. For a couple of hours we cut down trees, made levers, and dug before we were able to move on again. By now it was quite dark and we went very slowly, stopping at each puddle while one of us would wade ahead twenty or thirty yards to make sure that there were no deep holes. At about midnight we came out onto the Corumbá/ Campo Grande road running alongside the railway line, and almost immediately had to stop where a bridge had been washed away. A lorry was stuck on the short ramp of thick, sticky mud which was the only way round, and we had to wait for another two hours while a bulldozer was fetched to push the lorry out of the way. It was nearly three o'clock in the morning when we arrived at Miranda. Although we were all caked in mud from head to foot, we were given rooms in the enclosed court-yard of a small hotel, buckets of water in which to wash our feet, and bottles of iced beer, as though this sort of arrival was the most normal thing in the world – and I suppose in Miranda it is.

Anxious to reach Campo Grande in good time, as our aeroplane was due that day, I woke everybody at six and we drove on to Aquidauana, where we had breakfast. Aquidauana is an attractive old town on the river of the same name, with paved streets, a church and central square, and a very pretty colonial building which is a convent. The surrounding country is made up of magnificent views across undulating plains to rocky mountain ranges. We turned off the road to a large Terena reserve called Limão Verde (Green Lemon). The village, which was tidy and clean with well-ordered gardens growing flowers as well as crops, was in an almost fairy-tale setting. Sheer cliffs and wooded plateaux, out of which led wooded ravines, towered on all sides and the soil looked deep and fertile. The seven hundred and forty Indians had ten thousand acres which they were farming effectively, as we could see from the excellent crops growing on every open piece of ground. The young FUNAI administrator of the post and his wife, who was the school-teacher, mentioned in passing that they had not been paid for several months but otherwise seemed pleased with the way things were going. The Indians were cheerful, articulate, integrated and, although not yet fully accepted by the local population, they had much the same standard of living and were therefore less vulnerable to exploitation. This, combined with contact over a long period and a strong and resilient pride in their cultural background, makes them one of the very few Indian tribes in Brazil which has passed the bottom of the cultural depression and is now on the way up towards eventual full integration. We were told proudly that a Terena Indian had become the station-master at Miranda, which is, as far as I know, the highest post yet reached by a full-blooded tribal Indian in Brazil.

We drove on through superb scenery with wide, endless vistas, flat topped mountains and open plains. Even on the main road we stuck once or twice in deep pools of mud, and when we finally arrived on the outskirts of Campo Grande itself we had a puncture and had to finish the journey by taxi. At the FUNAI office there was no news of our FAB plane. Edson insisted that he must get himself clean and have something to eat before he would do anything, and so Marika and I drove out to the FAB base where I was eventually able to establish that no plane had arrived for us or was expected.

We had a chance the next morning to visit the Dom Bosco Museum in Campo Grande where there is a remarkable ethnographic collection and in particular probably the best Bororo featherwork anywhere. While looking at these, I met Padre Ventorelli, to whom I had a letter of introduction. He has an outstanding record as a fighter on the Indians' behalf, as much against abuses within his own church as those from other denominations or official bodies. He told me that the Indian should be allowed to develop according to his own best interests and not according to any dogma. The priorities were, he said, health and education, leading the Indian to a level at which he might feel the need for some sort of religious instruction in order to understand better the complicated modern world in which we live. It was wrong to attempt to catechize the Indian too early, and thereby only confuse him further. He drew me charts to illustrate his theories and I would have gladly spent much longer discussing the subject with him but we had to leave and, since our official plane was not forthcoming, catch a commercial flight to Cuiabá and the next stage of our journey.

Cuiabá

❧

IN Brazil there is a sharp contrast between the remote rural communities living in wild countryside and progressive modern industry in expanding new cities. This contrast makes the unusual and dedicated people stand out all the more clearly. On the one hand, there is a struggle for survival against the massive forces of nature, the distances and the isolation; on the other hand, there is an obsession with progress through technological means, to raise the standard of living and alleviate the poverty of overcrowded city populations. As a result, a preoccupation with material matters prevails at both ends of the scale. This is not to say that the Brazilian people are not gay and charming with varied and tremendously alive cultural traditions. They are. But, whatever their origins, they are caught up in their country's current 'great leap forward'. The black descendant of a slave who practises *macumba* and the German-, Japanese- or Italian-speaking Brazilian of the south, whose parents and grandparents may also have been Brazilian, but who still retains many of his mother country's customs and traditions, are equally a part of a developing and growing nation which longs to be rich. 'Order and progress', the words on the Brazilian flag, have never been truer of the spirit of Brazil than they are today. Never has there been such a feeling of national pride and such a desire to work at all levels in the country's interests.

The price of this is not always attractive. There is talk of torture in the prisons, police brutality and the repression of all opposition. Personally I found most disturbing the posters everywhere from large hoardings to car stickers, saying 'Brazil. Love it or leave it'. However, the occasional pencilled addition 'and the last one out turn out the light', went some way towards reassuring me that the Brazilians had not lost their sense of humour.

It also seemed to me that the policy was working. Most Brazilians I talked to were proud (sometimes perhaps a little too proud) of their country, and anxious to work to make it great. A staggering amount is being done and has already been done. Vast projects have changed the economy of whole regions and employed millions in the process. Now the talk is all of Amazonas and the far west. Those who take part in the development of the Amazon area are eligible for a seventy-five per cent grant, and so it is highly profitable to make roads and clear tracks of virgin jungle in order to set up agricultural communes and then sell off the land. About 170 000 000 acres, which was one estimate I was given of the amount of land being cleared each year, represents an appalling devastation of virgin forest, as most of the timber is simply burnt. Some of the areas consist of gallery forest, now becoming rare, where the tall trees keep out the sunlight from the forest floor and the ground is often bare and free of undergrowth. Gallery forests take two hundred years or more to evolve and they grow much of the finest timber, which is why they are so vulnerable.

Unless something of equal value replaces these eco-systems, then the exploitation of Brazil's hinterland is a backward step as far as the country's natural resources are concerned. Although some will undoubtedly become very rich during the process of exploitation, the pattern of subsequent settlement was all too often a sad and familiar one. Hungry, inexperienced, but hopeful people are brought from the overcrowded coast, and land which they, or the government, have bought is given to them. Some die in the first year, before their first crops are reaped. Most succeed in clearing their land and in the second year grow good crops. In the third year the crops are not so good and in the fourth year, if they have saved enough, they leave to return to the coast. The land is hostile and unfamiliar, and by the time they leave it is often also exhausted and good only to revert to valueless scrub.

In the southern Matto Grosso I had seen literally hundreds of miles of good rich farming land still undeveloped. This land, in a climate where the grass grows well, close to towns and markets and already intersected with roads, makes development a sensible idea. There have been some successful settlement schemes. But there is room for much more. So why this preoccupation with opening up the Amazon, at such vast cost to the nation? Is it part of a plan to give Brazil a common cause and so unite the country, at the same time taking peoples minds off other activities such as political opposition? Or is the commercial pressure from the huge construction and property consortia so great as to be able to push Brazil into this mad rush west? Perhaps there is also a fear that if Brazil does not settle, develop and exploit her own hinterland and resources, someone else will. Whatever the reason for it, the cost is enormous and all other government departments and agencies, FUNAI included, feel the pinch as a result.

The Indians of Brazil are outside this stream of the national consciousness. About half of them, like the Terena and the Kadiweu, are set irrevocably on the road towards civilization as we know it, and the materialistic ideals and aspirations that go with it. Their preoccupation to date is with achieving a reasonable standard of living in our world and holding on to the lands they have been given and which are small enough considering the vast territories over which they once ruled. The other half are not yet ready to face the stresses imposed by our culture. They live in a world which we have almost forgotten about, and which more and more we are looking to rediscover. Their existence in the world gives us hope that we may one day do so, not necessarily by forsaking our technological skills, but by learning to live with them. The Indians' survival depends upon their continued isolation from our abrasive and destructive influences.

There is something about the Indians of Brazil which, when it does not bring out a desire to destroy what is not understood, produces from time to time a level of selflessness and dedication seldom found in any other sphere of life. In this cynical and selfish world where material values dominate, it is, ironically, one of the most impressive achievements of the Indian that he can sometimes bring out the best in us. Nine miles outside Cuiabá there is a small country hospital for Indians. It only consists of three rough thatched buildings, the generator seldom works and the equipment is limited. But it is without any question the most valuable FUNAI service in the whole of that part of Brazil. This is entirely due to the diminutive thirty-four-year-old Japanese-Brazilian nurse in charge, Dona Cecilia. Outwardly meek, mild and docile, she radiates a determination and forcefulness which makes everyone from puffed-up petty bureaucrats to angry, naked tribesmen, do exactly what she wants without question. She is one of those rare people who holds together, with the sheer force of their personality and strength of will, a situation that would otherwise collapse.

The Chacara, as the hospital is known, is constantly short of medical supplies and funds, and has only a skeleton labour force of three or four. Yet it serves a vital and perhaps a unique rôle in Brazil in the fight to save the Indians from extinction. Invaluable help is given by the Peace Corps who have, ever since the Chacara was begun a few years ago, provided two American girls as laboratory assistants.

Alice came with us to the Chacara – a big, tough, extrovert girl on her second tour of duty from the States. She had a great love for the Indians, who constantly threw their arms about her in demonstrations of affection, and were given a judo throw to the ground or a hefty punch in the chest for their trouble.

The road out to the Chacara is very rough and sometimes impassable when the rain washes away the narrow plank bridges. As we neared the houses, we passed the corral where two milk cows are kept, providing the much-needed milk for the children suffering from tuberculosis but not enough for anybody else. Near-by was a vegetable patch where some recuperating Indians were working. As many as seventy Indians from the various tribes of the northern Mato Grosso have been cared for at one time in the Chacara, although this must make for terrible overcrowding. Our visit coincided with a serious measles epidemic among the Nambiquara groups along the Guaporé River, and so the hospital was very busy. In one group alone, the Sararé, it was estimated that half the tribe (twenty-five out of fifty) had died. Most of the deaths had been among women and children. This, of course, reduced the chances of the tribe surviving this disaster.

We saw several Nambiquara at the hospital. One man lay weak and emaciated on a bed, his apparently fully-recovered small son lying beside him. The wife and mother had died the day before. On the next bed another man lay flat on his back staring at the ceiling. His wife and two children had all died back in the Sararé village. An appallingly thin and wasted woman in a coma was being drip-fed intravenously. Her husband, a tall Nambiquara with a shaven head, was very agitated about the situation. While we were visiting the kitchen he came and took two burning logs from the stove and went to make his own fire outside the house. Once he had got this going he returned and tried to carry his wife out to sleep in the open beside him. Dona Cecilia explained patiently but firmly, in sign language and a few words, that this was impossible, but that he could come into the ward and sleep next to her on the floor. He looked round then and came over to Marika and me. We were standing together and I had my arm around her, which made him recognize us as a couple. With great emotion he put his arms around both of us, expressing his grief at being unable to embrace his own wife. Moving rapidly, with extraordinarily vivid miming and descriptive sounds, he told us in an unmistakable way how they had been brought to the hospital in an aeroplane, and how he missed his village and would like to fly back there with his wife. If he could not do this, then he would carry her and walk for many days through the jungle until they reached home. There he indicated that he had four children; one as tall as I, another a bit smaller, a third smaller still and the fourth only a baby. We were very moved by this demonstration, in particular by the way in which his love for his wife transcended all other feelings, overcame the strangeness of the hospital scene and rules, which must have been far more forbidding and intimidating for him than the most dragon-like matron in a London teaching hospital.

Dona Cecilia was busy all the time as she showed us round, changing dressings, taking temperatures and adjusting the drip. I longed to help and was grateful when she allowed me to give a glass of water to one of the weak patients who needed holding up. I glanced up while doing this and saw Edson looking at me. His attitude seemed to be that Indians, and particularly sick Indians, should be kept as far away from him as possible as they smelt and might bite. I felt this must surely be the wrong attitude in a man working for FUNAI, responsible for training its future employees.

Our meeting with the young lieutenant, who was the FUNAI delegate in Cuiabá, amused us a lot. During our talks in Brasilia, the General had specifically mentioned Cuiabá as being a place that we must arrive at on schedule as 'everything had been prepared in advance and all the plans had been made'. In spite of our plane failing to rendezvous with us in Campo Grande, we had, by taking a commercial flight, done so. Yet the young lieutenant, who looked like Harry Belafonte, and who greeted us courteously, had heard nothing whatever about us in advance, had made no preparations and seemed uninterested in our plans and the purpose of our visit. He either knew nothing about the condition of the Indians under his control or was not prepared to discuss it.

The Bororo

✦

We made our own arrangements to visit one of the Bororo villages south of Cuiabá, chartering at our own expense a light aircraft for the forty-five-minute flight. Alice, who knew this group of Bororo well, having lived with them for a time, came too, glad of the opportunity to pay them another visit. Edson chose to remain in Cuiabá.

The flight to the Bororo Indians was exciting. We had a crazy young pilot who asked me as soon as we had taken off whether I could fly. When I said that I had done a little he watched me take the controls, established that I was just about capable of maintaining straight and level flight, produced a comic from the map pocket of the aircraft, and began to read. He barely glanced up again until we reached the São Lourenço River on which the post of Gomes Carneiro is situated. Then, as if to make up for being inactive for so long, he took over the controls again, swooped low over the water, skimming it with the aeroplane's wheels, and then proceeded to launch into a series of acrobatic manoeuvres designed partly to drive some horses off the runway, and partly out of sheer exuberance. Marika and I rather enjoyed this performance but poor Alice, who did not like flying, was green by the time we landed.

From the air, the Bororo village made a perfect circle of twelve neat, thatched houses with a large men's hut in the middle. The post, a collection of five red-tiled houses, and the airstrip, were about two miles away. After speaking to the FUNAI employee at the post, who declined to visit the village with us, Marika, Alice and I set off down the long sandy track. As we neared the village, we called in on a young American couple from the Summer Institute of Linguistics who were living in a modern house and studying the Bororo language.

Ten years ago the Bororo were in a very run-down and degenerate state. Missionaries and SPI officials had prohibited them from dancing, manufacturing any of their traditional artifacts, singing their songs, smoking or practising any of their old customs. As a result, they had become completely depressed, had taken to drink and were being exploited to the point of starvation. When Helio Bucker was made head of the Cuiabá Delegacy and visited them, they told him that the tribe now had no future and that they intended to let themselves die out. No children had been born in the tribe for two years. He sacked the SPI man running the post and told the Indians that they were now free to return to their old ways and dance and smoke as much as they wanted. Food was provided and they were encouraged to grow crops and hunt and fish. At first they refused to believe him and continued to sit and do nothing. Then, when the moon was full, they had a small secret celebration at which they danced a Bororo tribal dance. When they found that this was not forbidden, more followed and they began to make feather head-dresses and necklaces to decorate themselves. He encouraged them in this, persuading them to let him sell some of the things they made on their behalf, and when he gave them the money that came from these sales and did not cheat them, they began to make more. Their enthusiasm and pride in their heritage grew rapidly, so that they were soon producing enough artifacts to be able to buy horses and guns, and so hunt more efficiently and provide more food for their families. Soon after this, children began to be born again and the tribe became healthy and thriving with their numbers increasing and everyone working. They were no longer poor, ignorant savages, out of their depth in a world which despised them, but tough and healthy Bororo with a heritage they were proud of.

About a year before our visit to the Bororo, Helio Bucker

had been transferred to Campo Grande and we were interested to see how the Indians were now faring. The FUNAI man at the post had not impressed me as he appeared from our short conversation to have little interest in the Indians' welfare and had not bothered to accompany us. It had been suggested to me that he was the same man who had originally been sacked from the post by Bucker some years before, but I was unable to establish this.

Our arrival in the village was boisterous and noisy. Children and adults remembered Alice's stay with them with affection. They welcomed her by hugging her and waltzing her around. Several of the children were decorated with feathers stuck onto the skin of their faces and arms. They were outstandingly beautiful. Their parents smiled and greeted us, although their smiles were rather spoiled by a noticeable absence of teeth. The first question most of them asked us was, 'Where is Snr Helio and when is he coming back to us?' When I told them that I had just been with him in Campo Grande and that I brought *abraços* from him I was hugged emotionally and told to tell him to come and see them. There was no question but that the rôle he had played in their lives had been a very significant one and that they regarded him as their lifeline.

We went into each hut in turn, distributing the presents we had brought and seeing what they were making. Several produced head-dresses, necklaces and combs which they had made and some were hard at work. But they told me that things were not well with them, and that life was becoming difficult again. Game was scarce so that they seldom ate meat, and they were prevented from fishing in the river. The chief was away from the village so I gave the two kilos of *maté* tea to Hugo, a solid, reliable man with an alcoholic nose and bad eyesight, for general distribution to the village. I also handed out quids from a metre of rolled black tobacco, which was barely enough to see me round the village, and I had a special present for the oldest woman in the tribe. This was Margarita Coaka, a remarkable, wizened old Buddha, sitting cross-legged in her hammock with a huge toothless grin. I had been told that her favourite vice was a nauseous patent medicine called *Biotonico Fontoura*. When I produced this she clutched it to her gleefully, nodding with pleasure.

Heavy black stormclouds began to gather and we had to hurry back to the airstrip in order to take off before the rain arrived. This also meant that we were unable to visit the other Bororo village at Pirigara but instead flew directly back to Cuiabá, the pilot once again burying himself in his comic and rashly leaving it all to me.

There was much to do in Cuiabá: many plans to be made and decisions to be taken. We had still heard no news of our FAB aeroplane and we were anxious to leave the town and visit as many Paresi and Nambiquara groups to the north as possible. We therefore arranged that Edson should remain in Cuiabá until our aeroplane arrived, or he was able to make contact by radio with Brasilia, and then rejoin us some four hundred miles to the north at Vilhena with the aircraft. Meanwhile, with the help of the Peace Corps Director, I had managed to secure the services of an honest taxi driver in Cuiabá called Garcia, whom I can confidently recommend to anyone passing through that town. Unfortunately his jeep was out of commission, but he kindly agreed to take us in his ordinary taxi at the rate of less than two cruzieros per mile. The road to Vilhena was notoriously rough at this time of year and he was only charging for the outward journey, after which he would have to make his own way back to Cuiabá, so this was a not unreasonable charge.

This road, opened in 1965, and leading from Cuiabá right up to Pôrto Velho, is the major factor affecting the Indians through whose territory it passes. It was therefore important to me to travel by the road and see some of the groups living on or near it. We left Cuiabá at five a.m.

on Tuesday the 16th February, having arranged to meet Edson again in Vilhena three days later. Nine hours' driving brought us to the beginning of the Paresi reserve.

The Paresi

❧

THERE are about four hundred and sixty Paresi left and the road is having a disastrous effect on their lives. The tribe has fragmented into small family groups, most of whom no longer hunt or fish or grow crops with much enthusiasm, but instead prefer to sit beside the road begging, or try in some other way to exploit the existence of all the potential wealth which the road represents to them. About half the tribe lives in the large Paresi reserve from which, with advice and help, they and the remainder of the tribe could well extract a living. But there is great rivalry between the groups and they are reluctant to travel far from the road into the further reaches of the reserve where there is more game and the land is, in places, richer.

Rio Verde, where we arrived first, is as bad a situation as any. Here the Paresi reserve begins on the northern side of the road and borders it for the next sixty miles. One of the largest Paresi villages, with about thirty inhabitants, is situated at this point. Exactly opposite it and a bare two hundred yards away on the other side of the road, is a petrol station and lorry-drivers' pull-in. As a result, the Indians spend much time hanging about the petrol pumps waiting for the occasional lorry to pass through and hoping that they can sell the driver some bows and arrows. Undoubtedly, this also leads to cases of prostitution. We visited the village where there was an unfriendly atmosphere and we were forbidden by the Indians to take photographs unless we paid exorbitant sums. I had messages for one of the Indians who had a little medical training and was entrusted with handing out medicines to this village and some of the surrounding ones. He had run out of supplies but told me that he was afraid to hitch-hike to Cuiabá for more as he had heard about the Nambiquara measles epidemic. However, he did not appear to understand the danger of infection from contact with every driver who passed through Rio Verde.

Father Adalberto, a Jesuit priest from Diamantino, was also visiting the village and we met him there. He has travelled and worked among the Indians of this region for several years and is well known as an expert on them. We talked for several hours and I was most impressed by his unbiased and liberal approach to the problem. He was not afraid to criticize much of what his Church had done with the Indians in the past, although he did insist that the Catholic Church had done far less damage in recent years than the Protestant missions. But he was against taking children away from their parents to educate them in special schools, as both types of missions have done, and said that it had never worked in Brazil.

'Far more important', he said, 'is to educate the Brazilian people in ways to understand and help the Indians. So few people in this country have any knowledge of what is needed that they are liable to do more harm than good. Therefore it is better not to try unnecessarily to contact unpacified Indians or change the ways of contacted ones but rather to leave them alone as long as possible and then move slowly.'

He said it was more important for us to learn what the Indians' needs were and then try to satisfy those needs than simply to impose change for its own sake. In the case of the Paresi, the Indians were in a mess because, in order to develop and exploit their reserve, they ought to introduce cattle and ranch them: this was the use for which the land was best suited. But the Indians neither had the capital to buy cattle nor any knowledge of how to look after them. In spite of fifty years of contact they were still hunters at heart, and the changeover to an economy dependent on agriculture required expert advice and study. Since this was not forthcoming, and game was increasingly hard to find, they had grown to depend on the road and to put all their confidence in it. But it produces practically nothing for them and they are left worse off than their neighbours to the south and to the north – the Terena who are acculturated and beginning to cope with the situation, and the Nambiquara, who, for all their other problems, at least have much of their tribal culture still intact.

Another interesting suggestion that Father Adalberto made was that urgent research should be undertaken into the Indian as a patient. At the moment they tended to run away when taken to hospital and it was difficult to treat them. Health, he said, was the first priority in the struggle to keep the Indians alive. His mission at Diamantino would gladly welcome a doctor for this or any other purpose, irrespective of his denomination.

There are six Fathers working in the Diamantino parish which covers 134 000 square miles and ministers to about six tribes as well as the Brazilian settlers and prospectors in the area. One of the Fathers is a doctor and all have some medical knowledge. They run a small hospital in Utiariti. The parish reaches far into the largely unexplored territory to the north where there are several groups of uncontacted Indians. The most important of these are the Cinta Larga, some of whom we were to see from the air later on, but he told me that he also knew of small groups of Apiaka, Irantze and Canoeras. He said that he was not working to pacify these as they were better left on their own for the moment.

We slept that night at the 'Transport Cafe' at Rio Verde where about twenty long-distance lorries arrived during the night, but no other cars. Starting again at five a.m., we drove on for ten miles and then turned right and followed a rough track for a further twenty-one miles into the reserve to visit another Paresi village called Sacre. There, only four small huts and very few Indians could be seen over a wide area. However, these were much more friendly and forthcoming than the ones on the road had been. They also told us that the American missionary, from the South American Mission to the Indians, was at his house on the far bank of the river. We were ferried across on a precarious raft – oil-drums attached to a wire cable – to find an incongruous, palatial, modern house of two storeys, with an astonishing fairy-tale castle built out of breeze blocks, painted white, near-by. This, we learnt, was a summer-house for the missionary's children. He and his wife invited us in for breakfast and we talked. He called the Paresi the Jews of the Indians and said that he was fed-up, after working for them for over six years, with little or no success. In his opinion the Paresi were lazy and had no desire to learn. It was vital that they should do so as their only hope lay in education and, since they refused to do it the easy way, the only solution left was forcibly to remove the children and educate them while making the adults settle and work. As far as his own efforts at evangelization went, he defended these by saying that what he was trying to do was not to change the Indians' beliefs but merely to alter them slightly. His theory was that they already believed in good and evil spirits but worshipped the devil because they regarded the evil spirits as stronger than the good ones. All he and other evangelists wanted to do was to make them change to worshipping the good spirits and gradually give them Christian names.

He was just about to return to the United States, where he intended to attend university and take a degree in philosophy, and he said he would probably be returning to Brazil.

The work of the Protestant missionaries in this and other parts of Brazil has often been criticized by anthropologists and others, and several of them, including the one we met, were for a time expelled and prohibited from working with the Indians, but they later returned. I believe it is now illegal for anyone, missionaries included, to live and work with Indians in Brazil unless they have a degree in anthropology, but it seems that this rule is seldom enforced. Another American belonging to the South American Indian Mission and working with the Nambiquara was described in the following terms in a report submitted by an anthropologist who had spent several years studying the Nambiquara.

'He is a missionary of the old guard; limited, intolerant and almost fanatical in his religious fervour ... his presence is now more prejudicial than helpful.'

The report goes on, 'the psychological state of the Indians is lamentable'.

The missionary 'prohibits all the Indians, whether they are *believers* or not from,

i performing the initiation rites of women;
ii piercing the lips of the men;
iii dancing;
iv singing in the Nambiquara language;
v playing flutes;
vi using necklaces or bracelets;
vii smoking.

'Since most of the Indians (perhaps all) still do not accept the missionary's religion, they remain, in fact, without any culture. They are no longer Indians nor are they *civilizados*. They don't know what they are.

'In fact, the missionary dominates the Indians through fear. Recently, the chief of the village wanted to get married. The missionary did not approve of the marriage and said that if he made this marriage God would punish him. Three days later a rattle-snake bit the chief and he died. The Indians understand little about the Christian religion and think that the missionary sent the devil, disguised as a snake, to kill the chief. Now they are incredibly frightened of the missionary because they think that he can kill any Indian he chooses by spiritual means.'

* * *

The International Red Cross team of doctors also criticized the work of some of these Protestant missionaries and it was officially announced after their visit that some of them were to be removed. We heard that most, if not all, of them had subsequently returned.

One of the problems facing those who criticize the missionaries – of all denominations – most severely, and suggest that they should all be removed, is that so much of the actual assistance being given to the Indians in Brazil does come from missionary sources. If it were all to be removed overnight, the Indians would be left without the medical and practical help and the protection to which they have grown used. Also, there is no question but that there are and have been many missionaries who have understood the Indians' needs very well and have not forced them to change their ways. However, in the long run I believe that missionaries have done more harm than good in Brazil, and that the Indians' interests would be best served by a corps of dedicated men, motivated by a desire to protect the Indians' own culture and beliefs rather than to impose an alien one. Although a few such people will appear whatever the sacrifices involved, enough to take proper care of the Indians will only be produced if sufficient incentives and rewards are forthcoming. Should the Villas Boas brothers be awarded the Nobel Peace Prize, this might inspire some people with idealism and ability to devote their lives to the same work but the solution lies ultimately in the hands of the Brazilian Government itself. Only by paying top salaries for this uncomfortable and difficult work, and by giving every encouragement to those who make it their career, will the necessary number of people join the service. With the eyes of the world upon Brazil and her remaining Indians, the cost of doing this would not seem too great.

The Nambiquara

❧

W E managed to reach three Nambiquara villages. At two of them we found young couples from the Summer Institute of Linguistics living on the edge of the villages in houses of their own construction, and at the third there was a young anthropologist and his wife living in an Indian hut. They, and the Indians, were all gratifyingly amazed and impressed to see us arrive by taxi and through them we were able to make the maximum use of our short visits.

The Nambiquara are quite different from any other Indians that we saw in Brazil. They look more like Australian aborigines or the Vedda of southern India, with wild straggly hair, thin taut bodies, and slightly splayed noses. Although some groups have been in contact for many years and were, in fact, studied by Lévi-Strauss (see *Triste Tropique*), others are only recently being contacted and there are still some isolated groups. There are about seven hundred Nambiquara in all. About two hundred live in the reserve which has been created for them north of the road. The remainder live in fiercely-independent groups scattered over a fairly large area in the jungles south of the road and between it and the Guaporé River. Several plans have been put forward in the past to create small reserves around these groups, but so far nothing has been done. The need for some sort of protection is very urgent as a large amount of settlement programmes are being encouraged in the region and most of the Indians' land has already been sold to property developers by the government.

It has also been suggested that the roughly five hundred Indians outside the reserve should be collected together and brought into it, so that all the Nambiquara could be together and protected. This would be totally disastrous and would almost certainly mean the extermination of the remainder of those who have survived this far into the twentieth century. The impetus behind this plan comes from the large profits available to the firms developing south of the road. Some of these firms have directors who are well connected in the government and the way in which they have managed to establish title to land clearly occupied and used by the Indians is a sad reflection on the way the System works in Brazil.

In order to be given development status, which legalizes their eligibility for grants, etc., firms need either to have a statement from FUNAI that there are no Indians on the land which the firms have bought, or else proper arrangements have to be made for providing sufficient land there or elsewhere for the Indians concerned. Instead, almost all the Indians' territory has now been sold including, in some cases, the very land underneath existing Indian villages. As the Brazilian constitution states categorically that land occupied by Indians is theirs in perpetuity and by inalienable right, this action is illegal. What happened was that in some cases FUNAI did not know of the existence of the Indians and gave the firms the necessary papers without first checking on whether there were Indians there, and in other cases they stated that the Indians had already been provided for, implying that reserves had already been set up for them. This means that in many cases the firm's title to their land is, under Brazilian law, invalidated by the discovery that it should never have been sold to them in the first place because it was already occupied by Indians. There seems no reason why the situation could not be rectified before it is too late, and the firms compensated where necessary. The current plan to move all the Indians to the reserve north of the road would mean that the Indians south of the road would lose all their traditional and sacred lands, their cemeteries and current crops, and it would in itself spell disaster for all the Indians involved.

This is because, although they are all grouped under the name 'Nambiquara' and speak related languages, there are nearly a dozen different groups involved, and they all hate and distrust one another. The move would involve what have been described as 'forced truck trips to enemy areas', and would result in murder and mayhem, food shortages for many years, appalling psychological shock and the probable fragmentation of many of those brought together as they ran away into the surrounding jungle.

The land in the reserve, which was the first Nambiquara area we visited, is very poor. At the distant end of the reserve, far to the north, there are areas of jungle, but these are largely unexplored and are known to be occupied by groups of Cinta Larga and Erigpatsa. These would certainly be hostile to any Nambiquara attempting to move into their lands and in any case it would surely be more sensible, since a reserve has been declared over the area, albeit known as the Nambiquara reserve, that the Indians who already regard it as their territory should be allowed to continue to do so.

We spent the night at Serra Azul in the house of the Summer Institute of Linguistics man who had been there on and off for six years. He had developed an elaborate system of barter with the Indians and throughout the evening Nambiquara men, women and children crowded into the American's small kitchen. They were usually wearing the object they wished to sell or trade and they would take these off and lay them on the table. An animated discussion would follow over the object's value. Payment was either in the form of exchange goods such as soap, aluminium pots or small plastic toys, or they could credit the objects to their account and eventually receive the money after it had been sold in Cuiabá through the FUNAI shop there. They also brought combs made out of cleverly-carved single pieces of wood, and nose flutes which I had not seen before. These the American would try out one by one as he received them, trilling a few notes as he held the flute to his nostril and assessed its quality and tone. Each transaction was then recorded in a filing system and the trade goods handed over or the credit written down.

I was impressed by the fair way this was carried on and by the Indians' obvious enjoyment of the whole business and the trust they had in the American. The quality of the goods was high and he said that he worked hard to maintain this, although it was difficult to sell all the objects he acquired in this way. FUNAI had more than they could cope with and the Brazilian market was limited in any case. We discussed the possibility of trying to find international outlets and certainly if this could be arranged it would be one of the ways in which the Indians could earn some money without abandoning all of their tribal skills.

We talked far into the night and I learnt that several Nambiquara had recently come to this village and that the population was now at, or perhaps even slightly over, its maximum. The Nambiquara do not take kindly to living in large communities and this one, of about seventy people, was as big as any. There are only small stretches of jungle in the region for the Indians to hunt and grow their crops; most of it is poor open *campo* or bare scrubland with a few trees. The Indians had to go further and further afield to find game to kill as meat for the tribe. If the Nambiquara are to survive in an increasingly confined area, new sources of protein must be found for them.

One of the problems about introducing stock farming, such as chickens, cattle, pigs, etc., is that there is a tribal tabu on killing animals which have been raised domestically or kept as pets. One of the other groups was given a small herd of cows some years ago. They immediately let them all loose in the jungle and then went and hunted them, bringing them back one by one on their shoulders. Overcoming this resistance and teaching them to keep domestic animals takes time, but there seems no alternative to it if they are to survive and adapt. Various proposals have been put forward and they would make the basis of a very valuable agricultural study into the Indians' needs. Goats have been suggested as a good possible beginning, as they appear relatively similar to deer and would live in the very rough terrain. However, the effect they might have on the countryside if they became numerous would have to be considered.

We swam at dawn in the little river at the bottom of the valley below the village. Several Indians joined us. The water was cool and clear, but they told us that there were few fish in the river, which was too small and overgrown to use canoes on. Later we visited the village, photographing and going from hut to hut. These were very primitive, being little more than simple shelters made out of palm thatch. They were dirty and untidy with a good deal of litter and squalor, but there was a cheerful busy atmosphere. The Indians, too, were unkempt with tousled hair and charcoal, ashes and dirt on their faces. But they seemed fairly healthy and some of the girls were very beautiful. Their fine features with wide eyes and high cheek bones, conformed much more to our standards of beauty than the rather flatter faces of most of the tribes we had visited so far. Several of the men had feathers through the septum in their noses, and others had long pieces of wood like fine knitting needles through their upper lips and sticking out in front. I had noticed, when we were swimming, that they removed these before going into the water.

As usual, the little children were very endearing and several of them were heavily adorned with necklaces and beads. One tiny girl was wearing heavy bands of thousands of strung beads slung across each shoulder. They were suspicious of being photographed and we had to be careful not to upset them. The American complimented us on the way that we did this, saying that a professor who had visited the village some time before had caused a great deal of trouble by making the Indians line up and stand still while he took a considerable time over each photograph. We had learnt to click away without making a fuss about it and move on as soon as anyone froze or objected. Most of the men were naked or wore only a small apron but all the women were dressed in ragged 'mother hubbards'. We saw one old woman frantically struggling into her dress as we approached her hut, where she had been sitting quietly tending the fire.

As it was early morning most of the families were loading themselves up, from old men to small children, with pots, pans, weapons and sacks of food. They were on their way to hunt or work on their crops and the American told us that they took almost all their possessions with them every day because they did not trust each other not to steal them in their absence. An anthropologist has since told me that he considered it more likely that, not knowing whether they might decide to continue on a long hunt or decide to stay away for several days, they preferred to be prepared. By the time we left, the village was almost empty and we could see the last of the small groups tramping determinedly off in all directions loaded down with their belongings.

The other two Nambiquara villages we visited were both members of the Mamaindé group who live to the west of the road. To reach one of these we had to walk for an hour along a track leading into the jungle, but the other had a side road running right past it to a *gleba*, or settlement project, which was alarmingly close to the Indian village.

Each of these villages had a young couple (one English and one American) living with them, and had it not been for the very limited amount of protection and help which they were able to give the Indians, it seemed likely that they would have been wiped out. Both had suffered from serious epidemics in the recent past and the threat to their land was a continuing and pressing one. Game was exceedingly scarce in the jungle surrounding the villages. Clashes with the frightened, and often discontented, successive waves of settlers were inevitable, and the possibility that some of them might retaliate by wiping out all the Indians in a group was far from remote. This had happened a few years ago when forty armed men went out and shot every single member of an isolated group of Nambiquara on the Riozinho.

The pressures on those trying to work for the Indians are very great. They are often caught between trying to do what they consider best for the Indians and at the same time trying to keep in with the pioneer fronts and the local police and militia upon whose goodwill their presence depends. This was illustrated by a story I heard of a Summer Institute of Linguistics man, in an area north of the Amazon, who had made contact with an isolated group of Indians and was the only person they trusted. The local chief of police had told him that he must speed up his pacification of these Indians as the local landowners wished to develop the area and would liquidate them if they put up any resistance. The difficult choice was presented to him of assisting in the pacification and movement of these Indians to another area where they would almost inevitably soon degenerate, or leaving them to their own devices when they would be shot.

The problem of the Nambiquara groups of Indians is a very pressing one as decisions taken now will have a fundamental effect on their future. In many ways, apart from the periodic epidemics which decimate them, they are in a fairly strong and healthy position. Their culture and traditions are largely intact and they have an independent spirit which, given the right conditions, would help them to survive. They are neither craving for free hand-outs wanting to be dependent upon them, nor have they passed the nadir of cultural contact and begun the slow process of integration and competition with the Brazilian population. Instead, they are in a somewhat unusual and fragile state where, unless ample and well-protected land is provided for them together with regular medical treatment and proper care and protection from outside influences, they will stand very little chance of surviving the inevitable shocks to come. Their land is part of what appears to be one of the main 'far western' development regions of Brazil. Whether the government decides that there is room for the Indians as well as this development remains to be seen.

The Cinta Larga

❧

GARCIA brought us safely to Vilhena. By now his taxi had lost its exhaust and rattled tiredly. Worse still, we learnt on arrival that there was no petrol available there and none expected, so that he looked like having a long wait before being able to set off on the return journey. But he made no complaint when I paid him the agreed amount, although we had made him do a great deal more than he had bargained for and the condition of the road had been exceptionally bad.

Vilhena is little more than a rough posting station on the road, consisting of a couple of bars and general stores, a few frame houses and a FAB post beside the airstrip. There is a derelict passenger aircraft, a DC3, in the long grass behind the huts. It crashed on landing some years ago and was not worth repairing. Little children climb in and out and play with the instruments in the cockpit. The commercial service between Cuiabá and Pôrto Velho calls here regularly, and Edson had arrived on this, there being still no news of our Beechcraft. He was waiting for us in a bar with Apoena Meirelles, the son of Francisco Meirelles, whose FUNAI Delegacy we had now entered.

Apoena had brought with him from Pôrto Velho a single-engined light aircraft in which he hoped to take us to visit the Cinta Larga camp the next day. We were tired after our three-day car journey and so talked little that night, but were taken to the FAB post where we were able to wash off the dust of the journey in a shower, and sleep in a barrack room between clean sheets.

In the morning Marika and I, taking only the barest essentials with us, flew off with Apoena to try to visit the

Cinta Larga. About two years ago a large party of men from this tribe suddenly appeared in Vilhena. They camped outside the village and appeared quite friendly and anxious to make peaceful contact. Unfortunately, there was no one present at the time with experience of Indians. An incident occurred in which one man was killed, and the Indians vanished again. On another occasion a group turned up beside the road and were seen by several lorry drivers, but again it was not possible to make proper contact with them before they disappeared back into the jungle.

In 1968 a large Indian reserve called the Indian Park of Aripuaná, was created between the Roosevelt River in Rondônia and the Juruena River in Mato Grosso. There are several uncontacted groups in this area, the largest of which is probably the Cinta Larga. Francisco Meirelles, who is well-known for his pacification of several other tribes, flew over the region and several Indian villages were located. A contact post with an airstrip, known as the '7 de Setembro' camp, was set up about forty-five miles east of the road and about fifteen miles from some villages seen from the air. Unfortunately, due to faulty mapping, both the camp and these villages are outside the area of the Aripuanã Park, although this should not affect the issue greatly as land occupied by Indians should, under the law, belong to them. However, development is taking place rapidly in this region and I was interested to see what was happening.

We were also hoping very much that we would be able to reach the Cinta Larga village. Since the '7 de Setembro' camp was established, the Indians have made regular visits to it, where they have been given axes and machetes and other goods, usually exchanging these for presents of their own. Apoena, who has spent much of his time at the camp and become very friendly with the Indians, told us how he had several times attempted to accompany them when they left the camp and returned to their villages. He had always been stopped and made to return to the camp, until a few weeks before our arrival, when he and another boy working for FUNAI had been allowed briefly into one of the villages. They had been made to take off all their clothes and had only been allowed to stay for one hour, but this represented a major breakthrough in Apoena's efforts to gain the Indians' confidence. He now planned to make a second attempt, taking us with him if the Indians would allow it.

We flew north for an hour, following the route of the road and were able to have a good look at the fringe development taking place along it. A few small settlements were dotted along the road with others scattered in the countryside far back from it. Near these were little rectangular blocks of cultivated crops. But most of the land on which the natural forest had been removed seemed to be going to waste and reverting to scrub. I saw almost no open country or land suitable for rearing cattle in large numbers. The cultivated areas all appeared to be on the edge of virgin jungle, waiting its turn to be cut down. The waste land left behind seemed valueless and I began to see what is meant by the destruction of the Amazonas forests. If it were possible to stay in one place and continue farming then the whole process would make more sense. Perhaps a way will be found of making use of the scrubland left behind and it will be possible to turn these growing deserts into valuable country again. Research is going on into this, or so I am told, but it seems a pity that so much irreplaceable raw material must be destroyed before a solution has been found.

It was only from an aeroplane that the full effect of the road could be seen. On the ground it had seemed like a thin fragile ribbon, hemmed in on either side by towering jungle, and with only very scattered and occasional habitations dependent upon it. From the air we could see better how great is the impact of this road upon the country through which it passes. The thin red ribbon of the road itself is often reflected in a wide band where many of the original trees have been removed and scrub has taken their place; or else where rectangular patterns mark the areas which have been clear felled. Every now and then tracks lead off to plots which are being cultivated or have already been abandoned, or to areas of forest from which the valuable timber has been extracted. The road was only opened in 1965 and undoubtedly it has served a most valuable purpose as a supply route and means of communication between Pôrto Velho, in the north-west of Brazil, and the capital and major cities in the south and east. Now a dozen more such roads are being driven across Brazil, bisecting Amazonas in all directions. The last great jungle in the world is being carved up. Although this is necessary and inevitable, the whole process cries out for planning and study so that what is being done may be controlled and Brazil (and the world) may end up better off once the operation is complete. If care is not taken, all that may be happening is that jungle is being changed into desert with a few quick profits made on the way.

At Pimenta Bueno we turned right and flew east away from the road. After about twenty minutes we came to some low hills, their bare rocky tops showing above the trees, and began to circle round looking for the camp. It was a cloudy day and there had been a lot of rain during the night. Black stormclouds growled and flashed on almost all horizons and we had already been forced to make some detours to avoid going through them. Without exactly being lost, we were at the same time not quite sure of our exact position. Apoena recognized a rock and told the pilot to fly south from that. Soon afterwards we saw a small river and on the edge of it a minute airstrip and a few huts. About a third of the airstrip was a darker brown than the rest and as we swooped low over it we could see a dozen men in a line pounding the earth to make it hard enough to land upon. We passed low over their heads several times and both Apoena and the pilot shook their heads and agreed that it would be another two or three days before the *pista* was in a fit condition. It might be possible to land but the plane would certainly not take off again until the ground had dried out. I tried to encourage them to have a go, feeling that this might be our only chance, and at least once we were down we could start walking to the Cinta Larga village and hope that the weather would improve. But the pilot was no fool and not about to risk his plane. It was even more frustrating for Apoena who had with him urgently-needed supplies for the post, including a couple of five-gallon cans of petrol with ill-fitting stoppers, the contents of which were slopping about our feet as he and Marika chain-smoked. This fuel was needed by the people on the ground to run the generator which drove the radio by means of which they could tell us when the strip was in a fit condition to land upon. Without it, the only way to find out was to make expensive charter flights from Pôrto Velho to see for oneself, because even if the weather cleared up enough in one area to dry out the land, this did not mean that at this time of year it was not pouring with rain fifty miles away.

We agreed to try again in two or three days and flew on eastwards to look for the Cinta Larga villages. After about ten minutes flying across the solid green canopy of trees hiding the ground, we came upon several large cultivated areas. These, Apoena told us, were Cinta Larga clearings and I was impressed by their size. Some seemed to be as much as one hundred acres, with tall crops growing among the blackened remains of burnt and felled trees. But we could see no people or houses. For a time we circled, looking. Due to the height of the trees, we had to be right over a village to see it. The first one we found was the same one to which Apoena had been brought and there were only two huts left standing, the remainder having been burnt. He said that the village had been abandoned since his visit and we cast about looking for the new one. A clearing flashed past beneath us and the pilot, turning the plane onto its side, returned, and began to circle it slowly.

Below us lay five of the largest *maloccas*, or communal

huts, that I had seen. They were not in a circle, or any pattern but simply grouped together with beaten earth between them. On this stood a large number of tiny figures. They looked dark, as though covered in urucu, and we could see that their faces were turned up towards the plane. We could not see their expressions nor did they make any gestures, friendly or otherwise. No arrows were loosed into the air. No fists or spears were shaken at us. On the other hand, no one waved in the friendly way the Xingu tribes had, whether we were about to land or just passing by. They just stood and looked.

The Cinta Larga are waiting for us to come to them. Some of them have been as far as the road, looked, and returned to their villages. Several of them have been to the '7 de Setembro' camp where they have been given machetes and knives and other things, but have always refused to eat. Already they have been abused by prospectors and rubber gatherers who have shot at them and given them poisoned food. Even from Apoena, whom they like and trust, they will not accept food. They know we pose a threat to their survival and yet we have things which, once having tried, they know they need; rifles and axes, fish hooks and matches are too useful to them to be ignored. We exist and we are coming closer all the time. What will they do?

Just how close we are coming, I was able to see a few minutes later as we swung away from the village and headed back towards the road. Barely five minutes later – perhaps ten miles from the village – we came to a modern town. At least, that's what it looked like at first glance, with corrugated iron roofs, a wide 'street' marked out between rectangular plots and straight roads leading off at right angles. I asked Apoena what it was.

'That', he said, 'is one of the proposed new towns for when this area is opened up. Already most of the land between here and the Roosevelt river has been sold, including that below the Indian villages we have just seen and the '7 de Setembro' camp. Soon there will be a road through the district and then the settlers will come.'

'But surely that's illegal?' I said. 'Everyone must know the Indians are there and they are supposed to own the land they occupy.'

'I know,' said Apoena. 'I wrote to the governor of Rondônia about it and both he and the government authorized the removal of all settlers from the area. Federal police were supposed to come and carry out the order but nothing has been done.'

'It's not the settlers' fault. Many of them are friends of mine and good people. It is their masters who break the law, the men behind the scenes who parcel out the land and then sell it or lease it. They are too powerful for the law to touch and so they get away with it.'

I later managed to get hold of a map produced by one of the development companies in the region (see end papers). The Cinta Larga we had seen are right in the middle of this map and if the scheme is to work it is clear that they must be eliminated. The sooner this is done the better for the companies as, once there are no more Indians in the area, the scheme will become legal and the land will become the rightful property of those who are at present illegally developing it.

Of course, the easy answer would be for the Cinta Larga to move away to the east and across the Roosevelt river, when they would be inside the Aripuaná Park. But that land is already occupied by other Indians who would not take kindly to the arrival of a large and hostile group. Also, the Cinta Larga themselves will have to be persuaded to leave their traditional lands and move away. This may not be easy as many Indians are involved. Apoena put the number as high as two or three thousand and some estimates go as high as five thousand. Of course, it might well not come to that as some contacts are already taking place and sooner or later an epidemic is likely to sweep through the Cinta Larga and reduce their numbers to manageable proportions.

If this happens before sufficient trust has been established with the '7 de Setembro' camp for them to allow themselves to be vaccinated and treated, then the problem may be removed altogether.

Clearly, the survival of this group of Indians depends upon swift and firm action. The land on which they live, as far as, and including, the '7 de Setembro' camp, should be added on to the Aripuaná Park and titles to any land within that area already sold should be revoked. If, at the same time, it could be explained to people like José Melhoranca, the entrepreneur behind much of this development, that land occupied by Indians cannot be bought and sold, then it might prevent the same thing happening elsewhere. It might.

Another problem is presented by the *garimpeiros*, or prospectors, in this area. Some of the rivers are rich in minerals, in particular diamonds and tin, and the tough lonely men who seek them are inclined to shoot first and ask questions later when they bump into Indians. Not surprisingly, the Indians in turn retaliate and so the situation becomes aggravated. The same applies to the *gateiros*, or skin hunters, seeking jaguar, ocelot or crocodile. As so much of the interior is not occupied by Indians, and clashes are inevitable when these people penetrate areas where Indians do live, it would surely be in everyone's interest for the boundaries to be clearly defined on available maps, and for the laws concerning illegal penetration of these areas to be enforced. If the Indian areas and reserves in Brazil were extended and new ones created to include all land genuinely occupied by Indians, or needed by them to support their way of life, the urgency of having to contact Indians in a hurry, with all the harmful side effects which this entails, would be removed, as would the need to transfer Indians to other and often less desirable areas. It would also mean that people would not be tempted to settle areas to which, if the law were properly enforced, they might find that their title was not good.

The Seringal do Faustinho

❧

As the light aircraft in which we had been flying over the Cinta Larga was not large enough to carry all of us on to Pôrto Velho, we returned to Vilhena, and Marika and I remained there while Apoena and Edson flew on. The commercial flight was not due until the next day, which gave us time to visit a group of Nambiquara Indians on the road forty-five miles north of Vilhena. I particularly wanted to do this as I had heard from several different authorities in Europe and America, as well as in Brazil, that they lived in a state closely resembling slavery.

We were driven there by an Air Force sergeant who had his own truck. By setting out at four thirty in the morning, he had agreed to take us, saying that this meant that he would be able to be back at the post in time to take up his normal duties.

The sun was up when we arrived at the Seringal do Faustinho and drew in beside the road. Three or four simple houses stood in a row with cattle crushes beyond them. There was no sign of life. On the far side of the road opposite us we could see, across a small marsh, the huts of an Indian village. A curl of blue smoke was rising into the still air, a few cows grazed at the roadside and a mule stood with its head hanging, asleep. The scene was peaceful and bucolic and it was hard to believe that the place deserved its notorious reputation.

The story was that in the late fifties one Alfonso de França was the SPI man at an Indian post called Espirro, some ten miles east of Vilhena. There he had been respon-

166

sible for the group of Nambiquara known as Tauandé, whom he was said to flog, torture and shoot as the mood took him. When his daughter married Faustinho he 'gave' him sixty of the Indians as a wedding present. They had been moved to the farm we were now visiting and although most of them had died from a measles epidemic in 1963, the survivors were still there. When the SPI was disbanded Alfonso's crimes were brought to light but he could not, apparently, be prosecuted as the only witnesses who could testify against him were Indians. They, under the law, are minors and cannot testify. Instead, he moved away from the post, which has not since been manned, and settled with his son-in-law.

We were now about to meet this reputed devil incarnate. I felt apprehensive; not because of his reputation, but because I did not know how one was supposed to behave in such a situation. Should I boldly accuse him of the crimes, demanding that he gave me his side of the story, or should I pretend that I knew nothing about his past and was simply paying a polite visit?

We walked across to the largest of the houses and knocked on the door. A crippled girl with a badly-twisted leg and frightened eyes opened it to us. Yes, Snr Alfonso did live there and she would fetch him for us if we would sit and wait at the table. We did so and looked around the sparsely furnished room. Earth floor and bare plaster walls. A faded photograph of an old woman – wife or mother? – and a religious picture in a frame were the only decorations. On a hook by the door hung a horse-whip with a long plaited leather thong. I found myself staring at this, and yet what could be more natural on a cattle farm?

The short, grey-haired old man who came into the room and greeted us politely did not look like an ogre. But then how should an ogre look? He offered us coffee and the frightened girl went to get it at a look from him. Once he had established who we were, he began to complain, saying that he had worked twenty-eight years in the Indian service but would not receive a pension unless he worked another two. He told us that four years previously he had had to retire because of ill health, and that he had spent some time in hospital. As he was now sixty-eight and would not be able to work after he was seventy, it was urgent that he was taken back into the service as soon as possible so as to complete the necessary two years. Perhaps we could get his job at Espirro back, or if not, he would be prepared to work anywhere else. I was too cowardly to say that this might be a bad idea, but instead asked him what he felt about working with the Cinta Larga. That, he said, he would not do under any circumstances, as they were cannibals. People might claim that they were not, but he knew for a fact that they were.

I asked him about Faustinho's Indians and he said that his son-in-law treated them well and gave them clothes in return for work. At this point, Faustinho himself appeared and we went outside to meet him. He was a much more villainous character in appearance than his elderly and almost distinguished father-in-law – unshaven and surly. He simply grunted something to the old man and walked off towards the corral. I asked if the Indians here were ever paid in money and he replied that they were.

'How much per day?' I asked.

'It's impossible to pay a regular salary to an Indian, as he may come to work for an hour or two and then go off to hunt and fish.' I had to be content with this.

We then walked across to the Indian huts. Alfonso told me that there were twenty-six men, women and children in the village, which was more than I expected, as I understood that no children had been born to the group for some time. In fact, during our visit, we saw only one child, of about three years old. This, of course, was the strongest indication that there was something wrong with the situation. Normally, an Indian village, even as small a one as this, is vibrant with the laughter and play of children. They are the first to run out and greet one or peer shyly

Paresi Indians begging beside the road

The Nambiquara village at Serra Azul

Seringal do Faustinho

The Cinta Larga village from the air

Apoena Meirelles making the first contact with Cinta Larga Indians
(*copyright: Jesco von Puttkamer*)

Tin mining camp at the Igarapé Preto

Nambiquara woman

Karaja girls

Nambiquara Indian with feather nose plug

Nambiquara (Mamaindé)

Kuben-Kran-Kegn boy

Gorotire girl with Amelia

Gavião woman at Mae Maria

Kuben-Kran-Kegn boy

A stretch of the
Trans-Amazonica
road seen from the air

Tirio girl

The Gaviões at Mae Maria

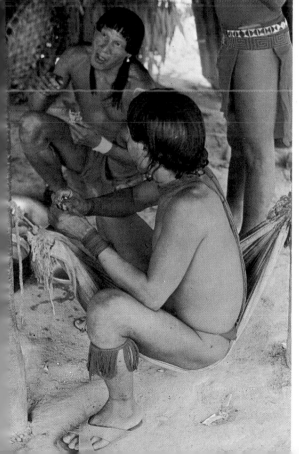

Tirio in the Tumucumaque Park

A Tirio hut

Tirio woman weaving a belt

out from around the huts. Babies roll in the dust and play with the dogs and, although they seldom cry, there is always a noise.

This village was silent as we walked into it. A thin, gaunt man in ragged shirt and trousers with bare feet walked towards us. Alfonso said that he was the chief. Marika and I went up to him and shook his hand, at which he looked surprised. We then went on to shake the hands of the other men and women in sight, but I watched to see what the chief and Alfonso would do. For a moment they stood looking at each other, and then the Indian went up to the old man and shook his hand, at which he scowled in obvious displeasure and embarrassment, and walked over to join us. Trying not to allow myself to be biased by what I already knew about the background to the village, I went in and out of the huts, which were clean though very bare. The Indians had no hammocks but slept on the floor on sacks stuffed with straw. The ground was low-lying and appeared to be liable to flooding, as a result of which most of the houses were on short stilts.

Another man sat on a bench outside his hut and did not turn his head as we approached. When I put my hand on his shoulder, he glanced up briefly and then went back to staring into space. One of the women had a pet coati, which was the first one we had seen, an inquisitive and charming animal with a long pointed nose and striped tail. Her daughter, the youngest woman we saw in the village apart from the one child, was lying in a hammock in their hut and we were taken to see her. Her face was badly swollen on one side and she was clearly in acute pain, groaning, crying and clenching and unclenching her hands. It looked to us like a mastoid, but Alfonso said that it was probably mumps as 'they often had that'. The mother asked if we had any medicines with us, but all we could do was to give her some pain-killers. She looked as though she ought to be in hospital or at least have a visit from a doctor, but Alfonso said that there was no doctor and that the nearest hospitals at Utiariti and Pôrto Velho were too far away and the Indians never went there.

His attitude towards the Indians was condescending and bored. He must have known them all intimately for many years, and yet there was no talk or discussion with them about problems or day-to-day matters and certainly there was no joking or laughter. If Edson had been with us, I felt sure that he would have been telling us how much Alfonso did for the Indians and what a responsibility it was to have them under his care. Just because he was not there, I tried particularly hard not to prejudge the situation, but the atmosphere of gloom and despondency was inescapable. Without having seen any direct brutality or oppression, I could not help feeling, as we left, that civilization was at a very low ebb at the Seringal do Faustinho.

Another forty-five miles up the road there was another farmer with a group of dependent Indians. These, I was told on good authority, were well treated and cared for, thanks to the generosity and humanity of the Brazilian patron. Although utterly dependent on him, it was said that he paid them fair wages and protected them from exploitation and abuse. Unfortunately, there was not time for us to go on and visit this place as we had to return and catch our flight to Pôrto Velho.

Three days after this, on February 23rd, the report of the International Red Cross medical mission to the Indians of Brazil was released to the press. It had been sent to the Brazilian authorities in November 1970. In it conditions at the Seringal do Faustinho were severely criticized. The Indians were described as being in 'a wretched state ... of complete dependence'. The report went on that the women did not want to bear children, because they were afraid that they would lose them owing to the hard work they did and because they felt that they would not be able to look after them. 'Abortion by means of a bark extract is commonly practised among them.'

Commenting on the report, General Bandeira de Mello was quoted in the Brazilian press (*Estado do São Paulo,* 26/2/71) as saying that all the recommendations had already been dealt with a long time before and that it just 'rained on wet ground' – a Brazilian expression meaning it was a waste of time. Among other action that had been taken, he had announced that Faustinho of Vilhena had been prosecuted by the federal police on the basis of an inquiry undertaken by FUNAI, and that the Indians had been moved to another post. Things just don't happen that quickly in Brazil and I would be interested to know whether anything has changed at the Seringal do Faustinho even now.

Pôrto Velho

❧

W E spent a frustrating and difficult week in Pôrto Velho, during which a combination of circumstances effectively prevented our achieving anything. The Governor of Rondônia and the commandant of the military barracks both received us cordially but were not able to solve our transport problem. It was carnival week which meant that most normal services came to a halt and it also poured with torrential rain for much of the time.

There was still no sign of our Beechcraft, although we had sent several cables to Brasilia informing them of our progress. There were several light aircraft at the small airfield almost in the centre of the town, but the pilots who were not enjoying the carnival were busy flying supplies in and out to mining camps. I did find two pilots who were prepared to try and fly us to the '7 de Setembro' camp, but we could not go until we heard on the radio from there that the runway was clear. Meanwhile, Apoena became elusive and enigmatic and he and Edson disappeared into the town for long periods at a time. Francisco Meirelles, Apoena's father and the Delegate for the region, was away at a conference in Brasilia. His son, whose specific job is head of the Aripuaná Park, was in charge in his absence. Plans were made daily for us to make an attempt to visit the Cinta Larga, but they never materialized. It was one of those periods when trying to get things moving was more exhausting than action itself. Although achieving little, we were also unable to rest and relax properly.

I did, however, have several opportunities to talk to Apoena and listen to his views on the Indian problem. He is a dark and intense person, named after the Xavante chief whom his father successfully pacified. His father is well-known in Brazil as one of the country's leading Indian experts, having also pacified the Pacaas Novas and Mekronotire as well as other groups. Unfortunately, several of these tribes have since been neglected and are now in a very poor state. In particular, the Pacaas Novas, in the region to the west of Pôrto Velho, are said to be practically destitute, begging beside the road and prostituted by prospectors and settlers.

Apoena feels very deeply about the Indians and it is clear that he has a remarkable gift of communication and sympathy with them. By all accounts he is the only person whom the Cinta Larga trust and will deal with, and he is prepared to fight fiercely on their behalf. He has grand plans for the Aripuaná Park and wants not to create another model of the Xingu system, but to develop an economically viable unit where the Indians, thanks to their rich land, are able to compete with the surrounding settler population. In this way he hopes that they will be able to by-pass the worst aspects of shock and move gradually but directly from their present state to one in which they are again self-supporting. This seemed to me an admirable ideal, but I was depressed by his stated belief that nothing of the Indian culture and way of life should or could be preserved. The eventual object should make them as like us as possible. We discussed at length the motives of people who wished to protect the Indians and keep them as they are. He was suspicious of any suggestion of human zoos or that the Indians should be preserved as objects for study, and yet he clearly admires and feels in harmony with their way of life and regards them, as do so many, as superior in many ways to the surrounding population. He was very outspoken about the lack of idealism in most FUNAI employees, referring to them as 'gigolos of the Indians', in that they regard their employment as a job like any other and, as a result, live off the Indians as parasites instead of having their best interests at heart.

I liked Apoena and found his company stimulating, when he was there, but I was not entirely happy with his plans for the Aripuaná Park. Although he himself will, I believe, work with dedication for the Indians of the region, the concentration on purely economic values is dangerous. Exploitation of Indians has, in the past, been the rule rather than the exception, and if the administration of the park should change hands the Indians would be likely to suffer. At the same time, the picture he painted of an exclusive company under FUNAI's supervision, devoted to the maximum exploitation of the region by the Indians themselves, conjures up a dangerous picture of alien values being imposed upon some of the most primitive tribes in Brazil.

Much of our time in Pôrto Velho was spent sitting on the terrace of the pink sugar-cake hotel built there by the British at the beginning of the century when the Maderia-Marmore railway was being constructed. The other guests who passed through were mainly pilots connected in one way or another with the mining operations going on in the district. They were a cheerful, hard-drinking lot and Marika persuaded one of them to take us to the largest of the mines and show us what was going on. His aircraft turned out to be a vast ex-US Army transporter, with the cockpit perched high up in front and enough room for two or three lorries in the cavernous interior. We flew due east for over a hundred miles, skimming low cloud, to the camp which was known as Igarapé Preto. This lay between the Rio Machado and the Rio Roosevelt and was the centre of a rich tin deposit. Due to the noise, conversation had been impossible during the flight, but we had been told that there was an Englishman working at the mine.

'I'll bet he's Cornish,' said Marika, and was proved right when Mr Trevorrow, a large engineer in shorts, introduced himself.

He told us that he had been there for three months installing a new tin-cleaning plant. The area was, he said, extraordinarily rich in tin, averaging seventy-five per cent in cassiterite over ten square miles. The tin was all on the surface, going to a depth of ten feet, and it was at present being worked on a more or less freelance basis by up to five thousand *garimpeiros* at a time. The rights were, how-ever, all owned by a millionaire in São Paulo, and Mr Trevorrow was there to begin the process of mechanizing production.

At that time two hundred tons a month were being pro-duced. This was flown out in planes ranging from the large transporter we had arrived in to small, light aircraft with a couple of hundredweight in the back seat. A road was being constructed to the mine and when the cleaning plant was finished four hundred and fifty tons *per day* would be produced – a really impressive figure.

The camp itself consisted of a few huts strung out on either side of the runway, which was wider and longer than other jungle airstrips I had seen, but otherwise undis-tinguished. It was only when we walked a few hundred yards off, under the canopy of trees, that we saw the driving force behind the place – a scene straight from the California gold-rush. Hundreds of groups of men were busily digging channels in the wet ground, heaping up the grey subsoil and working with primitive washing pans and sieves to extract the almost pure metal. The Cornishman, who lived in the only air-conditioned hut in the place, with three or four other engineers of different nationalities, told us that there were quite a lot of shooting incidents, but otherwise it bore little resemblance to the boom towns of the Far West.

Everyone agreed that there were no Indian tribes in the area although two or three families of half-caste Indians worked at the camp.

On the flight back to Pôrto Velho the clouds had cleared and we were able to see the land below us. Instead of the usual endless mottled green of jungle tree-tops, I was astonished to see desert. Parts of it were covered in light scrub, and the beds of streams were marked with denser vegetation making it look from the air more like the region south of the Sahara known as the 'sahel'; but there were large patches of bare sand and rock with no vegetation at all. I had not realized that any such areas existed in Amazonas and shouted questions to the pilot over the noise of the engines. He told me that the 'desert' stretched for about three hundred miles from north to south, and was up to one hundred miles wide.

'It's a useless place,' he said. 'Nobody lives there because there is no grass for the cattle and there are no minerals. Much of it is very wet and floods during the rainy season and not even Indians live there, although it is very rich in game. In fact, that's the only reason anybody goes there, to hunt – lots of deer, wild pig and partridges.'

I thought it looked a most beautiful place. Tall, rocky outcrops cast shadows over the sand and here and there lakes of open water, fringed by reeds, had formed. Perhaps one day I shall find an excuse to go back and have a closer look on the ground.

The day after our visit to the mining camp, our FAB Beechcraft finally arrived in Pôrto Velho. On it was Edson's girlfriend, Orchida, who had decided to join him and apparrently had enough influence in FUNAI to have been able to arrange this. The aeroplane, however, had been having problems and had broken down several times, which had not improved Orchida's nerves. We were now told that two or three days would be needed in Pôrto Velho to repair it. The charm of Pôrto Velho was waning for us and so, having discovered that our friends with the transport aircraft were flying to Belém for the week-end – a mere fifteen hundred miles – we persuaded them to take us too. In this way, I would be able to have meetings with the various people I wanted to see in Belém and so be ready to continue on the next stage of our journey when the Beechcraft caught us up.

PART FOUR

❧

Belém

Gorotire and Kuben-Kran-Kegn

The Kraho

The Gaviões

Altamira

Tumucumaque

Roraima Territory

Belém

❧

FROM the cockpit, where we perched behind the two pilots, we had a panoramic view of the Amazon basin. We flew for nine hours, always downstream, and stopping briefly in Manaus to refuel. With the help of the maps, we were able to make out each tributary as we passed it and some of them I was able to recognize from rubber boat and hovercraft days.

Occasionally we crossed sections of the Trans-Amazonica highway, slashing its die-straight route through swamp and jungle. 'A road from nowhere to nowhere' it has been called, which is unfair, as it clearly will do a lot to help in the development of the region. What concerns the critics of the road most, I believe, is the harmful effect it is likely to have on the ecology of the world's last great jungle. Wholesale deforestation, destruction of the fauna and the 'settlement', or movement, of the indigenous inhabitants all seem likely outcomes of the road. It is in itself a stupendously expensive operation and Brazil's resources are being stretched in the completion of it. Ideally, an equal amount of money should be spent on research into the potential of the scheme and its likely effects, and also into ways in which the maximum benefit can be derived from it with the least wasteful disturbance of Brazil's natural resources. Unless this is done, expensive and even dangerous mistakes are likely to be made. There is the now apocryphal story of the proposal to dam the mouth of the Amazon and so stabilize the water table in the whole of the Amazon basin. It would then be possible to cut down all the forest and begin to farm the whole region. This scheme was rejected (or perhaps only shelved?) when it was pointed out that the Amazon basin and its associated jungles now represent over a quarter of the remaining green matter in the world. As vegetation is necessary to support life, by converting carbon dioxide into oxygen, the elimination of this much of it could, theoretically at least, lead to the suffocation of all breathing animals, including man.

Flying over it, the jungle seems endless and indestructible, and yet the days of its virginity are numbered. Each road that passes through it causes ripples like the wake of a boat which travel for hundreds of miles on either side of the road itself as trappers, prospectors, settlers and farmers, push their way up side tracks. It would be easy at this stage to create reserves, but it is not being done. As time goes by more areas are opened up and explored, settled and exploited, with the result that the establishment of a reserve at a later stage causes far more complications and involves compensation and re-settlement.

We flew east with the setting sun behind us, over the mouth of the Xingu where it runs into the Amazon and over the island of Marajó, around and through which the Amazon reaches the sea. Belém, across the salt waters of the Rio do Pará, looked like a space-age city of skyscrapers as the modern buildings caught the last of the sunlight. The Hotel Excelsior Grão Pará was modern and luxurious. The rest of the town was elegant and graceful with colonial buildings and narrow, winding streets leading down to the market places. Painted fishing boats were anchored in the harbour.

We had been looking forward to getting some letters in Belém, but as the postal strike in England was still going on there were very few. I spent most of my time having talks in the Museo Emilio Goeldi where there is also a good zoo and botanical garden. They take up one complete block quite near the centre of the town, with giant trees shading the animal enclosures, museum and administration buildings. I was impressed by the way that some of the animals and birds ran wild in the garden, and I enjoyed seeing at close quarters others which I had previously only glimpsed in the wild. The gardens had a fairy-tale quality with little unmarked paths leading to enclosures with capibara, or tapirs, while the jaguars and ocelots in their cages allowed one to scratch their heads.

I was given a lot of useful advice in the museum about the next stages of our journey, although unfortunately Professor Galvão, the Director, was away in Rio having an operation. There was general agreement that the integration of the Indians of Brazil should be as slow as possible and that the idea of trying to speed up the process was 'absurd'. I also heard considerable concern expressed over the amount of deforestation going on.

While I was in one of the offices, a girl came round with a collecting box. I heard the name Nimuendajú mentioned, as the man I was visiting put some money in. I asked what it was all about and was told that the widow of Curt Nimuendajú, probably South America's greatest anthropologist, has lived in penury in Belém since he died in 1945. Her pension from the government was twenty cruzeiros a month (less than £2 sterling) and the staff of the museum had a collection every month to help supplement this. I made a contribution on behalf of Survival International and said that I would try and see if I could raise some further interest in Europe.

The other person who was most helpful to me in Belém was a Spanish priest who has devoted most of his life to working with the Cayapo. Padre Jayme is now an old man, his head bent over his chest by rheumatism. He has been forced by his superiors to retire to a seminary outside Belém where he teaches boys who may become priests, and chafes gently against being deprived of his former active life. His enthusiasm and love for the Indians with whom he spent so many years is clear as he talks eagerly about them, describing their virtues and their talents, and emphasizing how important it is that they should be protected from contact.

He showed us his collection of feather head-dresses and stone implements.

'How,' he said, 'can people who still have the patience and ability to make Stone Age weapons possibly integrate rapidly into our society?'

He gave me the names of several Indians to greet on his behalf, and he spoke highly and with extraordinary generosity of the work of the Protestant missions. For many years he had worked in competition with them, his church being on one side of the village and theirs on the other. This wholly unsatisfactory arrangement had, according to Padre Jayme, been conducted with great friendliness and mutual help. I could well believe that this was so in his case but was not surprised, though saddened, to hear him criticized later by some of those of whom he had spoken so highly.

He took me to see the Belém Casa do Indio which was a sad come-down from those we had seen in Rio and Cuiabá. There were no nurses in charge, although one was said to visit from time to time, and the Indians appeared to receive little benefit except for having a roof over their heads. The house is a long way out of town and hard to find. When we arrived there Padre Jayme was greeted warmly by several of the twenty or so Indians, and in particular by the old chief of the Mekranotire tribe from Kokraimoro. He was very ill with what was said to be 'flu but looked as though it was turning into pneumonia. He lay alone in a small side room in a hammock. The hole in his lower lip, which had originally held his lip disc, had been sewn up some time before in the Belém hospital, which made him look even more miserable.

The house itself simply consisted of an open-ended building with a table down the middle, where the Indians ate, and some bare rooms leading off it in which hammocks were slung and they slept. As a rest house for Indians passing through Belém, and to provide eating accommodation, it was adequate. As a hospital it was not.

When I arrived back at the hotel, I found that Marika, who had been shopping in the market, had acquired a baby coati from a man in the street. Animals of any sort were strictly forbidden anywhere in the hotel, as we were informed by several large notices. My first reaction was to say that we had enough problems without adding to them. It would escape in the aeroplane, we had no idea what to feed it on and it would be nothing but a nuisance. However, Amelia, as Marika had christened her, managed to charm me utterly within five minutes, poking her long cold nose into my ear and going to sleep curled around my neck. As it turned out, she was not only great company and very little trouble – except for a tendency to rummage through our clothes during the night – but she was also a useful asset and ice-breaker in Indian villages. Women and children always wanted to hold her and play with her. They also fed her a rich and varied diet on which she grew fat and healthy.

Gorotire and Kuben-Kran-Kegn

✣

THE FAB Beechcraft caught us up in Belém and we flew off to the south to visit some of the tribes living in the very south of the State of Pará and the northern tip of Goiás. This brought us virtually full circle as we were now once again not far from the Xingu National Park and the northern tip of Bananal.

The first villages we wanted to visit were those of the Gorotire and Kuben-Kran-Kegn, both Cayapo groups, related to the Txukarramai. It was considered that the airstrips at these villages would be large enough for the Beechcraft to land on, provided that the weather conditions were suitable. As we were in the middle of the rainy season, there was some doubt about this, and our problems were not eased by dense low cloud which made finding villages isolated in the jungle very difficult.

On our first attempt to reach the Gorotire village, we had to return to Belém after nearly three hours' flight when the strain proved too much for one of our pilots. He had recently had a very serious plane crash during a similar operation and his nerve had not fully recovered. Just as we were about to descend through the cloud cover, and start searching for our destination, his nerve broke and he asked to be relieved from the assignment. As soon as we landed back in Belém he boarded a military transport plane to Brasilia and was immediately replaced by another pilot.

This was tiresome for us as it wasted a precious day, but we felt very sorry for the young lieutenant who would probably never fly again. I should perhaps say here that I have nothing but the highest praise for the various Brazilian Air Force pilots who flew us during this journey. Apart from their skill and efficiency, which was the more remarkable for the very limited facilities often available to them, they were, without exception, likable and friendly men. I was frequently impressed by the way in which they never threw their weight about unnecessarily or demanded special treatment, and we never had any trouble in discussing together what was and was not possible while planning our next move. Unlike Edson, who invariably raised objections to anything which I proposed or which involved necessary variations to the original route or time-table, they had the experience and confidence to decide what should be done in the light of prevailing circumstances. At the same time they managed to avoid becoming involved in pointless academic arguments.

When we finally did reach Gorotire we found that most of the tribe were away collecting Brazil nuts in the surrounding jungle. The resident Protestant missionary, called Durval, came out to meet us as we landed, and invited us back to have lunch in his house. On the way we had stopped at Conceição do Araguaia where we had picked up an Indian woman who had been in the Catholic hospital there. She had never flown before and was very frightened during the flight, gripping Marika's hand throughout, but as soon as she stepped out she immediately began the familiar high-pitched keening over how awful it had been to be away for so long, or else over some relation who had died.

There were only a few women and children in the village, which was clean and spacious. They were cheerful and attractive and seemed to be in good health. Durval was proud of his medical record, saying that during the previous year twenty babies had been born to the tribe and none had died. His wife, who is a nurse, told us that most of the Indians had been vaccinated against tuberculosis and small-pox, but that twelve had died a couple of years before in a measles epidemic.

We stayed only briefly after eating with the Durvals. We walked through the almost deserted village, where the small

Catholic and Protestant churches faced each other at either end. A stream running past the village joins a larger river nearby which is a tributary of the Xingu. Navigation is impossible, however, due to rapids, and this has helped to preserve the Gorotire's isolation. But we had seen roads and the beginnings of fazendas from the air. Their independence will soon be threatened. Although a large and easily defined reserve was created for them and other Cayapo groups, the region is rich in brazil nuts and jaguars, and already infringements of the further parts of the reserve regularly take place. Unless action is taken to prevent this, the future of the Gorotire will be in jeopardy.

We flew on to spend the night at the Kuben-Kran-Kegn village, further west, another Cayapo tribe in the same reserve. The village is on the Riozinho, which, too, runs into the Xingu. Just beside and below the village are several impressive and beautiful waterfalls. The lowest one is large enough to create a substantial, permanent cloud of mist around it. They also have the effect of preventing large fish from going up the river, and limit the use of canoes to short stretches. We circled in and came down low over the village, which consists of two rows of wooden thatched houses, the landing strip simply being a continuation of the 'street' which these create. As we slowed at the far end of the strip and turned to taxi back to the village, the wheels of the aircraft suddenly sank into soft ground. After revving the engines powerfully for a few minutes to try and pull us out, which only succeeded in sinking us in deeper, the pilot switched them off. We climbed out to inspect the damage and watch the thin column of Indians running towards us from the village. The wheels were sunk in to half their diameter and it was clear that a lot of digging and pushing lay ahead of us.

One by one, the Indians arrived. Mostly they were women as once again the men were off gathering nuts in the jungle, but there were many more of them than there had been at Gorotire. They crowded around Marika when they saw that she was carrying a coati. Amelia now really came into her own, as the Kuben-Kran-Kegn women were very reluctant about being photographed but did not object while they were fondling or feeding the coati and passing her from hand to hand.

There were also a few vociferous old men with large lip discs who came and told us urgently exactly what to do. Later, an American girl working for the Protestant mission came and interpreted for us.

The next four hours were spent pushing the aeroplane out of the mud, only to have it sink back again a few yards later on each time. The Indian women, who were extra-ordinarily tough and sturdy, were persuaded to push against the wings, which they did with great enthusiasm, but seldom together. I found myself acting as a sort of cheer-leader to make them co-ordinate, which helped to sustain their interest and gave them quite a lot of amusement. I became known as 'one, two, three, heave!' and whenever I later went round the village they mimicked me. The young FAB sergeant/steward and I became coated with mud as we dug below the wheels. Everybody sweated and heaved to move the aeroplane to dry ground before evening. It was vital that we did so, as rain clouds were forming and once rain fell the plane would sink deeper and we would never get it out.

Everyone helped. Everyone that is except Edson who either got under our feet giving wrong and pointless orders to which nobody listened, or sat inside the aircraft, adding to its weight, munching bananas.

When at last we had done all we could, and the light began to fail, we carried our things through the village to the Protestant mission house. This was surrounded by a high stockade with a padlocked door in it and was being lived in by the American girl and the Brazilian wife of Arnoldo, the FUNAI man working with the Kuben-Kran-Kegn. He had gone off with the main body of the tribe collecting nuts, so his wife had moved into the mission building.

Beth Smith, the American girl, told us that she was only there temporarily, for a few months, while the resident German missionary girls were on leave. She said the worst medical problem was tuberculosis; there was little malaria on the Riozinho and health was generally fairly good. The season for collecting brazil nuts lasts for between two and three months. They are sold through FUNAI, taken to a point some distance downstream from which they are collected by boat.

Most of the tribe also leave the village for about a month in June, when they go hunting jaguars. They kill between forty and sixty on average at this time, and once again FUNAI arranges the sale of the skins at the equivalent of a pound or two sterling each and credits the money to the Indians. There had been great difficulty this year in persuading the Indians to go and collect nuts as they had not yet been paid for the previous year's Jaguar skins. There is clearly something wrong with the system and, whether or not corruption is involved at some stage, it seems wrong that the Indians should derive little or no benefit from the killing of a large number of animals of a now increasingly rare species. Since a government agency is responsible it should be possible to control the situation, so that fewer jaguars are killed and more is paid to the Indians for them.

Another very disturbing thing we learnt was that there had been a series of tourist visits to the village during the previous summer. Not only are these specifically prohibited time and again under Brazilian law, as they create a quite unacceptable health hazard for the Indians, but they accounted to a large extent for the bad atmosphere we found in the village. We felt strongly that we were disliked, immediately and on principle, when we arrived. There was a sullen, aggressive attitude, which at the same time never flared up into open anger nor vanished completely in laughter. This is so unlike the normal and natural Indian response to visitors that it made me very sad. Although the tourist potential is undoubtedly there where Indians are concerned, it is an unfortunate reflection on our civilization that we tend to corrupt the people we like to go and look at and never more so than where primitive societies are concerned. The Indians must learn in time to understand and accept many of our ways if they are to survive, but surely the best way for us to help them is for people who respect their culture to live among them teaching by example and learning from them at the same time, rather than for tourists to make fleeting visits bringing nothing but disease.

We went down to the river by torch-light and swam in the cool, clear water. The current was strong past the small, sandy beach, and threatened to pull us towards the first of the waterfalls roaring a few hundred yards downstream. The night noises were loud and the moon almost full. It was a glorious night which made us feel strong and glad to be back in the jungle again after too much time spent hanging about in towns.

Later, as we ate in the mission house, many of the Indians crowded in to lean over our shoulders and sing Brazilian and American folk-songs with us, accompanied by Beth on a guitar. Then the women and girls went outside to dance. They formed up in two lines, graded exactly from tallest to smallest, and then stamped and sung and swung the small end of the line round in a dance similar to the one we had seen performed by the Kayabi. Marika and Beth, both blonde and about the same height, were each fitted into one of the lines with much giggling and laughter, and then, clutched firmly around their waists, literally forced to keep in step and go on and on dancing.

Torrential rain fell during the night, but when Marika and I got up before dawn to go and see what had happened to the aeroplane, we found that it had stayed firm on the hard ground. We then walked down below the nearest waterfall and sat watching the churning masses of water boiling over the edge until it was time to go back and visit the village.

Pigs had been introduced some time before and these seemed to be doing well, but they made a lot of mess and caused a good deal of damage, rooting in and out of the houses and roaming almost everywhere without restriction. We were also told that, although they represented an important potential source of meat for the village, the Indians were usually ill after eating them.

The first thing I did as we walked around the awakening village, was to visit the old chief, who had not gone to collect nuts, and give him a bag of presents. This went some way to improving the atmosphere which had reverted to glum mistrust after the cheerfulness of the late party the night before. The Indians had worked very hard on the previous day to push the aircraft out and made it quite clear that they were regretting having done so with such enthusiasm and energy. Several of them grunted 'one, two, three, heave!' at me as I walked past. It was lucky we had finished the job of getting the aeroplane out of the mud the day before.

After a few anxious moments, during which the wheels again stuck briefly in the mud, we managed to take off and fly towards Maraba. Unfortunately, we were unable to land there due to thick cloud. So we diverted first back to Conceição do Araguaia, and then on to Carolina. Here I was able to charter a light monoplane to take us to visit the Kraho.

The Kraho

❦

IT was all something of a rush as our FAB pilots were anxious to reach Maraba that night. As it turned out we never had a hope of doing so, but it meant that everything had to be hurried.

My main reason for wanting to visit the Kraho was that I knew that J. C. Melatti, one of Brazil's best-known, young anthropologists, was living with them. I had with me his recently published book, *Indios do Brasil* and had found it invaluable as a guide. I was anxious to talk to Melatti and hear his views. We could see the Kraho village at which I was told he was staying from the air, about five miles from the clearing where the airstrip was.

There was no transport and so we walked to the FUNAI post, were caught by a rain-storm on the way and soaked to the skin. After a few words with the resident FUNAI man, during which I showed him my letter of authority to visit the Kraho, I left Marika there and set off running fast with an Indian boy towards the village. He had long, black hair to his shoulders, cut in a fringe in front and reminded me of Mekarão at Posto Leonardo. The Kraho have a reputation as fine runners, being one of the tribes which carry the enormously heavy logs called *toras* on their shoulders in ritual races. I was pleased to find that I was fitter than he was and able to outrun him, but he saw a snake that I had failed to notice and pushed me to one side so that I should not tread on it.

We forded two or three waist-deep rivers on the way, and at the last one, after we had been running for nearly an hour, we found a large party of Kraho men who had just arrived to take their evening swim. They were a good-looking and cheerful crowd who seemed healthy and fit. One or two were carrying small-gauge shot-guns, and they had a few birds which they had shot, but I learnt that game is very scarce in the area now and they seldom eat meat.

We hurried on and climbed a small rise to the village, which is laid out in a most unusual way, consisting of a very wide circle of houses with straight paths leading like spokes of a wheel to an open circle in the centre. The houses were square and thatched, and not far from the village I could see a cattle crush with a few cows beside it.

The Indian with me pointed out the chief's house and I burst in, to see an old Indian, with long greying hair and spectacles, seated in a hammock surrounded by several younger men and children. I began to apologize for arriving unannounced.

The chief greeted me politely in Portuguese before pointing to a Brazilian man in shorts sitting on a bench against the wall, whom I had not noticed. This was Melatti, and from the notebook and pencil in his hands, I saw that I had interrupted his work with the Indians. I apologized again, explained who I was and what I was doing; also that time was desperately short if I was to fly back to Carolina that evening. He grasped the situation calmly, and at once suggested that we set out immediately to walk back to the post together.

This gave me only a few moments to glance around the village while he put on a shirt and sandals. Once again I was struck by how clean and tidy a Kraho Indian village is compared to ones in which Western influences have been superimposed. Worst of all had been the regimented rows of houses on Bananal, not far from where we now were, around which the litter had often been almost knee-deep. Here, by contrast, my fleeting impression was that the neat geometric paths and houses in a circle reminded me of a well-raked formal garden. There was dirt and dogs, chickens and children and yet, in spite of the inevitable messes and grubby faces, there was no squalor.

Melatti, a heavily-built man in his thirties, told me a lot about the Kraho. He seemed not to draw breath as we walked. This meant that we had to go more slowly and, just after we had reached the post again and were setting off for the airstrip, our little plane took off and flew away, unable to wait any longer. As a result, we had to spend the night at the post, but it also gave me a chance to talk to the FUNAI man there.

The Kraho are in a very unusual position for Indians in Brazil, in that their reserve, which is very large – seven hundred and ninety-one thousand acres – is not their original tribal territory, but land which settlers were moved off at the beginning of the century and which was given to the Indians in perpetuity by the Goiás State Government. They have lived there ever since and are now slightly on the increase. Numbers have risen from five hundred and nineteen in 1963 to five hundred and eighty-three this year – a ten per cent increase in eight years. The FUNAI post provides some very limited medical assistance. There is no doctor or trained nurse, and occasionally food is sent to the post for distribution to the Indians. There was also an agronomist working out of the nearby town of Itacajá on a scheme to develop land on the edge of the reservation. In spite of all this the Indians are facing major problems, the greatest of which is simple hunger. Tuberculosis is also rife among them.

There are five villages, two quite large with about two hundred people in each, and three smaller ones of about fifty. The Kraho are not very good farmers, being hunters at heart, and consequently their crops are not usually enough to support them. As a result, a very peculiar pattern of behaviour has emerged, which seems extraordinarily unsatisfactory. Just at the time of year when they should be cultivating their plots and planting the maize and manioc and other crops, they run out of food and often eat the seed which they should be planting. Several of the men then go out of the reservation and get lifts on trucks to cities and towns as far away as Rio, Brasilia and São Paulo. Melatti said that in his village alone twenty-two men had done this in the last year.

Apparently what happens is that they travel with the truck wherever it takes them and then practise a very sophisticated form of begging by persuading the prefect of the town, or other important people, to give them presents. These are readily given, as attractive 'wild' Indians are a rare sight in Brazil. Then, having collected several shirts, knives and so on, they return to the reserve. These material possessions do not, however, solve the food problem of the village and so they again leave the reserve and trade them with the local settlers and poor farmers around the reserve for food. In this way they survive.

Some years ago an effort was made to introduce the Kraho to animal husbandry and two hundred and fifty cows were given to them. Unfortunately, they had little or no previous experience of keeping cattle and they were given no proper help in managing them. As a result, they killed them off too quickly so that numbers decreased and a series of diseases wiped out most of the remainder, so that there are now only about fifteen or twenty left. There is also a good deal of rivalry between the villages over who owns which cows, resulting in the unfortunate tendency that the safest thing to do with a cow whose ownership is in doubt is to eat it. There are now so few cows left that they contribute little to the Kraho economy. It is a pity that the experiment should be allowed to fail. Melatti felt that if the right person were to spend a year or so in the reserve, and more cows were brought in, they would learn how to look after them. This would go some way towards solving their food problems by contributing the necessary meat. He lived in the village on the same food as they did, and he said that they almost never ate meat, the basic diet being rice, farina and beans.

Another cause of dissent between the five villages was the indigenous guards – twenty-eight of them in this reserve.

They accounted for about a third of the total number of indigenous guards in Brazil, and as they are paid two hundred cruzeiros a month (about £17) they represented the main financial income of the tribe. As they are all Kraho boys, their money is given to the village chiefs or their own parents and used to buy food for the whole village. The trouble and jealousy is caused by one village having fifteen guards, another six and the others only two each. Apart from their salaries, they appear to contribute little as they are too grand to work in the smart uniforms with which they are provided. I heard of no development projects in which they can take part and there is next to no police work for them to do. Mostly they just sat around and lived off the village.

The most alarming thing I heard concerning the Kraho reserve was that a second Brasilia-Belém road has been planned, and that the proposed route runs straight through the middle of the reserve, dividing it in half. Work had not begun on the road when we were there, and there would seem to be no good reason why it should not be routed around the reserve. If it does go through, the effect upon the Kraho can only be bad. They will inevitably devote more of their time to begging and less to learning how to cope with the problems facing them. At the moment their condition is not desperate, and with luck it could improve. They are so well on the way towards learning to cope with the modern world that it would be a very great shame if all the progress they have made was wasted.

As with many other Indian groups, the main problem is teaching the Kraho to undertake the responsibility for their own survival. On his own, before contact, the Indian naturally does this, and the constant struggle for survival is in itself a reason for most of his day-to-day actions. The difficulty arises when, his self-confidence shaken by the shock of contact, he begins to allow others to take decisions for him. This process can very easily destroy his ability to cope and even when, as so often happens, only minimal assistance is coming from the most hopelessly inefficient and uninterested people, he will become wholly dependent upon this.

It is only when people like Helio Bucker and the Villas Boas brothers instil into the Indians in a slow and subtle way the will to look after their own destiny that they retain their pride and their culture, and with these the ability to adapt. I feel sure the Kamayura in Xingu, for instance, would in many respects be better able to withstand and cope with the undesirable aspects of a mining camp opening next to their village than would many much more apparently acculturated groups. For all their nakedness and lack of familiarity with modern technology, they have had time to learn to value their own ways and to overcome the temptation to abandon them for something they do not understand. This means that we who say that the Indians should be protected and isolated for the time being are not so easily to be accused of trying to keep them as animals in a human zoo, but are simply saying that this is the best method of integrating them into society as useful citizens who, in due course, will be able to contribute to that society by being sane and proud members of it; people with original thoughts and ideas; men perhaps of rare and necessary talents, far more valuable to the world than just more worker ants. The Indians do not make very good worker ants anyway, which is why it was necessary to import African slaves to South America. If this is true, and if we do not want the Indian of Brazil to die out, then we must also accept that in order to integrate him into society we must make use of whatever talents he has. Anyone who has come into contact with Indians living in a relatively pure state or who has lived in an Indian village for any time must be aware that Indians are intelligent and talented people with much to teach us, not only practically but also philosophically.

Saving the remaining Indians of Brazil from extinction, while at the same time preserving their knowledge and talents, will not be easy, but I believe that it is possible. There is still plenty of land available, and, because there are so few Indians left, the resources necessary need not be colossal.

I had been interested to read in Belém, in a copy of *The Times*, a comment on the recently-published International Red Cross report, saying that it 'makes clear that the general incapacity of the Brazilian authorities to deal with the problem of the Indians can be countered only by international assistance for the remnants of a primitive people who have suffered cruelly from the encroachment of "civilization".'

This applied mainly to the medical aspects of the situation but I knew by now that my report on the other aspects would be saying the same thing. The President of FUNAI could dismiss my report as well, in the same way as he had dismissed the Red Cross one, but I could only hope that there might be others in the Brazilian government big enough to accept and face the problem.

The Gaviões

❧

WE ate and slept at the post, talking till late, and were down at the airstrip again before dawn. One of the reasons we had had to hurry so much the day before was that I knew that the bush-pilot who had brought us to Kraho-lândia had had a flight booked for the next morning and so had not wanted to stay the night. As it turned out he had relations at Itacajá, only five minutes' flight away and had flown there. As the sun rose he came flying in from the west, picked us up, and took us to Carolina. He then very charmingly only charged us for the two flights which we had made (about £30), saying to me with a broad wink that the flight to Itacajá and the night he had spent there had been well worth it.

Edson and the pilots did not arrive from the hotel in Carolina until nine-thirty which meant that by the time we reached Maraba there was barely enough time for us to make the journey to the Gavião post at Mae Maria. Getting there involved a complicated piece of island- and river-hopping in which we used three taxis and two boats, passing through the centre of the prosperous little town of Maraba, going some six miles downstream to São Félix and then twenty miles along a new and very rutted mud road.

We found the FUNAI man asleep at the post having his siesta, but he agreed quite readily to take us to the Gavião village. We drove another three or four miles up the road and then turned in along a rough little track. It was only the third time that a vehicle had been up it. I expected, as we drove into the village, that the children would clamber excitedly all over it. Instead, we saw families of Indians sitting under rough shelters and barely turning their heads to look at us. Something was badly wrong.

There are thirty-five members of this group of Gavião and they had only been contacted, 'pacified' and persuaded to move to that spot about a year before our visit. Eleven men had gone off collecting brazil nuts, leaving behind five men, eleven women and eight children. The disproportionate number of men implies that many women and children died during the period of contact and that this is only the remnants of a much larger group.

They were a very terrible and depressing sight. Every single Indian there looked ill and seemed to be suffering from 'flu at the very least. The children were coughing and wheezing in an uncontrolled way which made me think of whooping cough. They all had runny noses and looked dirty and depressed. I asked the FUNAI man what was wrong with them and he replied, 'Nothing. It is the normal state for Indians to be in.'

Unable, on the spur of the moment, to think of a suitable. reply to this alarming remark, I asked him what the Gavião economy was based on. He laughed and said, 'It's based on hand-outs from me!'

Edson then decided to translate the last remark to me, and said, 'FUNAI supports the Gaviões.'

The brazil nuts which they collect are sold through FUNAI, and the proceeds go towards the cost of administering the post. It was hard to see what the Indians lived on. Two or three tortoises hung from the rafters tied with pieces of string and struggling feebly, but I saw no sign of any other meat. The FUNAI man said that they were not allowed to sell their artifacts beside the road, although when I pressed him, he admitted that they sometimes did. There were a lot of bows and arrows lying in the roof rafters and they looked well made and serviceable.

The whole situation depressed me more than any other I have ever seen. Here were Indians who, a short time ago, were free and wild. Whatever discomfort, hunger and fear they suffered there, it could not possibly be as bad as what we have replaced it with. The pressure upon them, which had caused them to agree to leave their tribal lands and put themselves in the hands of FUNAI, was our civilization, with its greeds and needs. If all that we have to offer is a slow and painful extermination, the Indians would have been better off to stay where they were.

One of the Gaviões was an epileptic whom we were told the other Indians tried to kill from time to time. There was a dirty bandage round his leg and he sat with his back to us behind a screen of bamboo stakes stuck in the ground. Two of the women were cooking some ears of maize in the embers of a fire, but most of the Indians were just sitting still, staring into space. I found the almost complete lack of contact and communication frightening, but the worst of all was when we came to the man whom we were told was the chief. He was lying in a hammock and made no sign of recognition or of pleasure or displeasure when I took his hand. He just gazed blankly through me and did not even look down when I placed my small offering of razor blades, soap, fish hooks and so on in his hand.

The International Red Cross Mission had visited this group the previous July. When I later saw their report I learnt that they too had found these to be the worst conditions of any they had seen. More worrying is the fact that they reported the number of the group as forty-eight, sent immediate supplies of powdered milk and beans to them, and cabled to Belém requesting protein-rich food supplies for the group. There was no indication that any of these had arrived. I suddenly remembered that these were the Indians that General Bandeira de Mello, in Brasilia, had referred to as an example of very successful rapid integration.

A male nurse had also come with us from the post. He was a small, wizened man with a face like a monkey and he seemed eager to help the Indians. He told us that he went to them by bicycle every day but that there was little he could do.

'What can I do without medicines? I have none and they need them. Please don't forget us. We really need help here.'

He showed me his 'medicine chest', which contained a few bandages, some ointment and malaria pills. His boss, the FUNAI head of the post, spent much of his time complaining that he had recently been prohibited from visiting Maraba without permission from headquarters, and that this often took several days to arrive. I could not make out why the restriction had been imposed and his preoccupation with it, rather than with the Indians, was irritating. He insisted, against the evidence of our eyes, that the Indians were in excellent condition, and he also told us that none had died during the previous year. I would have been more impressed if he had backed up his male nurse in saying how badly they needed assistance or if he had given any indication that the fate of the Indians was any concern of his.

As we left, two young Gavião boys walked with us to the jeep. On the way I tousled their hair and gave them each a sweet, something which always produces a friendly and cheerful reaction from Indian children. These two just stopped and stared wide-eyed after me, holding their sweets in their hands, as though I were a child molester.

I had given up expecting Edson to understand what I was trying to do, or to accept that a problem existed, but it still surprised me when on the way back to Maraba he said,

'What a pleasant and interesting visit that was! And how nice of the man at the post not to mind being disturbed during his siesta!'

Altamira

❧

FLYING westwards again after another night in Belém, we persuaded the pilots to land for a few hours in Altamira. Already this place is being marked on some Brazilian maps as a large city and we were surprised to find that it was little more than a village which, to Edson's distress, did not even run to a restaurant. It is one of the main bases from which the Trans-Amazonica Road is being built. About four hundred miles of the main east-west road is being surveyed from here through virgin jungle. A wide swathe is then cut by hand, after which the bulldozers and heavy machinery come in and build up the big earth road. The scale of the operation is staggering. The distances involved, the numbers of men and machinery required to build the road, and the physical obstacles to be overcome, such as the endless succession of rivers and streams running from south to north across the path of the road and the widespread flooding which occurs during the rainy season, make it a tremendous undertaking. Altamira is at the very heart of Brazil's 'leap to the west' and is scheduled to become one of the country's great cities of the future.

FUNAI's part in all this is, as far as I can see, to make sure that the Indians, and in particular the uncontacted tribes in the path of the road, do not delay its progress in any way. Concern for the Indians' welfare often seems to be secondary to this, which is why I several times heard Brazilians bitterly refer to FUNAI, the successor to the SPI, the Service for the Protection of Indians, as the 'Service for the Protection of Settlers'. The man in charge of the FUNAI headquarters in Altamira was a Colonel Rondon – a distant relation of the founder of the SPI. He was reluctant to answer many questions, saying that he regarded the whole business as a military operation.

'The Indians must be pacified and resettled before the road gangs reach them.'

The office was impressive, with large wall maps and a busy atmosphere. Fifty-seven men were, I was told, employed by FUNAI at Altamira, including officers, Indians, workers and the administration. This was many more than we had met or heard of during the whole of the rest of our journey through Brazil.

There was some confusion when we began to discuss what had been achieved. The Colonel said that the situation was completely under control and that the road workers were now in no danger. I asked him how he could be sure of this and he replied, 'Our pioneer fronts have cut paths for many hundreds of kilometres through the jungle and they have met almost no Indians.'

When I asked him to show me on the map where those which had been contacted were, and whether it was known which tribes they belonged to, he appeared very uncertain as to locations and names and had to call upon his staff to help him. One of these was a well-known *sertanista* called Cotrim, about whom several people had spoken highly as an expert on Indian affairs. He happened to be in the office between expeditions and I was glad to meet him and learn from him what had been achieved. Considering the expenditure in manpower and money at Altamira, the results were not impressive.

Cotrim talked about the Indians in a calm and serious way and, although quite young, clearly knew his subject well. I would like to have had time to talk to him for much longer than was possible. As it was, he was only able to give me a brief outline of the picture. He told me that so far only three groups of Indians had been contacted in the whole region. The first of these was a small Cayapo group called Kararão. They had been found about a hundred and fifty miles south-west of Altamira on a tributary of the Rio Iriri called the Cantinho. They were thought to be the descendants of a group formerly settled at an SPI post north of Altamira on the Rio Jarauçu, who had run away and reverted to a natural state. We were told that the plan was to move them back and reopen the post. Quite near to these, another group of either Jurunas or Araras had been contacted and were accepting presents. Cotrim said there were once again very few of these, as the area was much flown over and few villages had been reported. It looked like a small party of nomadic Indians, constantly on the move. The party who had made the first contact had had a Juruna Indian with them who had not been able to understand their language; it therefore seemed likely to him that they were Araras.

To the east of Altamira, along the route of the road between the Tocantins and Xingu Rivers, no Indians had been seen, but the most interesting of the contacts had been made by Cotrim himself, more or less due south of the town. He had travelled up the Bacajá River for six days by motor-boat and had then cut west towards the Ipixuna River. In this unexplored region of jungle they had met Indians who had invited him and two others back to their village, where they had spent two days. He thought that they were probably Tupi as they use a lot of Tupi words. The women wore skirts which they wove themselves, similar to the Juruna ones. The men used some urucu but no genipapo. Although they had one or two knives and axes that they had stolen from *civilizados*, they were otherwise totally unacculturated. There were about forty in the village which he had visited but, judging from the number of abandoned villages in the area and the extensive cultivated patches, he estimated that there might be two or three hundred Indians there, broken up into small groups for security. He said that their main diet was maize and bananas, although there was some game in the area which they hunted with bows and arrows. The name he used for them was Xipaya.

My main feeling on leaving Altamira was that the money and manpower could be better used. There are undoubtedly Indian tribes along the route of the road, and others will come across it, so that contacts of one sort or another are inevitable. FUNAI must be on hand to deal with these and to try to prevent workers on the road from shooting Indians and vice versa. But it seems wasteful to go and look for groups whose existence is not certain. Where Indian villages are known to exist or are seen from the air in the line of the road, then regrettably it will be necessary, if the planners cannot be persuaded to make a detour, to intensify efforts to make contact with those Indians and persuade them to move out of the way. Otherwise a highly mobile party of experienced Indian 'trouble-shooters', who could be on the spot rapidly as soon as Indians were reported anywhere near the road, would seem to be a lot more use. I could not help feeling that on their long and often arduous treks searching for Indians, the pioneer fronts must often be watched by groups who did not wish to be contacted, and simply kept out of their way.

More important still was the question of the allocation of FUNAI's limited resources. All too often FUNAI employees in other parts of Brazil had said to me, 'We never get paid because all the money available is going into the road programme.'

Of course, the answer is a greatly increased budget for FUNAI, combined with a genuine desire to protect the Indian and preserve his culture. As long as there are those who regard him as a barrier to progress, a barrier which must be removed, the chances of his eventual successful integration are small.

While in Altamira we paid a short and rather unsatisfactory call on Horace Banner and his wife. He is another living legend of the jungles of Brazil, a Protestant missionary who has been with the Cayapo for thirty years and who was the first man to contact several of their groups. He is an Englishman, now old and in somewhat ill-health, and Padre Jayme, who had for many years shared Indian villages with him, had spoken in highly flattering terms of his experience, which he maintained was far greater than his own. As soon as we mentioned Padre Jayme's name, however, Banner attacked him bitterly, accusing him of confusing the Indians with 'all that Roman Catholic nonsense, incense and crosses and so on.' He then showed me a photograph of thirty Kuben-Kran-Kegn, fully dressed, up to their necks in water being baptized by him.

Another point of disagreement arose when the Villas Boas brothers were mentioned. For Banner, the Xingu National Park was a den of iniquity where the Indians were exploited and corrupted and fortunes were made by the sale of articles to the *National Geographic Magazine*. It turned out, after much skirting about the subject, that what upset him most was that the Indians there were allowed to wear no clothes and, worse, photographs were taken of them in this state. He particularly objected to Jesco's postcards which are widely distributed around Brazil, and most of which were taken in the Xingu Park. It was only when he showed me some of his own photographs that I fully understood the depth of his puritanical abhorrence of nudity. Wherever naked Indians were shown, their genitals had been scratched out so violently that the nib of the pen had torn the paper.

The only comment he made on FUNAI was to say that where the SPI had regarded the Indians as devils, FUNAI now regarded them as angels, which was worse.

We disagreed politely but fundamentally on almost every subject that came up. It saddened and worried me that this should be the case when I was talking to a man with so much practical experience, and our conversation left me confused and uncertain. If he was right, then many of those whose opinions and beliefs I respected were wrong; and yet some of them had spoken highly of his work with the Cayapo and the success he had had in taking care of them. It was his intolerance of the work of all others which I found hardest to accept, contrasting as it did so ill with Padre Jayme's generous praise. I began to realize that I was in danger of falling into one of the errors for which I freely criticized many of those working with the Indians in Brazil – the danger of seeing everything in terms of black and white, devils and angels. The Indian question was more complicated. If I allowed that to happen it would be impossible for me to produce a balanced report at the end of my visit.

Tumucumaque

❧

W E spent two nights in Santarém, a pretty town protected by the clean, black waters of the Tapajós which sweep into the Amazon, permanently pushing the thick, white waters away from the river bank. As a result the town is surrounded by clean, sandy beaches and is relatively free of insect life. It must have seemed like paradise to the early settlers sweating their way up from the coast. The narrow streets, pantiled houses, some with imported painted Portuguese tiles on the walls and white marble statues on the roof, and the sizable fishing boats setting sail, reminded me of a Portuguese fishing port on the sea. There were top-heavy river-boats with row upon row of tightly packed hammocks, moored alongside the quay for the night, and the far bank of the Amazon was visible only as a thin line.

We visited the famous collection of Santarém pottery and ceramics, gathered over the years in the surrounding countryside by a shy, retiring lawyer. He kept it in his house. He had thirty-five thousand pieces ranging from tall tripod pots, heavily ornamented with figures like caryatids, to small clay figurines of animals. He had some very far-out theories about the civilization which had produced this pottery, considering it to be very much older than is generally accepted, and he was bitter because he was not allowed to sell any pieces except to the nation, who were considering moving the whole collection to Brasilia.

If time had not been so short we would like to have lingered in Santarém, a pretty and peaceful place, cooled by the breeze coming up the wide waters of the Amazon.

We would have liked to have gone by boat a little way up the Tapajós river, bathed from its sandy beaches and perhaps found some Santarém pottery. On the foreshore an old woman sold kakaka, the 'soup of the Amazon', in brightly painted gourds. A hot, glutinous jelly with a texture like frog-spawn, it has spices, shrimps and a slimy-green vegetable seaweed added to it. It is delicious.

But we had to get to Tumucumaque, and the next day we tried – twice. Twice we flew for nearly four hours, over three hundred miles up to near the Surinam border, only to meet huge cloud banks and rough weather. Twice the pilots tried to buffet the plane through, throwing it this way and that in their search for open bits of sky, while we in the back clung to our seats and felt sick.

That night in Santarém the pilots made their calculations and told us that if we did not make it into Tirio, the airstrip and main village in Tumucumaque, on the first run of the next day, we would have to fly on to Bôa Vista in Roraima, as the aircraft's hours would be up and it would have to be grounded. As it was they were a little worried about it due to the rough handling it had had when bogged at the Kuben-Kran-Kegn village. The undercarriage had been damaged and one of the propellors had touched the ground and was slightly bent.

They were to leave us in Bôa Vista and so, as this was the last time we were all likely to be together in a town, we took everybody out to dinner at the best of the two restaurants in Santarém. Our guests were: Captain Tommy Blower, the senior pilot, whose father had been English and who was beginning to grow fond of Amelia, the coati (in the end, being unable to take her out of the country, Marika was to give her to him to take back to his children); Captain Mario Jose, passionately dedicated to watching girls and a really first-class pilot; Edson, who, now that the end was nearly in sight, was beginning to worry less about my doing something subversive but still maintained that the Red Cross did not know what they were talking about and that there was no problem with the Indians of Brazil; Orchida, his girl friend, full of complaints about the dangers and discomforts of travel in the interior and genuinely terrified almost to hysteria each time she flew with us (she had remained in Belém during our flights to the south); and Sergeant Beal, the quiet and self-effacing steward-cum-mechanic on the aircraft, who, as the evening wore on, began to miss his young bride and shyly showed me a photograph of her. Marika had Amelia draped around her neck or crawling down her arm to investigate what we were eating. In the case of her mistress, this was, in the cause of culinary investigation, just about everything the restaurant had on its menu.

I watched them all and listened absently, tense inside at the thought of failing to reach Tirio the next day. It was important that I did so as Tumucumaque was the only place with which I could fairly compare the Xingu. Aripuaná was not yet really in existence and no one could honestly call Bananal an Indian park, with its ratio of eight thousand settlers to eight hundred Indians. The other Indians we had seen represented a hotchpotch of different situations and problems, none of them offering a basis of an overall policy for the future. If well-organized national parks were a possible solution, then it was important that I saw the other one.

It had been difficult to find out much about Tumucu-maque. Few people seemed to know of its existence, although it is larger than the Xingu. Protasio Frikel, the Franciscan priest and anthropologist who had been responsible for creating the park, had now, I knew, left the church to get married and was no longer in charge. What was the situation there now?

After covering so much ground, it seemed vital to my mission to get there so as to complete the picture. And when it was over and I had seen all I came to see, what would my conclusions be then? Was there a single theme running through the many different opinions that people had

expressed to me, or was I simply going to add to the confusion? What was I going to say in the report which I
would soon have to start writing? Would I have to criticize
sensitive Brazilian government departments and would
this mean that I might not be able to return to Brazil, or
were there ways in which I could simply concentrate on the
constructive forms of help international aid might take,
and so dodge the basic issues? I think it was then, towards
the end of our time in Brazil, that I began to realize the
complexity of what I had taken on, and what a long process unravelling all the tangled threads was going to be.

With an effort, I brought myself back to earth, laughing
as Mario commented on a pair of passing legs. As I did
so I realized with something of a shock that the issues with
which I was wrestling had become a part of my life and
would remain with me long after the journey was over.

We left early on our last attempt to reach Tirio, flying
west to Obidos and then due north at five thousand feet
for nearly two hours before dropping down through the
clouds to try to find the western Paru River. Without this
to guide them, the pilots dared not fly north as the Tumucumaque mountains lay in our path along the frontier with
Tirio just at their feet. If we were to overshoot in cloud,
we would not only cross the border illegally but probably
run into a mountain as well.

Through a tattered gap in a cloud we saw a narrow
strip of broken, white water between the ripples of green
jungle, and swung left to keep it in sight. We were so
low that, as I leant over between the two pilots giving them
moral if not much practical support, I could see a pair of
blue and yellow macaws flip past below us, and the water
in the river moved as it churned over the rocks. To reach
Tirio up the Paru River takes six weeks of constant hauling
over rapids. Since the airstrip was cleared it is a journey
that is seldom made, and this has helped to preserve the
Tirio Indians' isolation.

As we skimmed over the tree-tops the river suddenly

divided and, after a quick consultation over the maps, we all decided we knew where we were and that we should follow the right fork. It was a nerve-wracking business, trying to follow the river. If we flew too high we lost sight of it through the clouds, and if we flew too low there was a danger of hitting one of the many small, round hills which rose up out of the jungle.

Then the jungle gave way to savanna, and the clouds cleared so that we flew in bright sunshine over a dry grassy plain with the clear blue and white river running through it. By now we were in the park and it was simply a matter of finding the airstrip, to which neither of the pilots had been before. Ahead of us a solid wall of cumulus rising way above our maximum altitude, marked the mountains along the border. The airstrip had still not appeared when we plunged into this. Mario turned to me, and was just saying, 'I'm sorry, it's too dangerous, the mountains must be very near now', and, in fact, we had begun the turn to take us back again, when the plane burst out into sunlight and there below us was a corrugated iron roof glinting, and beside it the long, brown streak of the airstrip. The river ran past the end of the runway and beyond it was the tight cluster of thatched huts making up the Indian village. We landed.

As we did so, a Unimog, driven by a priest in a brown canvas Franciscan habit, and loaded down with laughing Indians, drove up.

During the flight I had shown Edson *The Times* article on the Red Cross report, which referred to the 'general incapacity of the Brazilian authorities to deal with the problem of the Indians'. He had counter-attacked by saying that the Red Cross had only seen the worst situations and that in any case these had now all been cleared up and FUNAI was in complete control, fully manned and operating efficiently.

'FUNAI does everything possible for the Indians and you must not believe these attacks,' he had said.

Edson was the first person to introduce himself to Padre Cyrille as we stepped out of the aeroplane, saying that he was from FUNAI. Immediately, before learning the purpose of my mission, of which he had had no prior notice, the Padre launched into the attack.

'You are from FUNAI? Then where are the medicines we have been promised for so long? Nothing, no resources, no equipment, no supplies have come to us from FUNAI for six months, nor have we heard anything from them. As far as these Indians are concerned, FUNAI might just as well not exist!'

Poor Edson then had the humiliating task of apologizing on FUNAI's behalf in front of me, saying what a difficult time they were going through and how short they were of resources and manpower. The Padre replied, 'FUNAI is now totally preoccupied with the Trans-Amazonica road and uninterested in any other help for the Indians.'

Padre Cyrille Hass, head of the Franciscan mission to the Tirio, then introduced himself to the rest of us, greeted us warmly and showed us to the large, tin-roofed building beside the airstrip which was a simple guest bungalow. Leaving our baggage there, we went with him to the village where he, another Padre, four nuns and two lay helpers live amongst the Indians.

The Tumucumaque Park was created in 1968 and consists of nearly ten thousand square miles of jungle, savanna and mountain, in a rough oblong with the Surinam border as its northern edge. The Franciscan mission which is based in Brazil, but has a college in Germany, administers the park officially, and Brazilian priests are being trained to take the place of the German ones there. FUNAI is supposed to contribute towards the running of the park but, as we had just heard, the help they gave was, to say the least, erratic. When the park was opened a commercial company donated a DC3 aircraft for the use of the park on the understanding that it should pay monthly visits there. It paid one visit and has not been seen since, being used now by the Ministry of the Interior.

The impression we received was that the Franciscans were doing an excellent job of running the park on their own. The village is an attractive mixture of different sorts of houses. All are thatched, some in the traditional Indian way with the thatch coming right down to the ground, while others have wooden sides or are raised on stilts. There is a round 'bee-hive' church with open sides and a similar school house.

There was a cheerful, relaxed atmosphere and the priests, nuns and other workers seemed extraordinarily well integrated into the life of the village. Their own houses were at first glance indistinguishable from those of the Indians, except that the store-rooms, dispensary and workshop were kept locked.

We were given a large and varied lunch, consisting entirely of home-grown or locally caught foods. As soon as it was over a party set out to continue working in the fields. Marika and I went with them, riding in one of the mission's two Unimogs. The airstrip lay at the extreme northern end of the savanna and across the river, on the side on which the village lay, the jungle began again. We drove for a mile or so along a rough track, crossing gullies and streams on well-made wooden bridges.

The clearing, which consisted of about fifty acres, had a sawmill, and there was a lot of varied agricultural equipment in another shed. Padre Cyrille's great interest in life is agriculture, and he took a delight in explaining his theories about the farm to me.

He is very concerned that the normal 'slash and burn' system of agriculture, practised in South America, is rapidly destroying the remaining forest areas. In Tumucumaque there is only a limited amount of jungle and this is vitally necessary to the survival of the Indians in terms of providing areas in which to hunt. He had therefore examined closely the theory behind 'slash and burn', which is that the land is weak, the goodness leaches out of it, and it will only grow crops for two or three years, after which it is necessary to clear a new site. He decided that this is not necessarily so in all cases and that what happened more often was that, in the dense shade created by large trees which provided a canopy, little undergrowth grows, and once the trees have been cut down and burnt, it is fairly easy to cultivate the soil and grow crops. After a year or two, the secondary growth begins to establish itself strongly, due to the sunlight being let in, and this is much harder to clear away, making it easier to go through the same process of clearing virgin forest again.

His policy was to clear the land completely of all tree stumps and roots, which he was able to do with his Unimogs, and then, by ploughing the land and cultivating it properly, prevent the secondary growth taking place. He was now cultivating this land for the fourth year and the crops already growing certainly looked strong and healthy, and the land due to be planted rich and fertile. He did not pretend to know all the answers and said that he would welcome the advice of a trained agronomist, but if his theories could be applied to even some of the rest of Amazonas they might well have the effect of halting much of the unnecessary destruction of the territory. A herd of cows was kept on the savanna across the river, and these provided a small amount of farmyard manure which was used on the land where seedlings and the more sensitive crops were grown. But otherwise no fertilizers were used, the cost of bringing them in by air being prohibitive.

Marika and I left the Padre to get on with his work and walked off down a narrow path which we were told led to another Indian village. Amelia, for whom the exercise was good as it quelled her inquisitiveness, struggled along behind us squeaking furiously if we went too fast.

After twenty minutes, we came out into another clearing and found a very different picture from the main village. A group of about thirty Indians, dressed in rags and living in some ill-constructed shacks, crowded round us begging for cigarettes and sweets, but we only had a few with us. We took shelter with them for a time during a short cloud-burst, and found out that most of them had recently come across the border from Surinam where the Indians were administered by an American Protestant mission. They had been warned to have nothing to do with the Catholic priests who, they had been told, were devils and would kill them. Several of them were suffering quite badly from coughs and colds but said they were afraid to go to the mission and ask for medicine. Later, when I told him about this, Padre Cyrille said that there was quite a lot of movement across the border between the two missions, which were only two to three days' walk apart, and that the rivalry between them was very regrettable. The Americans across the border, who belonged to the Unevangelized Field Mission, prohibited the Indians from continuing any of their own culture as well as from smoking and dancing. He said that he would go and try to persuade the new arrivals to take some medicine from him.

Back in the main Tirio village we wandered about freely taking photographs of the Indians whose lack of self-consciousness was something we had not seen since leaving the Xingu. The men, who were small and wiry with fine, sharp features, mostly wore loin-cloths with diminutive bright red aprons in front, and nothing else. The women had coloured print sarongs, leaving their breasts bare. The children played naked in the sand and laughed at us as we passed. No one begged or paid much attention to us and almost everyone was busy with some job or other, pounding and squeezing manioc, making arrows, or tinkering with a piece of machinery. The worst feature of the village was the large number of mangy, flea-bitten dogs which lay about everywhere growling as one approached their territory. Many of them were covered in open sores.

In the late afternoon, we went to visit Protasio Frikel, the ex-priest, who was living with his wife at a village about an hour's drive away, called Paimerú. We found a quite elderly, but jolly, round-faced and white-haired man, who told us that he now had nothing more to do with the running of the park, but was working as an anthropologist for the Museu Goeldi and studying the Paimerú Indians, who were also Tirio. He is the unchallenged expert on the Indians of Tumucumaque and I asked him how many there were.

'Impossible to say, exactly,' he said. 'They wander across the border. There are several groups around the edges of the park who come in and out, and there are even some uncontacted Indians in the park. In this region, however, we know that there are about three hundred, made up of two hundred and twenty-two Tirio, sixty-four Kaxuyama and thirteen Ewarhoyana-Kahyawa.'

I asked him whether many children were being born and he said that the population was increasing at a steady five per cent, which was very satisfactory. On the south-eastern edge of the park, on the Rio Xitare, he said that there were two large groups of Indians, which might amount to as many as five or even seven hundred. He referred to them as Vayena Indians and said that they were more or less controlled by a mysterious German called Manfred Rausebert who had been there on and off since 1957.

'They say he goes naked when he is with the Indians, used to have an Indian wife and family in Belém, and has now just married his white secretary. But that is all rumour.'

He was anxious about the dangers from cattle ranchers entering the southern end of the park and said that FUNAI should maintain a post there to prevent this. At the same time, he felt, the Indians on the edge of the park should be persuaded to move further in for their own safety, and other tribes from as far away as the Trombetas River to the west should be persuaded to come to the park.

As for the uncontacted Indians inside the park, he felt that they should be left to their own devices for the time being. One group, which may be Akurio or possibly even an isolated group of Tirio, appear from time to time around Paimerú. The Indians from there had bumped into them several times in recent months and had found that, while not hostile, the strangers had no apparent desire to establish contact. A few weeks before, the chief of Paimerú had come face to face with one on a path near the village. Without trying to speak they had both simply turned around and walked away from each other. Later, some women and children, washing down at the river just below the village, looked up to see Indians standing on the bank above them. Thinking they were their own people, they waved and shouted until they realized who they were when, after watching them for a few moments, they, too, simply turned and went away. Sometimes they came to the village when there was no one there, but they never stole anything and Protasio said that they did not appear to be afraid of anybody nor did they seem to be in need of anything. They still used Stone Age implements, except perhaps for a machete or an axe or two which they might have picked up.

The gravest threat that he saw to the park was the current proposal that tourism should be encouraged. He had recently seen an article in *Veja*, the main Brazilian news magazine, concerning the building of three hotels in the park with tourist accommodation. He was violently opposed to this and said that the idea should be quashed at once as it would be the worst possible thing for the Indians.

'At present they are healthy and making good progress,' he said. 'Bring in tourists, and all that has been done for them will be destroyed. They will lose their self-confidence, their pride and their ability to fend for themselves. They will become beggars.'

That night Padre Cyrille and I sat up talking until the small hours. He is a remarkable man of varied talents. Although a conscientious priest, whom it was clear that the

Indians respected and loved, he should really have been an engineer. His great interest and obsession in life was with things mechanical, and he is a highly competent, all-round handyman. It was through his abilities in this direction that he saw himself best able to help the Indians towards reaching a level on which they could compete with the modern world. Talking about the nature of the Indian, he told me that he believed him to be more intelligent than the *caboclo*, the usually half-caste backwoodsman of the Amazon.

'He takes to Western equipment more quickly and more intelligently than the *caboclo* and unlike him does not take kindly to being pushed about, learning best by observation and example. I have taken great care not to force any change upon the Indians but to allow them to watch me at work and see that what I do is sometimes better than their way, so that they may choose to imitate me.

When I first came to the village – this was ten years ago – I began by living in a house like theirs. Then I built a new house, still with a thatched roof, but with wooden sides which kept out the animals and insects and was more comfortable. Now you will see that about half the houses in the village have followed my example and about half have chosen to stay as they are. The Indians are choosing for themselves. One day the Indians will need stone houses and I am building one as a workshop down by the farm at the moment. My bishop wanted me to fly in cement and make concrete blocks to build this, but the Indians have no cement and it will be a long time before they will be able to buy any. So I am learning how to make bricks myself; they are learning with me and they will not forget.

The same applies to the bridges which we build, and the roads. At first, the Indians appear not to be interested, or they are scornful. But then they find themselves using our things and discover how much easier they make life. They are learning to work with my tools and to make things for themselves.'

A man of boundless energy and enthusiasm for new ideas, the priest told me that he was planning to install a water-pump so as to bring piped water to the village, and that he also had a much more ambitious scheme to dig a canal some four miles long, and develop a hydro-electric scheme. This, he said, would not only benefit the Indians directly by providing light for the village, but the dispensary would be able to sterilize its instruments, and other projects would follow.

As regards finance, he said that it was always hard to make ends meet and everything always arrived months late, but somehow they managed, although it was difficult to keep pace with the rate at which things developed. 'When I first came to the mission ten drums of petrol lasted us for a whole year. Now we use sixty or seventy, what with the two Unimogs and the small motors I have for running the machinery.'

We talked about integration and agreed that the Indians should be protected in their natural environment and prepared as slowly as possible. He felt that the object must be to raise the Indian to a level at which he can compete with the rest of civilization and that it was necessary to keep moving on this, as they might be faced with the need to use this knowledge at any moment. The Villas Boas brothers were not going fast enough, he thought, and so might be doing the Indian a disservice.

Although they are men of such very different talents, there was much in our conversation which reminded me of Claudio. The practical man and the philosopher, both in their separate ways, came to much the same ultimate conclusion concerning the Indian's welfare and his needs. They had never met and I encouraged Padre Cyrille to go and visit Claudio in the Xingu. I hope by now this may have happened.

Padre Cyrille's main interest is with the land and how

to make it produce enough to support the Indians. There are many problems. Horses which were brought in all died: the cattle and buffalo or zebu cattle have not done as well as had been hoped. There is a small herd of sheep, and fish and game are still plentiful, but the priest felt that the Indians' survival really depended upon their mastering crop agriculture. One of the problems in teaching them this was that under their traditional methods, based on manioc, sugar-cane and bananas, they seldom, if ever, stored food for any length of time, but used simply to go to the plots and collect what they needed and bring it back to the village. If they are to improve their economy, they must start learning to grow crops which need harvesting at a specific time, and which can then be stored. Inevitably, this must lead to a certain amount of co-operative work, in particular harvesting and planting. The difficulty about this is that the Tirio are very conscious of, and jealous of property. Although, when game is killed, it is usually shared out among everyone, personal possessions, even inside a family, are closely identified with the individual to whom they belong. When it comes to storing the food, communally, and sharing it out, there is trouble.

We could both, I think, have gone on happily talking all night, but at about two I felt I really must let the priest get some sleep. So, borrowing a raincoat from him as the night had turned wet, I set out to walk the two or three miles back to where we were sleeping. First I had to feel my way between the huts of the sleeping village. A few dogs growled at me and there were rustlings in the thatch, but I found the track leading down to the river and stood for a time leaning on the parapet of the long wooden bridge built across it. The river was wide and deep and cool and flowing silver beneath my feet. To my left lay the open savanna country, dotted with occasional trees, like parkland. To my right the soft contours of the houses in the village seemed to huddle together for security under the surrounding tall trees of the jungle. Beyond that again towered the high wall of mountains running along the frontier, standing out against the night sky. Rain clouds which had come all the way from the Caribbean, far to the north, drifted over the last hurdle on their way to the rain forests.

A few hours later, when we went to have breakfast and say good-bye, we found the priest giving Mass under the open thatched church. It was an impressive sight and a strangely touching moment, as we all joined them, standing at the back among some children who had come to watch. The two Franciscans in their brown habits and the nuns in theirs, grouped near the altar, the priest attended by two young Tirio warriors, their naked bodies glistening in the candlelight. The rest of the congregation, standing in respectful and curious silence during the ritual, and joining in the singing with surprisingly beautiful voices.

It was sad saying good-bye, as I had grown fond of Tirio and admired the way in which it worked. I had not the same depth of feeling for the people and the place as I had had in the Xingu, but I felt that there was much that each could teach the other, and nowhere else that we had seen came anywhere near them in achievement.

Roraima Territory

❧

THE Federal Territory of Roraima has a population of forty-seven thousand of which over a quarter is Indian. It therefore has far and away the highest proportion of Indians of any region of Brazil. Moreover, the Indians are divided between those who are isolated and those in various stages of integration in a way which is more or less similar to the pattern existing in the rest of Brazil. It therefore provides a very interesting model of the past, present and future problems affecting the Indians in Brazil.

Broadly speaking, the acculturated Indians live to the east and south of the territory in open savanna country, and the isolated ones to the west in jungle.

Linguistically, the Indians divide into three main families: Carib, Aruak and Yanomamo. The first two groups, most of whom are Makuxi and Wapixana respectively are all, with the exception of a small group of about three hundred Atroari in the south, going through various phases of integration. The last group, the Yanomamo, who are also often referred to as Waika or Xiriana, are all, to a greater or lesser degree, isolated. They form part of what is probably the largest remaining unacculturated tribe in the world, as there are rather more of them over the border in Venezuela. I would love to have been able to visit some of the groups in Brazil, particularly as it was while visiting them two years before on the hovercraft expedition that I had really begun to become interested in the possibility of doing something for them. Now I had come full circle and was back on the edge of their territory again. But unfortunately our own FAB aircraft had now left us and the two or three light planes at Bôa Vista were either grounded or unwilling to make the journey.

There was only a week left before we had to be back in England and, as the weekly commercial flight to George-town, Guyana, passed through Bôa Vista on the day after our arrival there, we decided that Marika should go on ahead and make her way home via New York, while I re-mained to see what more could be done.

I did manage to fly up to the Venezuelan border and have a very brief look at one Yanomamo village. I flew with Ernesto Migliazza, an Italian-American linguist and anthro-pologist, who had been working in the territory for several years, studying the various languages. Although in the throes of packing his house prior to moving to an American university, he devoted a huge amount of time to helping me with my various problems and telling me about the Indians of Roraima.

We flew up the Rio Uraricaa in foul weather, casting about between the stormclouds and mountains for the little brown slash of an airstrip in the jungle. A diamond prospec-tor lived there and not far away we passed over the single hut of a Yanomamo village. It was in the centre of a fork in the river, and looked like a Chinese coolie's hat or the big top of a circus. We flew low over the river and could see the people in their canoes, near the hut. But when we landed, we found that, after the heavy rain which had swollen the streams, it was three hours' walk away. The airstrip itself was a short switchback of slippery, wet mud and our pilot was anxious to get off again so that there was only time to talk briefly to the prospector and the two Yanomamo Indians sheltering from the rain in his hut.

There are about two hundred and fifty Indians in the area, which spans the Venezuelan border. More than half are on the Venezuelan side, living at the more active mining camp there and rapidly becoming prostituted and drink-sodden. The ones on the Brazilian side have, as yet, remained independent, although they came from time to time to the camp of the prospector, who expressed an unusual concern for their welfare, and their own village has been visited a few times. It was suggested that all the Indians should be moved so as to live close to the airstrip. They would therefore be easier to 'look after' but I felt that if the mining in the area should develop any further, this would be the worst possible thing for them. It would be an ideal situation for FUNAI to set up a post in order to prevent the same exploitation of this group taking place as is happening the other side of the frontier, and also to begin to study them with a view to setting up further posts.

But the extraordinary fact is that FUNAI has no posts in the whole of Roraima Territory. In fact, apart from a large farm north of Bôa Vista, which belongs to FUNAI and on which some Indians live – but few, if any, work – FUNAI does nothing in the whole territory. The help, protection and study of the Indians is almost entirely in the hands of various missionary organizations. Although some of these are undoubtedly doing excellent work, and without them the Indians would in many cases be very much worse off, they regard each other with the utmost suspicion, which confuses the Indians, and may sometimes result in them doing more harm than good. Also, they cannot concern themselves with such matters as land rights, vital to the Indians' future, and so the Indians' interests are not being properly looked after.

An international park would be the ideal solution for the whole of the Yanomamo region, most of which is largely unexplored and undeveloped as yet. Throughout it are scattered large numbers of related but unfriendly groups of Yanomamo; about three thousand five hundred in Brazil and perhaps as many as twenty thousand in Venezuela. They are very primitive, and trying to persuade them to move even a short distance off their accustomed land would be difficult and probably disastrous. Already, penetration of their territory is taking place. Their land passes over the low water-shed along the frontier, and is intersected with in-

numerable large and small rivers. Rival groups of missionaries, skin hunters, prospectors and smugglers are beginning
to move in. Soon it will be too late.

The idea of an international area, composed of Yanomamo country in both Brazil and Venezuela, is one which
would require courage on the part of both governments concerned, and the setting up of a joint and international institute to administer the region. Game parks which do this in
Africa have been a success. The wildlife and ecological
studies which could be carried on in an almost virgin area
such as this would be of the utmost value. Giving international experts and organizations an opportunity to work
directly with the Indians would help to quell criticism of the
two governments' treatment of their indigenous peoples, by
letting outsiders see how difficult and complex some of the
problems are.

However, in Brazil's current mood of enthusiastic chauvin-
ism, it is unlikely that such an idea would even be considered.

The missions working in Roraima are as follows: an
Italian Roman Catholic Mission, based in Bôa Vista, runs
one post with the Yanomamo and does other work with the
Makuxi as well as running schools, a hospital and an industrial school for teaching Indians in Bôa Vista; there are
three different Protestant missions, Baptist Mid-Missions,
Unevangelized Field Missions and Assemblies of God Missions, and they are assisted in their work by the Missionary
Aviation Fellowship, who maintain a pilot and an excellent modern light aircraft at Bôa Vista, without which
contact with their more far-flung posts would be impossible.

I went and saw the head of the Unevangelized Field
Missions, the richest and most powerful of all the above,
which maintains three posts in different Yanomamo regions
and also medical evangelistic programmes to the Makuxi
and Wapixana. I found him an intelligent and persuasive
man who did not, at least while talking to me, adopt extreme
evangelical attitudes. Talking about the more acculturated

Indians, he said that a very serious problem indeed existed with them.

'They have had a hard time but those who learn to speak Portuguese are beginning to break through. I think there is some hope of these people being accepted into Brazilian society.

Most of their dances are dying out, but their languages and beliefs still persist. We have managed to set up three Christian churches in Makuxi villages and taught them to pray in Makuxi.

We have been working much longer among the Yano mamo, but of course conversion has been much slower. The main difficulty with the Yanomamo is that their culture is largely based on killing and raiding each other and if this is removed they rapidly lose their pride. Their own name for themselves is "the fierce people".

Some of the young men and a few of the women are now beginning to turn away from this culture and refuse to go on raiding missions. I want them to remain as men and keep their manhood, but abandon the concept of vengeance.'

Another of the problems in working with the Yanomamo is the wide variety of dialects among the different groups These vary more between adjacent villages than, for example, Spanish and Portuguese. The Summer Institute of Linguistics, which is closely tied up with the Unevangelized Field Missions, does not do any work in the area and the study of these languages is undertaken by the missionaries themselves. I met, as he passed through Bôa Vista, one of the young missionaries, Donald Borgman, who impressed me with his fresh and unprejudiced approach to the problems. He was stationed in perhaps the remotest of all the posts, on the Uauaris River in a little finger of Brazilian land surrounded on three sides by Venezuela. He himself said that the 'rigid attitudes of the old timers are now being replaced by more modern ideas'. His intelligence and level of education made him highly-qualified for the job he was doing.

Without the courage and single-mindedness given to him by his religious background, it is inconceivable that he would have found himself in this situation at all, as he gave all the outward appearances of a successful, young business executive.

And yet for all this, when he said that the Yanomamo were 'difficult people to get to accept the gospel', I felt, without a hope of being able to convince him, that his desire to convert largely invalidated all the other good work he was doing. It seems to me wholly right that he should be moved in his work by a spirit of Christianity and charity, and that the eventual object should be to teach this to the Indians; but it should be the last and ultimate objective, after all the Indians' material and social problems have been resolved, which may take very many years. To start attempting to convert people from scratch adds a whole range of destructive prohibitions which could otherwise be left on one side. If the driving force behind the work is a desire to protect rather than convert, then it becomes unnecessary to forbid anything and every effort can be devoted to finding out what help is needed, as civilization approaches, and giving it.

The Brazilian Federal School Service supports several more schools in the interior, of which about fifty are in predominantly Indian villages. All are among acculturated Indians, living in or near settled agricultural communities. The facilities are usually extremely primitive and often the teaching is done by the most advanced pupil between the infrequent visits of the master. In Bôa Vista I met a young school-teacher who had done some work in this direction, largely in his own time and at his own expense. He was anxious to expand the whole service and badly needed funds to do so, but these never seemed to reach the territory. A top-heavy bureaucracy tended to prevent anything ever coming through to this remote and unfavoured part of Brazil. He told me a story about a time when he had been working at an Indian village and a man from the then SPI had come to ask what he needed to further his work. He prepared a long list of clothes, machetes, knives, medicines, books, a cartridge-maker and so on. The man had taken a lot of photographs and promised that everything would be arriving shortly. Three months later six small knives arrived and he said that this was one of the few occasions when he had known *anything* to filter through.

I was also able to visit one of the more remote, acculturated Indian villages. The Indians there were Ingarico, relations of the Makuxi. The village, which was on the other side of the Serra do Sol, was in the most beautiful setting of any village I visited in Brazil. The neat mud and wattle houses were grouped in a lozenge shape set on a knoll in the middle of a large shallow valley surrounded by high mountains. The views in all directions were superb and the initial impression of rural peace and charm was overwhelming.

A young Brazilian missionary from the Assemblies of God lived in the village and seemed to be popular with the Indians. They, on the other hand, were suspicious of strangers and faced quite a lot of problems. Health was fairly well under control except for tuberculosis, which was getting worse, but the main complaint was that game was now very scarce in the region. Although they were able to grow crops in the rather poor soil, they had no way of selling any surplus. The missionary felt that the Indians' lot would be best improved if a road came through to the village. Although this would bring all the usual risks and dangers, and settlers would move in along the road and start to take away the Indians' land, he believed that they were in a fit state to compete with the outside world, and needed this more than isolation. He may have been right, and the Indians appeared to agree with him, but it saddened me to think of lorries and electric light cables in that idyllic setting.

The time I spent in Roraima Territory helped me to put the Indian tribes we had seen in Brazil and their problems into some kind of perspective. The Indians with whom I was concerned constitute less than one per cent of the Brazilian population. If they were all brought together they would not fill half of Brazil's largest football stadium. They are only a small social problem compared to the other major issues of poverty and over-population in Brazil. But I believe they are a very significant one. I can see how irritating it must be for Brazilians, who are concerned in some of the biggest technological developments going on in the world at the moment, to have so much emphasis in the foreign press on this minute part of their country and population. However, if this interest and concern exists, what should the Brazilians do about it? There is clearly a temptation to eliminate the problem in one way or another as quickly as possible, but this would only serve to intensify the criticism and attacks. Better by far to devote a small amount of money and manpower towards trying to answer the criticisms and take some of the recommended action while at the same time modifying or delaying some of the development programmes.

About half the Indians in Brazil are already well set on the road towards integration. These suffer through being discriminated against. Their lands are taken from them and the future holds out little promise for most of them unless they are given special and concentrated help. They need medical help of a kind superior to that received by the surrounding population, because they are still at a disadvantage in relation to resistance to Western diseases. They need educational help, so as to be able to understand the position in which they now exist and to learn to stand up to oppression, and they need technological help in order to be able to compete on equal terms with those who regard them as inferior. If this is given to them, there is a chance that some of their inherited and handed-down tribal skills may be preserved and adapted so as to make them better able to cope.

The other half, those who are not yet much affected by the acculturation process, are in a quite different position.

Some are still isolated in the jungle while others have had a limited amount of contact and have received some modern tools and learnt to use them, but these have not yet destroyed their own culture which is still viable and intact. It may be many decades or even generations before they are ready to begin belonging to a technological world. In fact, it may well be that, in time, we will learn to respect aspects of their lives and will not be so anxious to change them. In the meanwhile, the slower the process of change, the less shock they will suffer and so they need protection and a degree of insulation against our world.

In Roraima territory, the Yanomamo Indian groups are still under no great pressure, but a branch of the Trans-Amazonica Road is planned to link up through Bôa Vista and Venezuela to the Pan-American Highway, and this must bring development to the region. There is no time to be lost in demarcating the areas which should be protected as Indian reserves. This should be done while the sole occupants still are Indians, and before it is necessary to remove settlers who will already have done untold damage.

It does seem quite extraordinary that FUNAI do virtually nothing for the Indians in the area in which their proportion to other members of the population is greatest. The very existence of Brazil's largest single tribe of Indians appears to be virtually unknown to them. As far as I could make out, no single FUNAI man had ever even been to visit the Yanomamo.

PART FIVE

Mount Roraima

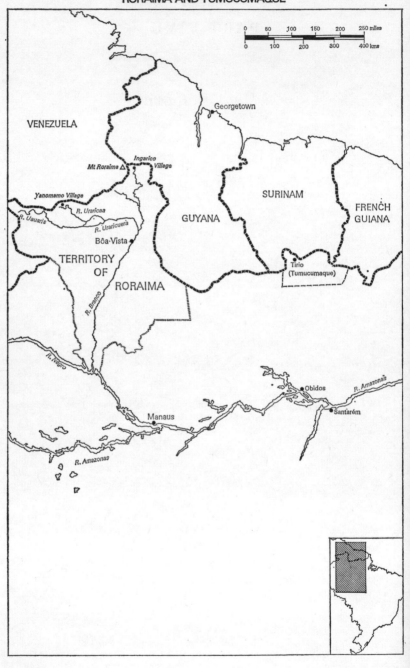

Mount Roraima

❧

MARIKA, who had been taking large quantities of photographs for an educational series for children on Indian domestic life, had flown to New York taking our film with her to have it developed. I made a couple of flights to Indian settlements in Roraima territory but now further flights out of Bôa Vista seemed impossible. Then I met a pilot who knew of a flat piece of ground near Roraima. He knew because he had recently dropped a party of Brazilians who were climbing the mountain and he was to pick them up again in four days. If I was back in time, he would fly me out too.

This was a chance not to be missed, not only to climb a legendary mountain, but also to have a quiet period of intense physical activity, and to give my mind a chance to unwind.

For nearly three months, Marika and I had been travelling over a large part of the interior of Brazil. We had visited over thirty Indian tribes and talked to innumerable people about the problems facing those pre-Columbian survivors. Each visit had been much too short and packed with new impressions and incidents, facts, theories and ideas. As one visit drew to an end, plans and preparations had to be made for the next one. There had been no time to rest and no time to think or to try and pull the whole jumbled, confused picture into a coherent shape.

Roraima is not a particularly difficult mountain to climb. The main problem is its isolation and inaccessibility. It has been climbed before a good many times but always, as far as I know, by parties supported by Indians carrying supplies. It had not been my intention to do it alone, but the bush pilot who had dropped me on a level patch of ground on a neighbouring mountain had suddenly discovered that he did not have enough fuel to fly on to the Indian village, at which he said I would be able to find Indians to accompany me. Rather than fly back to Bôa Vista, I had overcome his conviction that I would instantly be eaten by one of the jaguars which he assured me abounded there and had persuaded him to leave me.

After the shaky little single-engined aeroplane had bounced across the stony ground, narrowly missed a shoulder of the hill in taking off and flown away to the south, I sat for a while, looking around. Above me towered a steep, green slope culminating in a sheer, grey cliff which circled the summit like a crown of lamb. Over this poured a thin stream of water and a plume of cloud drifted away to the west. Near me a small river of clear water, ankle deep, splashed lazily over smooth rocks before disappearing into a green and shady copse. All around lay magnificent vistas. The wooded areas, elegant as if they had been land-scaped, set off the hills and rivers that stretched into the distance.

Only to the west was the view interrupted, by a bank of cloud. Somewhere behind it lay the mountain after which the whole territory – four times as large as Switzerland – was named: Roraima.

Having expected to be guided by the Indians who would have carried my supplies, I was badly overloaded. The worst item was a heavy magnum rifle which a well-meaning friend had thrust into my hands as I left Bôa Vista saying as he did so that it was extremely valuable and I would have to pay a small fortune if I lost it. Knowing that it was most un-likely that I would need to shoot anything, it was all the more annoying to know that I dare not be parted from it. I carried my possessions down to the edge of the river and laid them out one by one on a rock, making two heaps. There were two hammocks; one lightweight nylon jungle one and an ordinary Brazilian one which I had intended giving to one of the Indians as a present. Neither of those was likely to be vital to my survival during the next few days and so I put them on one side. My sleeping bag, on the other hand, would be needed as I intended to sleep on the top of the mountain where it would be cold and wet. One spare pair of shoes, too; and my cameras could not be left behind but my blanket and spare ammunition could.

In this way I reduced my supplies to manageable proportions and then spent some time working out the best way to carry them. They broke down into three – the rifle, my camera case and the rest wrapped in a waterproof cape. After an unsuccessful attempt to make a knapsack with some rope, but finding that the resulting straps bit into my shoulders, I ended up with the rifle and the camera case slung diagonally across each shoulder and the rest tied to the end of a stick and carried Dick Whittington fashion. In this way I could change shoulders every half hour without having to stop.

The things I was leaving behind I hid carefully in a dense thicket on an island in the river and then, wading to the far bank, I began to walk towards the mountain.

There was a faint track, but it kept dividing or disappearing. With part of my mind I had to keep deciding which way to go. The other part wandered in a way that had not been possible for a long time. There was so much to be re-looked at, conversations to be remembered, thoughts to be put in order. It had been an exhausting time mentally as well as physically.

Away from the need to plan and discuss and think and talk in Portuguese, my step lightened. I walked fast in this silent place. Insects buzzed around my head and birds cried in the patches of jungle.

It was hot and the sun beat down onto the hard burnt ground. Beyond the immediate hum of insect life and the stirrings and rustlings of the undergrowth, an overpowering silence lay over the landscape. It was lonely; a little frightening.

Impressions came back to me. Memories of the many people I had talked to, the people who had strengthened and confirmed my own conviction that the problem of the survival of the Indians is one worth fighting for. The people who convinced me that, in spite of all the difficulties and differences of opinion, there is hope. Memories of the silent Indians; the happiness and the despair, the rightness of their own ways and lives and the utter wrongness when our ideas and beliefs are carelessly and brutally imposed. I remembered the supreme peace of spending even a few hours in their world, where every act has a meaning and is part of a well-ordered but completely free system in which the simple joy of being alive is still something which can be embraced without shame.

I thought, too, of those who had been angry; those Brazilians who feel that the economic development and progress of the nation is all-important, and that bothersome Europeans, who have already destroyed most of the primitive peoples in their own colonies, have no right to interfere in Brazil's internal affairs, and are impeding that progress; the frightening number of ordinary decent people in the country who genuinely believe that Indians are inferior beings, lazy and dangerous, who have a limited use as labourers but would be better out of the way altogether; and the suspicious, doubting people, who suspected my motives, thought I was a dangerous revolutionary – probably communist, waiting to overthrow the regime – or a sensation-seeking journalist who would publish wild, unfounded attacks on Brazil in the foreign press.

And then the rewarding conversations with those who trusted me, and for whom my visit and the fact that people outside cared and wanted to help represented a new hope of success in what they were trying to do. 'Help us to fight for the Indian,' they had said. 'Teach the world to see what is best for him. Help us to prevent these people whom we love from being destroyed and vanishing off the face of the earth. Help them in the fight for survival. But above all help us with your voice which will carry weight in the world and make the world care.'

It was these conversations that troubled me most, these requests that made me feel afraid and lonely. The responsibility for what came next was mine alone, and was a heavy one. But through taking on the mission I had just completed I had acquired a burden of responsibility which would never leave me while there were still Indians in Brazil and people trying to save them from cultural and physical extinction. If I did nothing, or too little, I would be failing in my duty. If I did or said the wrong things I could easily do more harm than good. I felt inadequate to cope with such an enormous task, but then I had blithely accepted the chance of the journey and must now accept the responsibility that followed.

These were the thoughts and impressions which filled my head as I climbed. They seemed to draw me back across the vast wilderness stretching away below me to the south for two thousand miles.

My mind was so absorbed that I was barely looking where I was going. A slight movement made me focus on the path a yard ahead where a dark-brown snake had raised its head a foot from the ground and was preparing to strike. I stopped dead and we stared at each other for several taut moments. The snake, swaying slightly from side to side, seemed to be short-sightedly trying to decide what I was, while I was trying to remember the right thing to do in this situation. My stick was in use over my shoulder with my baggage tied to the end and I was only wearing light-weight canvas shoes.

In the end I stepped smartly sideways off the path and detoured around the snake, which silently slithered off in the opposite direction.

Towards evening I reached a thick belt of jungle. I felt sure a river must run through its middle. It was a few days from the Spring equinox and, Roraima being close to the equator, the sun had been directly overhead at noon. It had been very hot. I was thirsty again, and anxious to reach the river before nightfall.

A faint track led into the undergrowth. I followed it hoping that it was an Indian path and not the way to the lair of one of the pilot's savage jaguars. In the rapidly failing light, the possibility of stumbling upon an angry mother jaguar and her cubs did not seem at all far-fetched. The track vanished and I began to cut my way downhill in the direction of the river. Suddenly, there was space in front of me and I stopped myself falling over the edge of a small precipice by grabbing a branch. Unfortunately it was covered in thorns. There below me lay the river, cool, deep and inviting. But between me and it were thirty yards of tangled undergrowth which it was impossible to attempt at that time of night. There must, I felt, be a way round. I began to push through the bushes where they seemed thinnest. Thorns clung to my clothes and held me back, and razor-sharp grasses and reeds cut the flesh of my arms and face. As I was in danger of getting completely entangled in the undergrowth, unable to move in any direction, I decided to try a system I had found effective for penetrating the densest Cornish bramble patches. This was to put the waterproof cape over myself and all my possessions, and then fall backwards into the undergrowth progressing a yard at a time. Although more painful than anything Cornwall had to offer, I did manage to reach a part of the wood where the trees were larger and prevented the undergrowth from being so thick, so that I was able to walk forwards again. By now I was sweating hard, partly from the extreme heat generated by wearing a water-proof cape and taking violent exercise, and partly, I have to admit, from the fear that at any moment I might fall on a litter of jaguars.

Now, as I looked about me, a different sort of fear began to take over. Darkness had fallen rapidly as one is always warned it will near the equator. I could no longer see where I was going. The river was no closer, and, abandoning any hope of having another drink that evening, I decided it was time to get back into open country again. Having decided that, it suddenly began to seem infinitely desirable to leave the cover of the trees and reach open air again. I began to feel like Mole in The Wild Wood, and the temptation to run blindly in what I hoped was the right direction was very strong. A different set of noises from the friendly daylight hum and buzz of insects now began. Squeaks and rustlings in the undergrowth seemed much louder and very close, and it was easy to imagine hundreds of little eyes watching me from the black patches of shadow.

By turning my back on the sound of the river, I reached open country again with a great feeling of relief. I began to walk back in the direction from which I had come. It was lighter in the open and I could make out the shape of the termite heaps which littered the floor of the valley. Feeling conspicuous now, and not wishing to draw attention to myself by blundering around in the dark, I laid down my baggage on a flat piece of ground, hacked up some of the sandy earth with my hunting knife so as to make it softer to lie on, laid the cape over the top of this and, after eating a couple of bananas, lay down and went to sleep.

I woke from time to time to hear the varied noises of the night. It wasn't necessary to use the torch to look around me, and so draw attention to my presence, as light clouds were trailing across the high full moon. I could see the outline of the hills across the valley. Once I heard the gruff barking of a jaguar, and a little later a few drops of rain fell.

I had been sleeping soundly when, at about midnight, I became aware of a loud ticking beneath my right ear. At first I thought it was my watch, and was about to roll over onto my other side when I realized that my left hand was not underneath my head.

Sitting up very slowly I reached for the torch and shone it on the plastic bag containing some bananas, which I had been using as a pillow. The whole bag, the ground surrounding it and much of my head and shoulders were covered with long-legged black ants between one and two inches in length. They were moving about methodically, picking up scraps of squashed banana in their pincers, while smaller red and dark brown ants scurried about among their feet. For a long time I simply sat still and watched, unable to make up my mind what my next move should be. So far I had not been bitten and I did not want to precipitate anything by acting hastily. I was later told by a Brazilian, who probably exaggerated, that this particular variety of ant was known locally as 'the twenty-four hour ant' because one suffered from a racking fever for twenty-four hours after being bitten. He also said that it was extremely painful. Fortunately I did not know this at the time, but I had my suspicions that if it came to armed hostilities they could make life very uncomfortable for me.

At last, I decided that I couldn't sit and watch them all night. I stood up slowly in the sleeping bag and brushed them gently off my body, trying not to squash any in the process. This I managed to do fairly effectively although some of the smaller ones fell down my neck and subsequently bit me. After hopping a few yards away, I extricated myself from the sleeping bag and gave it a good shake. I then returned, picked up the ground sheet and shook that well too. Taking only the rifle and torch, I walked away for fifty paces, and spread out the ground sheet and sleeping bag again. After a good look round to see that all the ants which had accompanied me had been disposed of, I climbed into my sleeping bag. But, after a few moments' thought, I climbed out again, went back to my original camp, took a banana out of the plastic bag, opened it, and left it on top. Returning to my sleeping bag, I got in, pulled it tight over my head and hoped for the best.

Four hours later I woke up with a start but found that no ants had joined me. I was able to lie peacefully watching the pre-dawn darkness gather, as the moon set and a chill dew fell before the sun rose. In the first glow of light I went to examine what damage the ants had done. To my surprise it was hard to tell that they had been there, except that my 'pillow' was clean and there was no trace of the banana I had unpeeled for them. All the ants, large and small, had vanished, and none of my possessions was damaged. I gathered everything together, heaved my assorted packages on to my now stiff and aching shoulders, and set off again.

One of the effects of my night with the ants was to add to my thirst. Having failed to reach the river on the previous evening, it was now some thirteen hours since I had last had a drink. And, as I was warmed by the first rays of the sun, I began to look forward to reaching the water. Although I was now walking back downstream along the top of the river bank, I was still separated from the river itself by a steep and densely overgrown slope. Before forcing my way through this, I wanted to see if I could find the point at which the track to Roraima crossed the river, as the thick belt of jungle on the far bank looked impenetrable.

I was fairly unclear as to where exactly I was at this point, but guessed that either this river marked the boundary with Venezuela or I had already crossed the border some time before. It seemed likely, from its size, that this river was the Arabopo which is one of the sources of the Caroni River. This in turn joins the Orinoco shortly before it runs into the Caribbean. Mount Roraima is also the source of the Rio Cotingo in Brazil, which runs eventually into the Rio Branco, and so to the Amazon. On the Guyanan side of the mountain is the Mazaruni, which joins the Essequibo near Georgetown. The cleft to the top of Roraima is on the Venezuelan side, so that although the three-way boundary between Brazil, Venezuela and Guyana is on the top, only Venezuela has access to it. I understood that border patrols seldom visited the region, and hoped that this was the case, as I had no current Venezuelan visa. It would be inconvenient to be arrested and taken to the nearest Venezuelan town as this was several days' walk away and would mean that I would miss my flight home from Bôa Vista.

At last I reached the point at which a track led down to the water's edge and I was able to scramble down it. I waded across the river, waist-deep in places, and left my possessions on the far bank. I then stripped off my clothes and plunged in for a very refreshing and welcome swim. The water was cool, clear and fast flowing, and there were few mosquitoes and flying insects at that early hour. A light mist rose off the surface upstream where some flat rocks held back the current to form a deep pool. In front of me lay the dark forbidding stretch of jungle. In its depths a bell-bird was calling monotonously. It sounded like a metal axe-head striking. The peace and solitude almost seduced me: I could gladly have stayed there for the day, avoiding the long journey ahead.

Following the faint track through the dense undergrowth was not easy and I took several wrong turns. But at last I burst out into the sunlight again and saw ahead of me the path winding along a narrow ridge gaining height all the time. Here, in open country, it was clear and easy to follow. Roraima grew closer with every step and although I could not make out the cleft leading to the top, I began to hope that I might reach it before nightfall.

I came to a divide. The path ran off clearly to my left – away from the mountain. Ahead of me lay a few dried up ravines and across bare, burnt country was a small 'sugar-loaf' mountain with the grey walls of Roraima rising up behind it. I should have known better than to leave the path, but I did, convinced that it led not to the mountain but to some Indian village. When I reached the top of the small mountain, having scrambled across country which proved to be much more difficult than it had looked from a distance, I saw two things. The first was a deep and overgrown valley between me and the base of Roraima. It was clearly impassable and meant that I would have to detour right back almost to the point at which I had left the path. But my annoyance at having added a good two hours to the climb was overruled by another sight. Barely five yards from me was a giant ant-eater. It was an unmistakable creature, tapered at both ends like a flattened croquet hoop. Its long thin head and snout were probing into anthills. Occasionally it cuffed them open with the long claws on its front feet.

Although I was coming downwind, it failed to see or smell me, so that I was able to watch it for some time before walking up to almost within touching distance. Suddenly it stopped dead, looked at me for a moment, and then began to shamble off down the hill rather slowly, as though its corns hurt. It seemed embarrassed at being taken by surprise and glanced nervously from time to time over its shoulder, while at the same time waggling its tail as though expecting a bullet at any moment. I felt sorry for the poor ungainly creature and, as we two were alone on the mountainside, spoke aloud assuring it that the last thing I wanted to do was to shoot it. In fact, after my experience with the ants, I regarded it as a close friend.

Of course, an Indian would have shot the ant-eater without hesitation. He would have done this partly because he needed the food to feed his family, and partly, instinctively, because it was too good a chance to miss, even if he did not, at that moment, need the food. This is a difficult and uneasy problem and one which becomes more acute throughout the world as certain species of wildlife decline in numbers. Conservationists concerned with the setting up of wildlife parks often dislike the idea of allowing primitive tribesmen to live in the parks as they may destroy the wildlife. They will do this more effectively if they are provided with modern weapons by us and they need these weapons if they are to survive in a more confined and less rich environment. However, we must make no mistake in realizing that the fault for this is ours. In his natural state the Indian will never exterminate a species deliberately, but will always prefer to move on to new hunting grounds as game becomes scarce. The rarer an animal, bird or fish becomes, the more we value it and hunt it down. The Indian prefers to leave it be and move on, perhaps returning in a few years when stocks have built up again. It is we who have surrounded him and prevented him from doing this.

At last, the way up the mountain came in sight. A diagonal blur of green vegetation stretched across the cliff face, visible, once I had reached the right side of the moun-tain, from a good distance. As I came closer, I could see some streams of water pouring over the lip of the rock-face high above, barely checking as they passed through this green band, before continuing their sheer drop to the ground below.

Only the last half-mile or so before reaching the base of the cliffs was jungle, and here the ground rose steeply. I plunged into the undergrowth, following the now clearly-defined path. I was glad that I was not having to make a path as I went. The water which poured over the edge of the mountain and the mists which swirled around it every day had created a rain forest at its feet. Everything was wet and overgrown, lichens hung from the twisted trees and the ground was wet and muddy underfoot.

My legs and feet were very tired from walking. Now, instead of simply having to put one in front of the other in order to go forward, I had to climb. The temptation to stop at the bottom and postpone the climb until the next day was very strong. But I was afraid that I might be so stiff that I would never make it and the top, directly above me, now seemed so very close. Besides, the Brazilian Expedition was up there somewhere and I looked forward to their company – to say nothing of the food they would undoubtedly have prepared. My own bunch of bananas had long since turned to pulp, and the idea of a square meal encouraged me.

From a distance, the cleft had looked like a regular slope. In reality the path ascended the side of the cliff in a series of switchback ups and downs. Much of the time it was necessary to pull myself up hand over hand by creepers and tree roots before slithering down the next muddy slope. I was soon soaked through and filthy dirty. At the same time my thirst increased. I remember at one point lying on my belly in the mud and reaching in under the cliff to drink from a clear spring while the mist swirled wetly over me. It had begun when I was about halfway up, a solid, grey wall which moved along the side of the mountain, bearing rain and completely blotting out the sky, the view, and the sheer cliffs above and below. This, and the two or three feet of vegetation between me and the edge, made me oblivious to the fact that I had a gradually increasing sheer drop just to my left. Every now and then the rain suddenly poured harder for a few yards and I realized that I was walking through one of the waterfalls.

My legs ached abominably by the time I reached the top, and it was also beginning to grow dark. As I scrambled on all fours up the last rock fall, bare now of vegetation, two shapes loomed out of the mist ahead of me. They were the skulls, complete with curving horns, of two oxen which General Rondon had had carried up the mountain to feed his men on the boundary commission in the thirties. Below them were some signs painted on the rock, and beyond them the ground levelled off.

It was now late in the evening and I was very tired. My feet were sore and covered in blisters, my back ached, my shoulders ached and I kept getting cramp in my calves.

I had not counted on the fog. Actually, it was more like a cloud, swirling over the top of the mountain and drenching everything in its path with particles of water. It soaked through my clothes to the few parts of my body which had remained dry, except for sweat, during the climb. With the mist and darkness came a dank chill and the rock on which I sat felt cold to the touch, making me shiver. Around me rose grotesque pinnacles and outcrops glimpsed fleetingly behind curtains of mist.

Climbing to the top of the highest point I could find, I stood and shouted, 'hallooed' and yodelled as loudly as my lungs would stand towards the four points of the compass. Silence, except for the faint fluting of the breeze in the rocks. Scrambling down from my pinnacle, I slipped and rolled the last few yards to lie in a shallow puddle, cursing my bruises and quaking at the thought of broken bones in the midst of such desolation.

I groped on through a mad, moon landscape in which strange distorted rock shapes leaped up on all sides; blank cliffs, their tops invisible, forced me to change direction; and water lay everywhere in pools whose depth it was impossible to gauge. My sleeping bag, though wet like everything else, was probably still dry inside. I considered getting into it and waiting out the night. But how to get myself a little drier first? And where to lay it when all around was wet, slippery rock and mud and water?

There were no caves that I could see and no overhangs. An extraordinary rock, balanced upon the point of another like some gigantic toadstool, looked hopeful, and I scrambled up the side of it. But there was nowhere flat and nowhere dry. The angles were all wrong.

Before reaching the top of the cleft I had seen footsteps in the mud and knew that they must belong to the expedition. They had vanished on the bare rock of the plateau and, with little hope of success, I made my way back to where I had last seen them and began to try and track them further. By now I could only see the ground by the light of my torch, a small one with weak batteries. For fifty yards from the last footprint there was nothing but bare unmarked rock. Then came a narrow channel full of mud separating me from the next stretch. Casting along this, bent double, and examining the ground with intense care, I came to a place where the mud was slightly marked, as though a stick had been trailed through it. This gave me a line and brought me to the next patch where a small cactus had been crushed. A few hundred yards on I found a clear footprint and, as it was not my own, knew that I was on the right track – that is, unless I was following the trail of one of the expedition members who had gone off to walk the ten miles to the far end of the plateau!

For an hour I groped and searched, guessed wrong and

retraced my steps. Never has an Indian tracked anybody with more care than I did, having convinced myself that my life depended upon success. Wet, cold and very tired, the twelve soggy hours to daylight seemed like a death sentence. What slimy creatures might not find me if I lay down now? Or was I near the edge and might I step over it at any moment and fall back three thousand feet down the cliff? Fear kept me awake.

I must have walked a mile before I thought of shouting again. This time there was an answer. A few minutes later I saw the light of a torch. The Indian carrying it looked at me as though I was an apparition from the dead or one of the spirits known to haunt the summit of Roraima. When I had reassured him that I was not, he began to laugh and, giggling and shaking his head, led me to where the others were camped.

They sheltered in a shallow cave under an overhanging cliff. Over a roaring fire there bubbled a stew of spam and beans, more welcome to my nostrils than all the spices of Arabia.

The figures silhouetted by the fire rose as I came towards them. For a moment I hesitated, suddenly shy of human company and wondering whether I would be welcome. They looked at me in frank amazement and then we all began to speak at once.

As far as they were concerned, it was just not possible that I could be there. They *knew* that they were alone on the top of the plateau, and indeed that there was no one else in the region for several miles around its base. They knew that darkness had fallen over an hour before, and that there was no other camp on the top. So what was this Englishman doing appearing out of the fog?

It was impossible that I could be there. But they welcomed me generously, pushing a mug of hot chocolate into my hands, and listening while I told them where I had come from and how I found them.

'But where is the rest of your party?' they asked.

It took some time to convince them that I was alone and had been since the beginning of the climb. This was the part that amazed them most, and in particular the fact that I had slept by myself in the open. For most Brazilians this is a situation to be avoided at all costs.

They were a tough lot that I now shook hands with, unshaven and wrapped in blankets against the cold. Byron, a farouche character with drooping moustaches and the clothes and bearing of a Mexican bandit, who was a lawyer from Bôa Vista: Jaime, a *garimpeiro*, or prospector, who had spent most of the last twenty years looking for diamonds in the rivers between the Orinoco, the Essequibo and the Amazon. He was obsessed by diamonds and almost immediately started telling me how good the chances were of finding them on Roraima. He was wearing the jacket of a wet-suit, which surprised me, until he told me that much of his time in the rivers was spent deep below the muddy water at the end of a crude air-pipe, gathering stones from the mud at the bottom. The third member of the party was Raoul, a government geologist who was a powerfully built young man and looked as though he were always about to drop off to sleep.

Seeing them, and thinking of food ahead of me, I was once more filled with energy and, stripping off the soaking muddy clothes, I rubbed myself down with a dry towel. As I had no other dry clothes, I climbed, as I was, into my sleeping bag. Lying as close as possible to the fire, I ate and drank my fill – they even had some wine with them! – and then stretched out on the foot or two of dry ground under the ledge, which was all the cave consisted of. The others climbed up higher, to a place where they said there was a deeper recess, but I was content where I was near the fire with the Indians.

I slept little, turning over and over inside my sleeping bag on the hard ground and trying to find a part of my body which did not ache. It was bitterly cold and several times I had attacks of cramp in my legs and feet. But the

joy and relief of being in safety was so great that none of
this seemed much to have to suffer. At least I was sheltered
and dry. Outside, the rain sheeted down and the wind
howled, making the mist swirl around us. It was a horrible
night and I was glad and thankful to be safe.

The cold woke me. Although it was eight degrees centigrade
(forty-six fahrenheit), after what I had been used to it felt
well below freezing. The rain had blown away and the
clouds parted so that a shaft of early morning sunshine
was striking the rocks above the cave. A hundred yards
below it there was a deep pool of clear water. Its whole
floor was covered in shining white crystals.

As I was still filthy dirty from the day before, I hobbled
down there, threw off my towel, and, feeling excessively
brave, plunged into the icy water. It was not quite as bad
as I expected as the air temperature was lower than that
of the water. As I had soap with me, I had a thorough wash
and scrub. I looked up to see my Brazilian friends emerging from their blankets and looking down with some
surprise at this further manifestation of insanity by the
mad Englishman.

The wash and swim made me feel ready for anything
again, and when I returned to the cave and found that
they were cooking porridge for breakfast my joy in the
morning knew no bounds.

We went our different ways to explore the top, I to the
west, where I climbed on to an outcrop overhanging the
yawning space to the green forest floor below. There I sat
and looked out across to Kukenaam, Roraima's twin, and
watched the clouds play hide-and-seek with it.

For the first time since setting out to climb the mountain
I could relax. Now, too, the jumble of ideas and impressions
resulting from the previous three months was at last beginning to fall into shape. Somewhere in the back of my
mind a pattern was emerging, but the edges were fragile.
If I tried to define it too sharply I lost it and again became

confused. Putting the 'problem of the Indians in Brazil' into words and trying to spell out solutions in itself tended to cloud the issue.

If I criticize the actions and policies of some Brazilian government departments, then I am accused of being no friend of Brazil, a nation whose country and whose people I love. If I praise the work of some more than others then I am biased, and if I care more about the Indians than about the common people, then I am a fool. All I know is that there is a problem in Brazil – a problem which many would like to say does not exist, or has been solved, or does not matter. It is a problem which has no one easy solution, no single panacea, but which depends for its humane solving upon an enlightened and civilized respect for the fragile cultures of people emerging from the Stone Age – a respect often lacking in those who first come face to face with it.

More and more I come to feel that the amazing world of the Xingu National Park not only works best in practical terms, but comes nearest to satisfying the basic needs and desires of the people we want to help. In a world desperately unsure of its own desires and destiny, where values and attitudes change with each succeeding generation, what possible right have we to destroy knowledge and happiness in the name of Progress?

While I was in Brazil I spoke to many people, and it was through them that I learnt. Many did not agree with what I believed. Some resented the fact that a foreigner should come and make such a fuss about a tiny problem. I tried to explain to these that if they continue their present policy towards the Indian, and either integrate him completely into society or exterminate him in the process, they will in time come to regret it. This is because they can at present see no further than the immediate benefits of their very understandable obsession with progress, and with the raising of the national standard of living. They refuse to accept even the possibility that this philosophy does not apply to the Indian.

They will regret his passing, not only because he will no longer be there to study and enjoy as an exponent of a pure and beautiful culture, but also because the example of a way of life possibly superior to and certainly quite different from the end product of a materialist philosophy will have been lost.

The Indian is not motivated by the desire to acquire wealth and power greater than other men. He is content if there is game in the forest, fish in the river and crops growing in his clearing. He is not concerned with growing or killing a surplus with which to trade, and so build up wealth for himself or for a community. He does not desire to leave possessions to his offspring. The land on which he lives is enough.

Therefore the land is fundamental to the Indian question. If we leave him in possession of his lands – and this means parks and protection – there is no need for rapid change. Medical protection is the only vital necessity. But if we are going to take away his land, if the Trans-Amazonica Road and its tentacles are going to spread eagerly to every corner of the country, even through the middle of the Xingu National Park, then we must set about changing not only the Indian's material state, by teaching him to farm and trade and work as a labourer so as to be less wasteful in his land use, but we must also change his whole psychological state by instilling into him the acquisitiveness and material ambition of our society.

There is much of Paradise in the Xingu and elsewhere in Brazil, where the innocence of knowing no shame still lives in the Indian's eyes. Of course there is pain and savagery, ignorance and cruelty, too, but can we honestly say that what we have to offer in our world is any better? Are we still so uncivilized that we must destroy even this last remnant of the Eden from which we were banished aeons ago? Can we not let it survive a little longer and perhaps learn from the remaining residents a thing or two about our own chances of survival?

Summary of Tribes visited in Brazil

JANUARY–MARCH 1971

After preliminary visits to Rio de Janeiro, São Paulo and Brasilia, thirty-two tribes or groups of Indians were visited in Brazil.

A rough system of coding has been used to summarize their relative conditions.

Against each tribe, village or group visited the following information is added:

1. Name of tribe or sub-group (if generally known as such).
2. Name of village (if different from name of tribe or group).
3. Approximate number of inhabitants of village or members of group.
4. Area of Reserve, if known, in Hectares (1 Hectare equals 2.47 acres).
5. Date or dates on which visited.
6. Classification.

CLASSIFICATION OF TRIBES VISITED

It must be emphasized that this classification is based on brief visits to a selection of the Indian tribes of Brazil. It is not an anthropological classification and is useful only as a guide to this book.

CONDITIONS: 1, very good; 2, good; 3, fair; 4, poor; 5, very poor. STAGE OF INTEGRATION: A, isolated; B, intermittent contact; C, permanent contact (FUNAI/missionary); D, permanent contact (general population); E, integrated.

Tribes (including separate villages or groups of the same tribe).

1. Yawalapiti	CI	17. Terena/Limão Verde	E2
2. Waura	BI	18. Bororo	C4
3. Kuikuro	B2	19. Paresi	D5
4. Kamayura	CI	20. Nambiquara/S. Azul	C4
5. Txikao	C2	21. Mamaindé/Fifano	C5
6. Trumai	C2	22. Mamaindé/Cpt. Pedro	C5
7. Kayabi	CI	23. Tauandé/Faustinho	D5
8. Suya	B2	24. Cinta Larga	A?
9. Juruna	BI	25. Gorotire	C2
10. Txukarramai	B2	26. Kuben-Kran-Kegn	C3
11. Karaja/S. Isabel	D4	27. Kraho	D3
12. Karaja/Fontoura	C5	28. Gavião	C5
13. Terena/Buriti	E4	29. Tirio	CI
14. Kaiwa	E3	30. Paimerú	B2
15. Kadiweu/S. João	D3	31. Ingarico	D3
16. Kadiweu/Bodoquena	D4	32. Waika	A & B2

PART TWO

XINGU

The Xingu National Park consists of an area of 8 900 square miles in which live approximately 1 500 Indians from 15 tribes.

It is broadly divided into two areas – the southern half administered from Posto Leonardo and containing the eleven Upper Xingu tribes, and the northern half administered from Diauarum and inhabited by four other tribes.

Posto Leonardo
Administration. Six FUNAI employees administer both Posto Leonardo and Diauarum. These are Orlando and Claudio Villas Boas, their nephew Agnello Villas Boas, two nurses (Sara Orlando Villas Boas and her sister) and Captain Hausen, the pilot. At each post there is also an Indian responsible for administration who receives a small wage. Both these Indians

who, in addition to their other work, operate the radio link between the posts, are men of outstanding calibre.

Medical Assistance. There is a well-equipped clinic and dispensary and further assistance is provided by a doctor and nurses sent by the São Paulo School of Medicine for two-month tours of duty.

Facilities

1 light aircraft. 3/4 seats, very old but serviceable.
1 jeep.
Radio.
1 ancient motor launch.
2 outboard motors and canoes.

There is a small airstrip beside each Indian village and regular medical inspections are made.

TRIBES VISITED

1. Yawalapiti (60). 23rd and 24th January. C1. Ten minutes from Posto Leonardo by jeep.

2. Waura (115). 24th January. B1. Ten minutes' flight from Posto Leonardo. Famous for their pottery which they trade with other tribes in the region. Both large pots used in the preparation of manioc and smaller zoomorphic bowls were being made.

3. Kuikuro (150). 25th January. B2. Fifteen minutes' flight. A large village on the edge of open savanna country rich in game.

4. Kamayura (130). 25th and 26th January. C1. Twenty minutes by jeep. Had recently rebuilt their village close to the very large lake which provides the fish requirements of this tribe.

5. Txikao (58). 24th and 27th January. C2. Ten minutes' walk from the post.

6. Trumai (26). 23rd to 27th January. C2. We also flew low

over the Kalapalo (120) and Matipu (25) villages en route to the Kuikuro and met members of these tribes as well as some Aweti who came to the post.

On January 28th and 29th we travelled by boat down the Xingu River from Posto Leonardo to Diauarum, a distance of some 100 miles. No Indians were seen until we were close to Diauarum. This part of the park, though visited by Indians of the Upper Xingu on hunting parties, contains no permanent settlements. It consists of dense jungle with no open areas.

There is a Brazilian Air Force jungle training camp some way below Posto Leonardo and in from the river bank, but there is little or no contact with either the post or the Indians.

Diauarum

Administration and Medical Assistance. These are the same as Posto Leonardo, due to the radio link and airstrip. There is usually a nurse and Claudio Villas Boas spends much of his time there.

Facilities
Radio.
2 outboard motors and several canoes.

TRIBES VISITED

7. Kayabi (230). 29th January and 1st February. C1. We visited two Kayabi villages on the Xingu River, one south and one north of Diauarum.

8. Suya (125). 30th January. B2. One hour by canoe up the Suiá Missu River. Only contacted in 1960/61, many Suya died at that time from disease. Recently 40 Beiço de Pau, the remnants of a related group from the Upper apajós River, were brought to the Suya village and have integrated into the tribe.

9. Juruna (60). 7th February. B1. Five hours by boat from Diauarum down the Xingu and up the Manitsauá Missu River.

10. There were several Txukarramai at Diauarum discussing the new road and the possibility of moving the tribe to the

south of it. The tribe consists of over 280 members inside the park and about the same number outside.

PART THREE

BANANAL

The island of Bananal (8 600 square miles) on the Araguaia River is an open reserve, sometimes also called the National Indian Park of Araguaia. There are about 800 Indians and 8 000 settlers on the island.

Santa Isabel do Morro

Administration. This is the base of the 7th Regional Delegacy of FUNAI, from which the Karaja, Xerente, Kraho and Xavante tribes are administered.

Indian Guards. There is a detachment of Indian Guards on Bananal (9 at Santa Isabel and 7 at Fontoura). These are Indian youths from the Karaja, Xerente, Xavante and Kraho tribes, 84 of whom had been taken to Belo Horizonte and then returned to their tribes as a native police force.

VILLAGES (ALDEIAS) VISITED

11. Karaja, Santa Isabel (240). 3rd February. D4. The two rows of mud and straw huts on brick bases, with a couple of brick huts in the middle, were separated from the administration building by a barbed-wire fence.

12. Karaja, Fontoura (237). 4th February. C5. Three hours downstream from Santa Isabel. 5 hours return. The village is administered by a Seventh Day Adventist Mission with occasional visits by a FUNAI doctor or nurse from Santa Isabel.

Southern Mato Grosso

The Headquarters of the 9th Regional Delegacy of FUNAI are at Campo Grande.

13. Terena, Buriti (735). 2 000 Hectares. 8th February. E4. *Assistance.* FUNAI through missionaries; divided equally between Catholic and Protestant, the latter being at the FUNAI post.

14. Kaiwa, Guarani and Terena, Dourados (old name Francisco Orta) (approx. 1 900). 3 600 Hectares. 9th February. E3. *Assistance.* FUNAI employee at post. *Medical.* Modern Protestant missionary hospital on the edge of the reserve to which tuberculosis patients from a wide area are sent. FUNAI pays for treatment of some Indians. The main health problem was the after-care of tuberculosis patients.

Kadiweu Reserve (425). 364 000 Hectares. 10th and 11th February. Difficult access by jeep over rough tracks through swamp, forest and grassland areas of Pantanal. There is an airstrip at Bodoquena, but it was not considered serviceable. We visited both the villages in the reserve and the cattle station at Nalique.

15. São João (Aldeia Tomasia) (207). 10th February. D3. *Assistance.* Occasional FUNAI visits. No resident or medical help. The village comprises small groups of huts scattered over a wide area.

16. Bodoquena (Campina) (218). 11th February. D.4. *Assistance.* Resident, untrained, FUNAI employee at the post. No facilities (radio had not worked for two years and airstrip unserviceable). Some medical help given by nearby Protestant missionary.

We also visited the cattle station at Nalique, where a man employed by FUNAI looks after about 100 head of cattle.

17. Terena Aquidauana (Limão Verde) (740). 4 000 Hectares. 12th February. E.2. 15 miles west of Aquidauana. *Assistance.* FUNAI employee and school-teacher wife at post in the village.

Northern Mato Grosso

The Headquarters of the 5th Regional Delegacy of FUNAI

are at Cuiabá where there is a well-stocked shop selling Indian artifacts from the tribes in the region.

Medical Assistance. Thanks to the tireless work of a dedicated Brazilian nurse, assisted by two Peace Corps girls, medical help is given to the Indians who can be brought to Cuiabá. The hospital consists of two rough buildings and an isolation building some distance away.

TRIBES VISITED

18. Bororo (Gomes Carneiro) (120). 15th February. C4. 45 minute flight to strip next to the post on the São Lourenço River. Half-hour walk to the village.
Assistance. Resident FUNAI employee at airstrip. An American couple from the Summer Institute of Linguistics was living near the village.

From the 16th to the 19th February we travelled by road between Cuiabá and Vilhena, visiting Paresi and Nambiquara villages on the way.

19. Paresi (Rio Verde) (30). 16th February. D5. About 180 miles north-west of Cuiabá on the Cuiabá-Pôrto Velho road.
Assistance. Occasional medical supplies from Cuiabá and visits from the Catholic Mission at Diamantino.

There are about 460 Paresi in all living in about 17 villages which represent little more than family groups.

There is a large Paresi reserve, but less than half the tribe lives in it.

20. Nambiquara (Serra Azul) (70). 17th February. C4. About 270 miles from Cuiabá towards Vilhena and 20 miles north-east of the road. Inside Nambiquara Reserve.
Assistance. Summer Institute of Linguistics.

21. Nambiquara. Mamaindé (Fifano) (50). 18th February. C5. About 30 miles before Vilhena and 1 mile west of the road.
Assistance. Summer Institute of Linguistics.

22. Nambiquara. Mamaindé (Captain Pedro) (50). 18th February. C5. 5 miles south of Fifano and 6 miles in from the road.
Assistance. None. An American anthropologist and his wife

were living in the village and giving what help and protection they could.

23. Nambiquara. Tauandé (Seringal do Faustinho) (26). 20th February. D5. 38 miles north of Vilhena on the Pôrto Velho road.

24. Aripuaná. A large Indian park called the Indian Park of Aripuaná was created in 1968 between the Roosevelt River in Rondônia and the Juruena River in Mato Grosso. There are several uncontacted groups in this area, the largest of which is probably the Cinta Larga. About 35 miles east of the road is the '7 de Setembro' camp, a contact post with airstrip, set up by Snr Francisco Meirelles, FUNAI delegate for the region. Unfortunately both the camp and these villages are outside the area of the Aripuaná Park.

PART FOUR

SOUTHERN PARÁ & NORTHERN GOIÁS

Belém is the FUNAI Headquarters of the 2nd Regional Delegacy.

Medical Assistance. There is a 'Casa do Indio' in Belém, on the outskirts of the town. Facilities were minimal with no trained staff or equipment, although a nurse was said to visit occasionally.

TRIBES VISITED

25. Gorotire (100). 4th March. C2. About three hours' flight from Belém with a stop to refuel at Conceição do Araguaia. *Assistance.* Resident Protestant missionary whose wife is a trained nurse. Both are Brazilian. Also some visits from FUNAI and a Catholic mission.

26. Kuben-Kran-Kegn (300). 4th and 5th March. C3. *Assistance.* A resident FUNAI employee and resident American Protestant mission, both providing medical help. The Catholic mission was no longer resident, but made periodic visits.

27. Kraho (583). 320 000 Hectares. 5th and 6th March. D3. 40 minutes' flight from Carolina.

Assistance. Resident FUNAI employee and staff at the Kraho-lândia post which administers the whole reserve. Very limited medical supplies and no trained nurse. The main function of the post seemed to be to run the herd of cows which belongs to FUNAI and from which the Indians derive little or no benefit.

There are five villages in the reserve, which is not the original tribal land of the Kraho but was given to them at the beginning of this century by the then Goiás State Government, the settlers being moved off.

28. Gavião (Mae Maria) (35). 6th March. C5. 20 miles west of São Félix which is half-an-hour by boat from Maraba. One mile off the Maraba-Altamira Road.
Assistance. Resident FUNAI employee at the post three miles away. Medical assistance is provided by a male nurse with some training but very limited supplies of medicine.

Altamira

On 8th March we visited the FUNAI pacification base at Altamira. Here 57 FUNAI employees (many more than we encountered in the whole of Brazil) are working in connection with the Trans-Amazonica Road programme.

Tumucumaque

The Tumucumaque Park was created in 1968. It consists of nearly 10 000 square miles in the extreme north of the state of Pará on the border with Surinam. There are about 300 Indians from three tribes, being 222 Tirio, the predominant group, 64 Kaxuyama, and a very small group of 13 Ewarhoyana-Kahyawa. There is also some fluctuation across the international border.
Administration. The park is administered by a Roman Catholic (Franciscan) Mission based in Brazil but with a college in Germany. Currently the park is run by German priests but Brazilian priests are being trained. There are also three Brazilian nuns there. FUNAI is supposed to contribute medi-

cines and other supplies but has not done so during the last year.

Medical assistance. A well-stocked dispensary entirely supplied by the missionaries is run by a Brazilian volunteer male nurse who also undertakes dental work and minor operations.

Facilities. Two Unimogs and a lot of agricultural equipment. Radio. One outboard motor and canoe.

VILLAGES VISITED

29. Tirio (150). 10th and 11th March. C1.

30. Paimerú (4). 10th March. B2. A small village about 20 miles from Tirio, where Protasio Frikel, a well-known anthropologist and previous administrator of the park, lives.

Roraima

The Federal Territory of Roraima, consisting of 90 000 square miles, has a population of 47 000 of which over 25 per cent is Indian. It therefore has far and away the highest proportion of Indians of any region of Brazil.

The majority of Makuxi, Wapixana and a few minor groups, are in permanent contact and going through various phases of integration. The remainder, some 4 000 in all and made up mostly of Waika (Yanomamo), with a few Maiongong and Atroari, are either totally isolated or in intermittent contact with missionaries or others.

Assistance. Various bodies give assistance in one form or another to the Indians.

31. Ingarico (Serra do Sol) (100). 17th March. D3. 45-minute flight from Bôa Vista.

Assistance. Resident Brazilian missionary. Assemblies of God.

32. Waika Yanomamo (Rio Uraricaa) (50). 18th March. One hour flight north-west of Bôa Vista.

DEFINITION OF AN INDIAN

A brief comment should be made on whether the evidence suggests that the depopulation of Indians has, in general, come about through actual physical extinction or through assimilation.

Much has been written on the question of what constitutes an Indian in Brazil. For further study of this subject reference should be made to the publications of Darcy Ribeiro (in particular *Os Indios e a Civilização*, 1970) and J. C. Melatti (*Indios do Brasil*, December 1970). Many Brazilians have a greater or lesser element of Indian blood in their veins but I have dealt with those groups of individuals who consider themselves Indian and are considered Indian by the surrounding population.

In 1957 Ribeiro divided the 143 Indian groups up as follows:

Isolated	33
Intermittent contact	27
Permanent contact	45
Integrated	38

and stated that 87 groups had become extinct since the beginning of the century, reducing the population from about half a million to about 80 000. In spite of small successes in some quarters, the decrease has continued and the population is now estimated to be nearer to 50 000.

Melatti (1970) states, 'There are two ways in which an Indian society disappears: through the assimilation of its members into Brazilian society and by the death of its members. In the first instance, the indigenous society disappears but the individuals which comprise it survive as members of Brazilian society; in the second instance, both the society and the individuals disappear. The second instance occurs much more frequently than the first.' This is due to disease and the failure of those coming into contact with the Indians to understand their needs and the problems involved.

Numbers in the remaining tribes are so greatly reduced that

their survival will only be secured by the provision of massive medical aid, rigorous protection and careful study of their needs. Any attempt to speed up the process of integration or to allow indiscriminate contact will, according to past experience and all available evidence and informed opinion, lead not only to the destruction of their society, special knowledge and culture, but also to the physical annihilation of most of them.

Further information on Survival International and copies of my report, from which this Appendix is a brief extract, can be obtained from Survival International, 36 Craven Street, London W C 2.

On the 12th July 1971 a presidential decree removed from the Xingu National Park all land north of the BR 080 (Xavantina-Cachimbo) road, which had by then cut the park in half. 3 210 square miles of forest was declared no longer exclusively Indian land, although it was still occupied by the bulk of the Txukarramai tribe.

3 600 square miles were added to the south and south-west of the park, thereby making it larger technically. However, the new land consists of poor *campo* with little game or fish, parts of it were already occupied by cattle farmers and some of it had been burnt. No Indians live there and the terrain is totally unsuited to the Txukarramai who refuse to leave the tall jungle to the north. In spite of their international reputation and intimate knowledge of the Xingu region and its Indians, the Villas Boas brothers were neither consulted nor officially informed until after the event.

At the same time FUNAI's attitude appeared to undergo a complete reversal. Whereas the road was originally justified as a means of bringing help and civilization to the Indians (*Veja* 26.5.71), their land was now taken away in order to prevent clashes with road workers and settlers. Now plans have been drawn up for a new road to cross the park near to Posto Leonardo.

In May 1972 Cotrim (see p. 203) resigned from FUNAI, saying that he could no longer go on being a 'gravedigger for the Indians'. In an interview with *Veja* (31.5.72), he said that all possible forms of dialogue with FUNAI had failed and that agreements made with the Indians had not been fulfilled. 'Our society's experience ... cannot be transmitted in an instant form.'

Index

❧

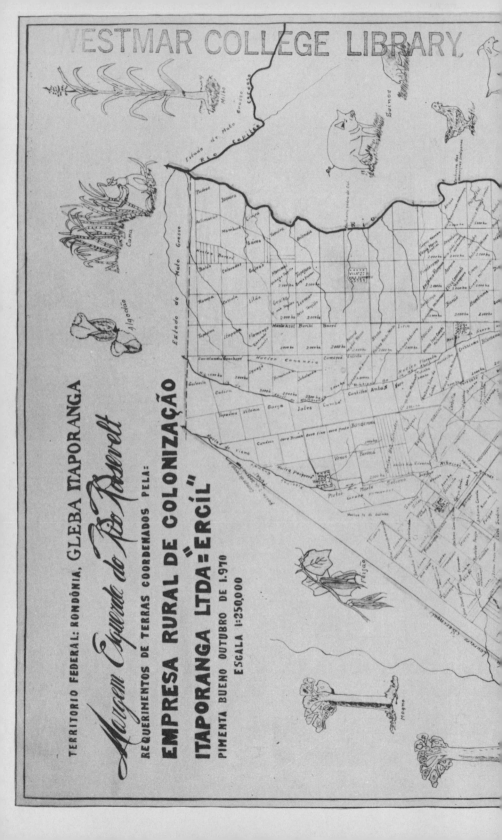

TERRITORIO FEDERAL: RONDÔNIA, GLEBA ITAPORANGA

Margem Esquerde do Rio Roosevelt

REQUERIMENTOS DE TERRAS COORDENADOS PELA:

EMPRESA RURAL DE COLONIZAÇÃO

ITAPORANGA LTDA="ERCIL"

PIMENTA BUENO OUTUBRO DE 1.970

ESCALA 1:250.000